D0205823

COMMUNITIES IN MOTION

Recent Titles in
Contributions to the Study of Music and Dance

COMMUNITIES
IN
MOTION

Dance, Community, and Tradition in America's Southeast and Beyond

Edited by SUSAN EIKE SPALDING and JANE HARRIS WOODSIDE

UNDER THE AUSPICES OF THE CENTER FOR APPALACHIAN
STUDIES AND SERVICES

Contributions to the Study of Music and Dance, Number 35
ROBERT E. DENTON, JR., Series Adviser

GREENWOOD PRESS
Westport, Connecticut • London

Library of Congress Cataloging-in-Publication Data

Communities in motion : dance, community, and tradition in America's
 Southeast and beyond / edited by Susan Eike Spalding and Jane Harris
 Woodside under the auspices of the Center for Appalachian Studies
 and Services.
      p.   cm. — (Contributions to the study of music and dance,
 ISSN 0193-9041 : no. 35)
  Includes bibliographical references and index.
  ISBN 0-313-29428-3 (alk. paper)
  1. Folk dancing—Appalachian Region. 2. Folk dancing—Southern
 States. 3. Appalachian Region—Social life and customs.
 4. Southern States—Social life and customs.   I. Spalding, Susan
 Eike.   II. Woodside, Jane Harris.   III. East Tennessee State
 University. Center for Appalachian Studies and Services.
 IV. Series.
 GV1624.A7C65   1995
 793.3'1974—dc20   94-30928

British Library Cataloguing in Publication Data is available.

Library of Congress Catalog Card Number: 94-30928
ISBN: 0-313-29428-3
ISSN: 0193-9041

First published in 1995

Greenwood Press, 88 Post Road West, Westport, CT 06881
An imprint of Greenwood Publishing Group, Inc.

Printed in the United States of America

∞™

The paper used in this book complies with the
Permanent Paper Standard issued by the National
Information Standards Organization (Z39.48-1984).

10 9 8 7 6 5 4 3 2 1

To my parents, James and Claire Eike
—SES

To my favorite dancing partners:
Jack, Jessica, Christopher, and Nicholas
—JHW

Contents

Figures and Tables

FIGURES

TABLES

Acknowledgments

We wish to thank all the members of the Center for Appalachian Studies and Services staff as well as the staff of the Sherrod Library at East Tennessee State University for their help. In particular, we would like to recognize Richard Blaustein's encouragement at the outset of this undertaking and to thank Jean Haskell Speer for her invaluable advice and support at its conclusion. We would also like to single out several other individuals who were important to this project: Beth Hogan of the Sherrod Library for her interlibrary loan assistance; Dr. Jack Higgs of ETSU's English department and Gail Matthews-DeNatale for their editorial advice; and Pat Arnow, Kim Boyd, Tim Bradshaw, Amy Cutshaw, Sandra Collier, David Dixon, Kim Durham, Nancy Fischman, Margaret Huang, Melanie K. Hutsell, Penelope Lane, Charles Moore, Jamie Pennington, Sandra Sanders, Frieda Souder, and Paula Whitman, all of whom gave considerable time and effort to this endeavor.

Introduction

Early on, we believed it was possible to confine ourselves to "old-time dancing in the Appalachian mountains"—to unassailably "traditional" dances that were distinctly Appalachian and that had come to us in an unbroken line from a distant past.

Our narrow focus was immediately challenged by the authors. These were individuals whom we first got to know while organizing East Tennessee State University's Center for Appalachian Studies and Services conferences on vernacular dance in 1989 and 1990—conferences that inspired us to commission the articles for *Communities in Motion*. For example, folklorist and dance ethnologist Colin Quigley finds intriguing similarities between Appalachian and Newfoundland dance forms. These similarities suggest that communities do not simply preserve whole, entire dances that have been handed down to them, but actively and creatively combine elements of dance traditions into new forms. Phil Jamison shows the ways in which the Green Grass Cloggers, a dance group begun in the 1970s, built upon several regional traditions, added innovations, and invented a new vernacular performance form. This new form then fed back into some of the regional clogging traditions that served as their inspiration. For example, many Appalachian precision clogging teams now incorporate into their routines the high kicks that originated with the Green Grass Cloggers.

Furthermore, it soon became clear that not all vernacular dance forms found in the Appalachian region were indigenous to the region. All the dances discussed in this book occur in the Appalachian region, but some are local versions of national or international dance styles. In other cases, we detect the influence of forms such as Appalachian square dance on the dance of other regions. Or we see the influence of dance forms found nationwide, such as Western club square, on Appalachian dance. Therefore, we have judiciously included discussion of dance forms from other regions that contribute to understanding the vernacular dance found in the Appalachian region and other parts of the South. Also, not all of the dances can trace their pedigrees back for generations. Clearly, vernacular dances are more complex affairs than we first assumed.

We ultimately replaced the term *old-time*, with its emphasis on dance belonging to the past, with *tradition*. We view tradition primarily as a process; we understand it to be a very fluid concept that includes both discontinuity and continuity, one that accommodates the notions of preservation and invention.

In addition, we have eschewed the word *folk* mainly because of its association with recreational folk dance programs. Beginning with the work of dance educator Elizabeth Burchenal in the first decades of the twentieth century, these programs extracted traditional dances from their contexts, then radically simplified them, often beyond recognition, and introduced them into schools and recreational settings.[1] Thus, we use *vernacular* as a more accurate term for the dance forms included in this book.

Vernacular situates the dance in communities of people who, while serious about dance, are not professionals. This linkage of the dance with community is vitally important. Each of these vernacular dance forms has always had a close relationship with its community. At times, the dance expresses the outlook, values, and needs of a long-established community, while in other instances, dance serves as a catalyst for the formation of a community.

We view *vernacular dance*, then, as dance that is community based and is shaped and perpetuated by the traditional process; it can be either social or performance oriented in character. Many of the authors deal in some fashion with trying to understand better the complicated and fascinating relationships between community and tradition. They pay attention to how communities influenced dance and how vernacular dance in turn shaped and expressed communities. This became the major unifying theme of the collection of research essays, methodological papers, and interviews.

Scholarly interest in American vernacular dance has been sparse until recently. Today, scholars are approaching issues of vernacular dance and cultural identity among diverse groups in every corner of North America. These scholars come to the genre from a variety of different fields: dance ethnography and dance history, physical education, folklore, and anthropology, to name a few.

In *Communities in Motion*, the authors, by and large, present case studies that attempt to establish an emic point of view; in other words, they try to reflect the opinions, beliefs, and values of the dancers themselves. Such studies stand in stark contrast to the work of important and dedicated pioneers such as Cecil Sharp. Since several authors use Sharp and his work as a touchstone, it is worth our while to provide a brief summary of the impact he had on dance research.

When he came to the Southern Appalachians just after World War I to collect folk ballads and, less copiously, folk dance, he came with a well-formed, preconceived theory. He believed that the vernacular dance in the Southern Highlands preserved earlier, purer, more vital forms of English folk song and dance than existed back in the mother country itself; he was particularly excited to discover these "purer" Anglo-Saxon forms since he feared that in England, such indigenous art forms were on the point of disappearing entirely. When he came across a circle-based dance in Kentucky, which he termed the "Kentucky Running Set," he immediately assumed that the dance was a remnant of a very old tradition that had been preserved intact by isolated and conservative mountaineers. By focusing only on folk songs and dance that he judged to be of English origin and by manipulating and interpreting the material according to his biases, he promoted a largely erroneous Anglo-centric view of the Southern mountains. He came armed with a theory that allowed him to assign a meaning to the material without paying close attention—in fact, any attention at all—to how the dance actually functioned within its twentieth century Appalachian context.

While we acknowledge the importance of making comparisons among contemporary and historical vernacular dance forms and then drawing conclusions as Sharp attempted to do, we believe that such comparisons and conclusions need to be based upon solid, in-depth ethnographies of dance communities. These ethnographies need to take the dancers' points of view into consideration as much as possible. Consequently, each of the first three parts of this volume incorporates scholarly case studies *and* interviews with the dancers. We have not only included interview excerpts in which dancers themselves describe and reflect on the vernacular dance forms that have had such deep and abiding meaning in their lives, but we have also selected studies written by dance researchers who did not venture to draw conclusions until they had listened, carefully and respectfully, to what the dancers had to say.

The case studies—with European American, African American, and Native American forms as their subjects—suggest the cultural diversity found in the Appalachian region in particular and in the southeastern United States in general. In addition, Parts 1 and 3 include methodological discussions. Part 1, "Continuity and Change," deals primarily with dance forms that have developed more or less organically within a community. The main impetus for change has come from within the group itself or from the group members themselves having decided how to respond to an external factor precipitating some modification in the dance. Part 2, "Conserving Tradition," considers the conscious efforts of people from a particular culture to maintain a type of vernacular dance in the face of change. Part 3, "Inventing Tradition," examines both so-called revival dance and historical reconstructions. Often such groups build on existing traditions that they have adopted from other groups or cultures and then go on to create new forms or styles. The divisions among the three categories of dance discussed in this book did not prove to be nearly as clear-cut and simple as they first appeared. Overlaps and cross-currents abounded. Finally, Part 4, "Practical Suggestions for the Documentation of Traditional Dance," is intended to benefit readers who are inspired to go out into their communities and try their hands at research and documentation themselves.

The core purpose of the book is to stimulate dialogue and further research on American vernacular dance. It is our hope that this work will give rise to more good in-depth ethnographies and comparative ethnologies upon which to base theoretical and methodological studies. We will also be pleased if it helps to raise increasingly sophisticated and subtle questions about the nature and the complex relationship of dance, tradition, and community.

We believe that this book benefits from the deepening understanding of vernacular dance we acquired as a result of having pondered the often surprising connections and complicated issues that emerged as we read the scholarly studies and the words of the dancers over and over again. The end of the project felt like the end of a journey. By the time we reached our destination, we developed an appreciation for the often fluid and dynamic, always complex and intriguing world of vernacular dance and its connections to tradition and community.

NOTE

The 1989 and 1990 Center for Appalachian Studies and Services dance conferences served as special topic conferences of the Congress on Research in Dance.

1. See for example, Elizabeth Burchenal, ed. and trans., *Folk-dances of Denmark* (New York: G. Schirmer, 1915); Elizabeth Burchenal, *Folk-dances of Finland* (New York: G. Schirmer, 1915); *Dances of the People* (New York: Schirmer Music, 1913); and *Folk-Dances and Singing Games* (n. p., 1909).

Part 1

Continuity and Change

In these studies we have the opportunity to observe how people in communities make choices about vernacular dance. These choices then feed back into their senses of community and personal identity. Community, tradition, and the relationship of both to vernacular dance: these are the themes that emerge in "Continuity and Change," themes that will continually recur throughout the book.

Part 1 gathers together two types of dances that fit the popular conception of "traditional" dance quite easily—square dancing and solo percussive dance called, among other things, clogging. In addition, we include a dance form that may seem too "modern" to qualify as traditional: the African American fraternity step show.

First, a number of different but related versions of old-time square dance is the subject of the articles by dance ethnologist Susan Eike Spalding, caller Veronia Miller, and folklorists Paul Tyler and Colin Quigley. This family of closely related social dance forms goes by many names: old-time or big circle, the Kentucky Running Set, Appalachian or country-style. Most often danced to the accompaniment of live string band music and directed by a caller, the dance generally starts out with any number of couples "all joining hands" and forming one big circle. They then work their way into two-couple sets that execute a figure or figures, often with such evocative names as "cage-the-bird" or "lace-the-shoe." To conclude the dance, the caller usually maneuvers the group back into yet another large circle, and the dance ends.

The forerunner of Appalachian square dance was probably a blend of the dances of European settlers—predominantly Scots-Irish, English, German, and French

Huguenot—and those of Native Americans and enslaved Africans. The blending occured during the generation or more that all these groups lived in close proximity along the Eastern seacoast. It continued once people of European and African descent came into the southeastern mountains and interacted with cultures such as those of the Choctaw and Cherokee.

Old-time square dance should not be confused with the more well-known Western club square, danced by men in modified cowboy garb and women in short skirts buoyed up by layers of crinoline. Western club square has the four-couple square as its basic configuration and is invariably danced to recorded music. This twentieth-century form is much faster paced, complex, highly organized, and more mentally demanding than its more sociable Appalachian cousin. Although it is a very popular vernacular dance in Appalachia, it is essentially a national and international phenomenon, complete with highly organized club chapters and a series of lessons, which become progressively more challenging.

In addition, dance ethnologist Spalding describes the various types of percussive solo dance. From community to community, this group of similar solo dance forms goes by many names, such as flatfooting, buckdancing, and clogging. These different terms can indicate subtle or not-so-subtle stylistic differences. Their common denominator is the use of the feet to tap out complex rhythms. Spalding provides descriptions of what she calls "rhythm-making with the feet" (borrowing the phrase from dance ethnologist Frank Hall[1]) in three different areas of southwest Virginia. This is yet another form that many people from within and outside the region closely identify with the Appalachian region and the Southern states.

Folklorist Elizabeth Fine and college administrator Charles Collier both speak about African American stepping. Found in African American fraternities and sororities across the country and throughout the world, this performance-oriented dance combines singing, speaking, chanting, and highly precise, synchronized movement. On the one hand, the dance form does indeed have very strong African American folk roots. Fine makes the case for its being able to trace its origins back to ring shouts, a Civil War-era sacred dance, as well as to the dance that enslaved Africans brought with them to the New World. And, as Fine clearly points out, stepping incorporates a pervasive tradition of verbal dueling and word play. In addition to drawing on such longstanding cultural patterns, stepping also makes use of contemporary elements such as the latest rap and top-40s hits, advertising jingles, and television theme songs. Blending together traditional and contemporary elements, stepping has evolved into a complex and exhilarating performance event.

DISCUSSION

Vernacular dance shows the potential to play a variety of different roles as we move from community to community. For example, dance ethnologist Susan Spalding demonstrates how different types of old-time dancing in the Blue Ridge and in the Coalfields of Virginia grow out of existing communities. But dance can also be instrumental in creating a sense of community. Spalding found dance performing this function, at least to a limited extent, among the old-time dancers at the Chilhowie, Virginia, Lions' Club as they met several times a week to dance. Note the comments of Veronia Miller, who calls old-time square dances each week at the Beechwood Family Entertainment Center in Fall Branch, Tennessee. She observes that the old-time square dancers who come to the Beechwood grow to become "just one big family." Speaking about the square dancers of Hoagland, Indiana, folklorist Paul Tyler concludes, "More than an expression of community spirit, square dancing defines the Hoagland community. It helps bring the community into being."[2]

Similarly, folklorist Elizabeth Fine shows how in the case of the African American fraternities and sororities at a Virginia university, stepping helps bring the community into being and imparts to that community a sense of "differential identity." As we learn from college administrator and Alpha Phi Alpha alumnus Charles Collier, part of the pledging process consists of the new members learning their organization's particular movement style and then staging a step show. However, vernacular dance is not always about community cohesion. It can also express the stresses and strains within a community, as Fine demonstrates in her study of the cultural politics of stepping in Virginia.

Spalding makes the observation that at a given point in time, three southwest Virginia communities located in close proximity to each other interpret old-time square dance quite differently. Those differences in dance structure and style reflect each community's particular history and circumstances, values and needs. In contrast, Tyler, in his history of traditional square dance in Indiana, demonstrates how the dance remained relatively stable as the community expanded and redefined itself over time. "Where does community come from, and where does it go?" asks Tyler. "It goes with people as they interact in new settings, conserving old relationships while dealing with changes that affect their daily lives."[3]

Tyler's characterization of community as a flexible and fluid concept also captures our sense of tradition as a process. We do not see tradition as a quality inherent in a particular cultural form or as the exclusive property of a certain group of people. We do not view traditional dance as something that is handed down whole cloth. Instead we agree with folklorist Colin Quigley. He regards tradition as a process by which a community-based art form is created out of a repertoire of dance movements inherited from the past. It then continually evolves according to coordinating principles, rules that determine the proper ways in which these movement elements can be combined into a dance. Factors internal and external to the dance community, as well as the creativity of individual dancers, influence this process. In other words, tradition is the process—and vernacular dance is a medium—by which people in communities try to maintain continuity with their past while dealing with changing circumstances in their present. Dance we now call "traditional" exists in the present as the result of generations of change; it serves in turn as the source of future forms and styles.

The dancers described in Part 1 do not spontaneously discuss the issue of tradition a great deal. For example, Blue Ridge square dancers never mention the subject of tradition. Paradoxically, then, the more outside observers tend to see dance forms such as old-time square dance as solidly traditional, the less the dancers themselves seem to exhibit an awareness of tradition. Exceptions are the African American steppers and Clifford Steffey, the coal miner in southwest Virginia who took up the old-time percussive flatfoot dancing he had learned from his father during the 1989–1990 Pittston strike. He saw his dancing as a form of protest against management. In both cases, the dancers come from cultures that have been denigrated by others in mainstream society; in both cases, therefore, the assertion that they have traditional art forms worthy of respect is important to self-esteem.

Rates of change vary. The African American steppers and the old-time dancers of the Blue Ridge represent opposite poles on the continuity/change continuum. Fine shows how the ground rules of what does and does not constitute appropriate stepping respond rapidly to the Greek organizations' instituting a public competition. In contrast, Spalding depicts the dance of a stable Blue Ridge community slowly changing over a period of decades. While some of these case studies try to pinpoint the moment of change, all of them attempt to understand the critical factors affecting change and continuity. And they clearly illustrate the fact that "tradition" and "change" are not mutually exclusive realities.

This part also includes "Anglo-American Dance in Appalachia and Newfoundland: Toward a Comparative Framework" by Colin Quigley, a chapter that concentrates largely on the question of how scholars should study vernacular dance. Quigley is working toward the development of a sound comparative methodology for traditional dance. Although based on European American dance traditions, his efforts have relevance to other dance traditions as well. He begins with the structural analysis of movement itself and then moves outward, first to the dance event and then ultimately to the larger social context. Quigley's methods resemble a sociolinguistic approach, taking into account ever more minute units of movement, principles of coordination (or syntax), and the context, or nonmovement elements, of the dance event. He stresses the need to build comparisons on solid ethnographic case studies.

Two specific analytic tools are represented in this section: Laban Movement Analysis (qualitative analysis) and Labanotation (structural analysis). Both were initiated by Rudolf von Laban in the 1920s and have been developed since then by practitioners to become the most widely accepted systems of movement analysis. Spalding's study uses as its basis Laban Movement Analysis, which identifies movement themes and core characteristics by describing specific actions of parts of the body, dynamic qualities such as forcefulness and lightness, use of space, and ways that movement shapes the body and its parts. Quigley bases his conclusions on Labanotation, which uses symbols on a staff and results in a score describing direction, level, timing, and part of the body for the movements in sequence. Both are meticulous analytical tools and may be used together, but neither is sufficient for understanding vernacular dance. Quigley stresses the importance of understanding dance in the terms of the people whose dance it is. Researchers arrive at that type of understanding through interview and participation, taking care at the outset to examine their own expectations and assumptions. Such expectations and assumptions can easily color the investigator's perceptions and get in the way of a true understanding of vernacular dance.

Taken together, the chapters in Part 1 illustrate how complex and dynamic these vernacular dance forms, which are usually cited as solidly "traditional," can be. Clearly, *traditional* does not mean stagnant.

NOTES

1. Frank Hall, "Improvisation and Fixed Composition in Clogging," *Journal for the Anthropological Study of Human Movement* 3 (1984–1985): 200–17.

2. See Tyler, "Square Dancing in the Rural Midwest," in this volume.

3. See Tyler, "Square Dancing."

Chapter 1

Frolics, Hoedowns, and Four-Handed Reels: Variations in Old-Time Dancing in Three Southwest Virginia Communities

Susan Eike Spalding

When I tell friends or colleagues that I am researching Appalachian vernacular dance, their immediate and almost universal response is "Oh, clogging," accompanied by a quick tattoo of footwork. What they picture is precision clogging teams performing synchronized steps, with the girls wearing short skirts ballooning with crinolines. Other colleagues have somewhat different ideas about Appalachian vernacular dance. Some assume that I am talking about teams of college students wearing old-fashioned calico and gingham dresses and overalls and performing "big circle" dances at folk festivals. Still others translate "square dance" into Western club square dance, a type of dance learned in schools in the 1950s and practiced today by formalized clubs. Or they think back to the type of dance they saw on the last episode of "Hee Haw." Even people who realize that an indigenous tradition of old-time dance exists in the region tend to romanticize that tradition. They view it, like the log cabin, as a carryover from a subsistence farming lifestyle that has survived from the past among people cut off from mainstream American culture. What all these colleagues and friends have in common is the notion that there is one form, and one form only, of Appalachian dance.

Two authors, Jerry Duke[1] and Richard Nevell,[2] while obviously enjoying the dance forms and wanting to promote interest in them, add to such oversimplifications and generalizations. The representations in their two books correspond to a popular perception that Appalachian dancing consists of fancy footwork, almost like tap dancing, with lots of high kicks and team figure dancing including high energy swings and twirls. They fail to distinguish between dancing that is a truly local, community-based cultural expression, and that which is learned and taught strictly for performance or competition.

Some scholars have devoted attention to traditional Appalachian dance. Burt Feintuch,[3] Gail Matthews-DeNatale,[4] and Thomas Burns and Doris Mack[5] have each found relationships between structural or stylistic features of old-time dancing and sociocultural factors or value systems within a distinct geographical area. Paul Tyler,[6] Colin Quigley,[7] and Frank Hall[8] have done similar work with related dance forms outside the Appalachian region. However, even serious scholars who recognize the subtlety of style and form and its cultural relevance refer to Appalachian dance at times as if it were a single art form. During a 1989 conference on Appalachian traditional dance at East Tennessee State University, researchers from West Virginia, Virginia, North Carolina, and Kentucky refuted this monolithic view of Appalachian dance. They, in fact, found striking contrasts among the styles and forms from each of their states, although all were within the Appalachian region.

My own fieldwork quite clearly establishes the fact that within a very small area of southwest Virginia, three communities separated from each other by a drive of only about one hour exhibit real distinctions in dance repertoire, structure, context, and movement style. Old-time square dance caller Veronia Miller first called my attention to this fact. Pointing out a gentleman's stomping footwork and highly lifted knees, she said, "You can tell he's from Grundy [Virginia]."[9] Following her lead, I visited dances across southwest Virginia and discovered three distinct stylistic areas corresponding to geographical areas from west to east: the Coalfields area bordering Kentucky and West Virginia; the Valley; and the Blue Ridge. (Figure 1–1.) The dancing of all three areas does have certain common origins in the dance of colonial Americans, of Scots-Irish, German, and Free Black early settlers, and of the Cherokee. But it is also equally true that differing social, cultural, economic, and demographic factors in each area have influenced dance's evolution, resulting in distinct dissimilarities. This chapter attempts to delineate some of the factors affecting the development of the specific dance structures and styles and to demonstrate ways in which their impact is evidenced.

DEFINITIONS

For the purposes of this study, I chose to examine the two dance genres that local consultants report as being the oldest.[10] They refer to both of these dance genres as "old-time dancing."

The first of these is the "dance of rhythm-making with the feet,"[11] to borrow dance ethnologist Frank Hall's graphic phrase. Such dance is called *flatfooting* in the Blue Ridge, *clogging* in the Valley, and simply *dancing* in the Coalfields. In this genre, dancers hold their torsos relatively still, and their arms make few, if any, specific gestures, while their feet make rhythmic movements or sounds on the floor.

The second genre is old-time square dance. This type of dance begins and ends with patterns[12] involving the entire group of dancers, which may number a hundred or more. Patterns include "circling right and left," variations on the "grand right and

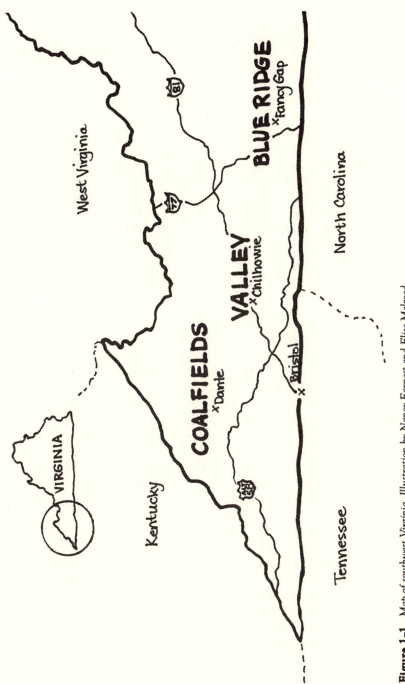

Figure 1-1. *Map of southwest Virginia. Illustration by Nancy Earnest and Elise Melrood.*

left," and "the London Bridge," in addition to snake-like and spiraling patterns.[13] In each area of southwest Virginia, these patterns have their own names, characteristic manner of performance, and placement within the dance structure. The middle portion of an old-time square dance consists of patterns by two couples joining together, with everyone dancing at the same time. Again, these have different structures, formats, and names in each community.

In general, old-time square dancing and flatfooting seem to have existed, at least in living memory, predominantly in farming communities. Dancers in the coal camps or in the larger towns did very little square dancing. Valley resident Louise Widner, born in 1899, remembers the term *country dancing* as the name used for square dancing and flatfooting in her youth. Town residents only danced the waltz.[14] Blue Ridge musician and dancer Calvin Cole, born in 1909, differentiates old-time dancing from the two step and the Charleston, which he termed "city things."[15] Coalfields consultant Nova Deel grew up in the country and, after moving to the coal camps, had to return to her country home for old-time dancing.[16]

Consultants born before 1925 in all three areas use the word *reel* to refer to what dancers now call old-time square dancing. Each also remembers his or her own version of a four-handed reel danced by two couples together, either alone or as part of the larger group. This four-handed reel is reminiscent of the traditional Scottish dance by the same name[17] and, at the same time, foreshadows the contemporary two-couple patterns.

Old-time dancing is currently popular among only a small percentage of the population of each area. Other population segments enjoy other types of dancing, such as ballroom, Western club square, rock, hiphop, and international folk.

METHOD

For purposes of comparison, I focused on a representative site in each geographical area. These sites had several factors in common. In each location, old-time dancing had been a regular weekly event for a number of years. The dances are community-based, serving as fund-raisers for worthy local causes. All ages are welcome, with restrictions on drinking enforced in order to create a family atmosphere. The dances feature live music, and the dance floor is almost never empty, except during the singing of one or two ballads during the course of an evening.

The specific sites of my fieldwork were the Dante Fire Hall in the Coalfields; the Chilhowie Lions' Club in the Valley; and Fancy Gap Elementary School in the Blue Ridge. During the course of the study, a United Mine Workers' strike began, a development that affected the Dante site and its dancing practices. Some of the documentation and interviews came from strike rallies. At each site, I made several visits; during one of these visits, I arranged for a professional film crew to videotape the dance. In addition, I interviewed several individuals in their homes and talked informally with many more. Perhaps most importantly, I participated in the dancing and experienced the learning process in each location. The dancers' responses to the finished video documentary[18] and to the rough footage provided invaluable information.

In each community, I studied the dance event, its internal structure, and its context. I based my analysis of the dance and the dance event on my observations of the dances during my visits and on my scrutiny of the videotapes. In each instance, I looked first at the overall style of those people dancing to glean an unspoken aesthetic. I then focused on those identified by others in the community as being good dancers and examined specific details of movement quality, posture, footwork, and arm and leg gestures. I refer to the other dances in the repertoire of each dance community only as a means of establishing context and the relative importance of the two genres I am considering.

I briefly outline the history of each area and of its old-time dancing tradition and then draw connections between social, cultural, and historical factors and the contemporary appearance of the dancing. It is impossible to know how the genres known today as flatfooting and old-time square dancing evolved prior to this century. I rely on the accounts of older consultants to give an indication of the appearance and context of these forms in living memory for comparison with current expression. Because it is the goal of this article to demonstrate the diversity within a relatively small geographic area and within only two dance forms, the exploration of each of the three areas is necessarily less extensive than it might be in a single ethnography. Because, like all vernacular art forms, old-time dancing continues to evolve and change, a visitor to any of these dance venues is likely to observe structural, stylistic, and contextual differences from my descriptions.

DANTE, RUSSELL COUNTY—THE COALFIELDS

History

Located among the many folds of the Cumberland Plateau area, Dante is west of the Virginia Valley and a few miles from the Kentucky state line. Taken together, the Cumberland Plateau of Virginia, eastern Kentucky and southern West Virginia is a major coal producing area. Although there are farming areas in the Coalfields, the coal mines and their support systems—railways, electrical lines, and the timbering that preceded the opening of the mines—have for most of this century provided the primary wage-paying jobs in the region. Therefore, it is the coal industry that in some way employs most of those who dance.

Although the winding roads have prevented rapid travel in and out of the Coalfields until the last two decades, it is the most culturally diverse area of southwest Virginia. This is due to the wholesale importation of workers for the timbering and coal mining industries, an influx that began in the 1890s. Among these imported workers were thousands of African Americans who were predominantly from Alabama and eastern North Carolina. In addition, mine owners brought Italian, Hungarian, and Polish immigrants to work in the mines. The difficult living and working conditions of the coal camps had a leveling effect among the various groups. Residents report mixed ethnicity dance halls and big band dances, resulting in cross-fertilization of art forms.

Conditions in the Coalfields have always been unstable, with a boom-and-bust economy, frequent strikes due to bad working conditions, and sudden deaths and prolonged illnesses resulting from the work. During periods of high unemployment, such as the fourteen to eighteen percent level in 1989, out-migration is rapid, but when jobs are available people return and newcomers arrive, bringing new customs with them. As a result, the population sometimes changes in size as much as 200 percent from one decade to the next.[19]

Old-Time Dancing History

Although square dancing is popular in the Coalfields of Kentucky, flatfooting, or "dancing," is currently the only old-time dancing in Dante. This was not always the case. Former dancer Nova Deel, born in 1914, remembers her uncle calling "hoedown dances" in her childhood and youth. At that time, people always held hands for the "reels," or two-couple patterns. The couples in the circle were counted off, and exact performance of the reels was very important. Just as in the Blue Ridge during the same period, one couple danced with every other couple in the ring and then the next couple took their turn and so forth. Besides square dancing, individuals did flatfooting and buckdancing, which always involved many specific steps, each with its own name. Nova Deel recalls the back step, or "buck and wing," as being the hardest.

In the 1920s, square dancing and flatfooting occurred at all weddings, during Christmas holidays, and at corn shuckings, molasses stir-offs, and other workings in the farming areas near the Coalfields. The primary instrument accompanying dancing at the time was the banjo, usually joined by the fiddle, guitar, and French harp.[20] This is the only area of the three included in this study where the banjo was the main instrument, perhaps reflecting the recent strong African American influence.[21] Most of the time, all ages danced together, although occasionally only the younger dancers danced with each other, and at times only the older ones were on the floor. People danced once a month on the average, less in the summer. Coalfields residents held dances either in the home or, quite frequently, in empty houses standing on their property.

In the coal camps of the 1920s and 1930s, old-time dancing did not usually occur, although there were occasional dances held in the school house. Still, other types of dances took place. For example, the Hungarian community held an annual Grape Arbor Festival and invited other coal camp residents to enjoy Hungarian music, dancing, and food. Coal camps also had dance halls or places like sweet shops with a band or, later, a juke box for popular dancing, and African American buck dancers filled the streets and porches on weekends and in the evenings.

At coal camp movies, silent short films shown before the feature demonstrated two new Charleston steps each Saturday afternoon, complete with subtitled directions. By practicing diligently, girls could learn over one hundred steps. Today, all Coalfields consultants, even one born in 1954, cite the Charleston as the basis for all dancing; they say that clogging is simply an updated version of the Charleston. Since many individual flatfoot and buck dance steps were already in the repertoire, it was undoubtedly enjoyable to learn more. The Charleston, emerging into the mainstream popular culture from Harlem, found fertile ground in an area so strongly influenced by African American culture. Perhaps its wildness met an expressive need in the stressful working and living environment of the Coalfields.

In the farming community of Brushy Ridge, people who gather on the porch to make music still do old-time dancing. There was no public place for old-time dancing until 1984, when the Dante Fire Hall began sponsoring country music and cake-walks[22] to raise money to buy a fire truck. These weekly country music evenings proved to be very effective fund-raisers, and subsequently the proceeds of these ongoing events have paid for two trucks and a rescue squad vehicle. Some consultants felt that people who will not go to the dances are not really interested in their community. Because of its fund-raising function, residents have come to associate old-time dancing with support for and commitment to the local community.

The Dance Event

Residents describe this regular event at the Fire Hall/Community Center as "having country music." The event is held in the fire house where the trucks are kept, with tables set up in front of the trucks, facing the dance floor and the band. Dress is casual, usually jeans. Pete Cassell and the Phillips Brothers is the regular house band, although once in a while organizers bring in another band. The style of music is essentially country rock,[23] with such tunes as "Johnny B. Good." Among the people attending, some have been dancing all their lives, like those from Brushy Ridge who everyone says were "born dancing." Many, however, have just started dancing since the Fire Hall/Community Center began having music. Consultants say that there are few other opportunities for recreation in the area and cite as a primary source of entertainment taking the family to the mall in Bristol, Tennessee-Virginia, or Kingsport, Tennessee, an hour drive away. The trip to the mall and the Friday night dances are family outings, and as a result, those who participate include teenagers, babies, great-grandparents, and adults of all ages.

A typical three-hour evening usually has six or eight cakewalks because these increase income, with the remainder of the time divided almost equally between two-stepping (couple dancing in the ballroom position) and the "dance of rhythm-making with the feet," known here only as "dancing." People say the reason there is no square dancing at the Community Center is that there is no one they can watch to teach them how it is done. Upon viewing the videotaped footage of the dancing, area residents talk nostalgically about old-time dancing and discuss finding a way to teach it to their children.

Structure and Style

The Coalfields dancing has an emphatic, almost explosive appearance and seems to provide residents with the opportunity to release tensions. The area's high energy style takes up more space than similar dancing does in the other two areas; it involves a stomping motion, with the heel digging into the floor for each step. The foot and lower leg swivel out to the side as the leg rotates inward on the gestures so that the foot comes off the floor. The torso is tilted almost forty-five degrees from the flexed hip joint. The torso exhibits great mobility with the upper and lower portions folding toward each other on the same side as the leg that kicks outward to the side. The arms sometimes even move above the head, and legs swing far out to the side. Dancers in the other two areas, the Blue Ridge or the Valley, do not use such expansive gestures or movement within the torso. Some Coalfields dancers rhythmically pat their thighs, chest, and arms with their hands, reflecting the cultural exchange between African Americans and others in the coal camps.

Some individuals or small groups take the dance floor, but most dancing and two-stepping is for couples and is associated with flirting. When I commented to a Coalfields resident that although at the other two locations I was frequently asked to dance, I was never asked in Dante, she said, "They would ask you to dance if they wanted to take you out." For the entire duration of each dance, the partners maintain eye contact and constantly circle each other while moving toward each other and then away, nonverbally expressing the courting function of the dance. The couple establishes a mutual rhythm but does not attempt to relate rhythmically or spatially to the other dancers. Because they presently do no square dancing, there never is a large patterned group in which to submerge the individual.

During the course of the study, the United Mine Workers' strike was taking place. The strike had the effect of bringing out old-time dancers and musicians at the rallies and on the picket lines. Some, who would never flatfoot before because it was too old-fashioned, began to dance with vigor as an expression of their support for the strike. Dancer Clifford "Redbone" Steffey, born in 1946, says his father was an excellent dancer, but he himself never danced until the day the strike began. He says he did it as a protest, to help draw a crowd, and to show the talents of the people of the area.[24] In a comment that illustrates the expressive nature of dancing in the Coalfields, Steffey said that dancing eased him when he was troubled by events in the strike. When asked what he thought about when he was dancing, he replied that he imagined "getting hold of them scabs [non-union replacement workers] and stomping on them."[25] Old-time dancing, therefore, is associated with cultural pride and serves as a means of identifying oneself with the common good.

CHILHOWIE, SMYTH COUNTY—THE VALLEY

Chilhowie's History

Chilhowie is located in the southern portion of "the Great Valley of Virginia," east of the Coalfields and west of the Blue Ridge Mountains. It stands in a major traffic corridor running from Pennsylvania to Tennessee, a corridor that has brought immigrants and new ideas to the Valley ever since the arrival of the first white settlers. During the first half of this century there were already several large towns in the Valley, and by the 1920s roads were so good that it was not unusual for people to travel up to thirty miles by car to reach these towns. Carnivals came regularly to the Valley town of Marion, and the citizens of Abingdon were drafted to participate in plays directed by outside professionals at the Opera House. All these factors resulted in a mobility and exposure to outside influences unparalleled in either the Coalfields or the Blue Ridge. Valley residents have developed a taste for change and variety and a faster-paced lifestyle than those of the other areas.

Several industrial parks have been built in the second half of this century, serving as a major source of employment for residents of the area. Before that time the Valley was essentially agricultural, and tobacco continues to be an important cash crop. Many dancers work for one of the school systems as teachers, custodians, or groundskeepers, or own private businesses such as nurseries, garages, or construction companies.

Old-Time Dancing History

By the beginning of this century, old-time square dancing was similar in form to the contemporary version. Louise Widner, born in 1899, describes most of the patterns danced today as being done in her youth. The whole circle would break into small circles of two couples; all the small circles danced at the same time and then changed partners. Each two-couple circle "made puzzles" by continuously holding hands with each other and going under each other's arms all during the execution of the patterns.[26] Around 1912, people in the Valley held dances in different homes every night for two weeks at Christmas time. The dancers were high school students and young adults, though young children were in attendance. The fiddlers and callers were older. In the mid-1920s, dances were held in homes more or less weekly year-round, in addition to the periodic dances that took place in conjunction with quilting bees, corn shuckings, and barn raisings. The fiddle—accompanied by a banjo, guitar, and bass—was the main instrument used by the musicians.

Consultants tell of square dancing acquiring a bad name by the 1930s because of the drinking and roughhousing associated with the dances. Musician Bill McCall, born in 1927, recalls that his father played for dances but would not let him attend them in his youth. In fact, "a boy carrying a guitar was considered trifling," he says.[27] Chilhowie High School sponsored regular square dances attended by young adults during the 1940s, but by this time the students preferred popular dances like the jitterbug and folk dances such as the Texas Schottische and the Patty Cake Polka taught by ministerial students from Emory and Henry College. They also felt ashamed of "hillbilly music" made by performers such as early bluegrass musician Ernest Tubb. As a result of these two factors—cultural embarrassment and negative associations—very few young people born after the late 1920s learned old-time dancing from their families.

This accounts for the fact that even though they are lifetime residents of the area, many of those who dance at the Chilhowie Lions' Club have only learned since 1981, with the opening of the predecessor of the Lions' Club dance. It is common to hear praise of how much one or another of the dancers has improved. Evelyn

Sturgill hypothesizes that this resurgence of interest in old-time dancing is part of a growth in regional self-esteem. "We have learned to appreciate all the things we were ashamed of. We get out our old quilts and things we used to make. We have had a revival of appreciation of our heritage."[28]

Dancing has become the primary recreation for many Lions' Club dancers. There are at least a half dozen places to dance elsewhere in the valley, the furthest being about an hour from Chilhowie. Most who attend the Lions' Club on Fridays go to one of these other establishments on Saturdays and take clogging or waltzing lessons one or two nights a week. As Gene and Jane Salyers responded when asked about other types of recreation, "I don't know what we *did* do before we danced!"[29] Old-time dancing, then, is both a novel recreational pastime and a connection to the regional heritage in the Valley.

The Dance Event

The dance takes place in the Lions' Club building, which has a pleasant restaurant-like atmosphere; opposite the tiled dance floor are wooden tables on carpeted floor. Couples dress up to attend, with some men wearing Western shirts and string ties and many of the women wearing full skirts and peasant blouses. Each week, organizers book a different band with a style ranging from country to bluegrass, and from old-time to country rock. Attendance varies according to the popularity of the band. During an evening, two or three different callers take the microphone for the square dances, and even those who have never done so before are welcome to try.

Along with an occasional waltz, the preferred dance form at the Lions' Club is two-stepping, which occupies over half of the time. The evening also usually includes two or three square dances of fifteen minutes each, one or two Paul Jones mixers,[30] and clogging—sometimes done as a polka or jitterbug. Couple dances predominate, with square dances providing an opportunity for couples to interact with each other in dance.

Structure and Style

The repertoire at Chilhowie is more varied than at the other two locations. In both the square dance and clogging styles, skill and variety are paramount.

After the initial "circle left and right," "swing," "promenade," and a large group pattern such as "grand right and left," each square dance includes at least six different two-couple patterns; the conclusion involves two to four large group patterns. In the two-couple patterns, couples join with other couples nearby on the periphery; they only cross the circle if no couple is available next to them. They frequently enter the circle next to others with whom they would like to dance and may "circle up four" with the same couple throughout the dance.

Almost all two-couple patterns in the Valley involve all four dancers holding hands and going under each other's arms in various ways and staying on or close to the starting position. An example is "the corkscrew," which begins with two couples holding hands in a circle. One man lets go of the hand of the woman to his left and leads the others under the uplifted arm of that woman and her partner, going around behind the man in a clockwise circle. He then goes under the arms of that man and his own partner in another full clockwise circle. Returning to his place, he joins hands with the other woman, and the other man then repeats the process. Each man then swings first the other woman and then his own partner. The caller may then call another four-person pattern before a short promenade followed by another sequence of two or three "circle fours."

Throughout the "circle fours," the caller keeps up a rhyming patter which results in all the dancers moving in unison at a fast clip. For the "corkscrew," he might say, "Everybody do a little soft shoe, First gent do the old corkscrew. . . . Now the next gent do that too." These patter calls are similar to Western club square dance patter or hash calls,[31] and in fact, some of the Chilhowie dancers participated in the Western square dance clubs popular in the Valley since the 1950s and 1960s.

Clogging, the Valley name for the "dance of rhythm-making with the feet," emphasizes variety in footwork. Dancers arrange themselves in groups of two to six and maintain the group throughout the clogging tune, establishing a rhythm with the small group. The torso is tilted somewhat forward from the flexed hip (but less far forward than the Coalfields tilt) and held very still, drawing attention to the footwork. The whole foot is placed on the floor for each step; the legs rotate inward each time the foot is lifted behind on the "and" beats and rotate outward for the placing of the foot on the floor for the main beats. Dancers accomplish this rapid, accented in-out rotation with extreme quickness. Most of those identified as good dancers take clogging lessons where they learn specific steps to incorporate into their Friday night dancing.

The dancers value formality in appearance. In the swing and promenade holds, attention on the hands gives a sense of distance between partners. For the promenade, only the hands make contact, with left hands clasped in front of the waist and right hands grasped either beside the woman's right shoulder or in front of the waist. Kirby Smith, who has called and taught old-time dancing for fifty years, says, "If you want to hug [after the dance event], that's fine. But on the dance floor, be a gentleman, be a lady."[32] The variety in repertoire, in clogging steps, and in square dance patterns reflects a love of change and stimulation on the part of the Valley dancers, which has developed over generations of living in a travel corridor. The rapid speed of the square dance and its many quick changes may be seen as reflecting the faster-paced lifestyle in the Valley, while at the same time making a connection with the area's agrarian past since, as mentioned earlier, historically it was done only in the country, never in towns.

Residents cite dancing as a source of fellowship. A community of dancers—interest-based rather than geographically based—has developed as a result of the dancers' seeing each other several times a week at dances and lessons. Dancer and musician Bill McCall recounts the unexpected condolences he received from other dancers on the death of his mother. He says, "I think people are as congenial as they ever were. I think the reason we don't show it is because we don't visit [as we once did].

I think this [dancing] has sort of overcome some of that."[33] Although dancing with many different people is not a primary goal of the evening, participants do take care that everyone is given an opportunity to dance. Bill McCall says, "My wife's not jealous. She *wants* me to dance with the widows and single women!"[34] Caller Kirby Smith says, "If you don't have someone to dance with, come on your own. We'll make sure you get somebody."[35]

Because dancing fills the role of a primary recreation or hobby among the Valley dancers, those who participate in it are inclined to improve their skills, trade ideas with each other, and find new outlets and opportunities. At least some of the dancers have gotten interested in performing. A group from the Lions' Club began offering demonstrations at the 1990 Virginia Highlands Festival and went on to perform at the Smithsonian Institution's 1993 Festival of American Folklife.

FANCY GAP, CARROLL COUNTY—THE BLUE RIDGE

History

Fancy Gap is located a few miles from the North Carolina border atop the Blue Ridge Mountains of Virginia; the Blue Ridge runs from the northeast to the southwest and lies east of Virginia's Great Valley and west of the Piedmont Plateau. Carroll County is essentially rural, with numerous cabbage and sheep farms. The primary sources of livelihood for the dancers are the furniture and textile factories that came to the area in the early part of this century. Women are also teachers or aides in schools and rest homes. Many people own or work for private businesses and then farm on the side for additional income. When the Blue Ridge Parkway was built, it provided jobs for many local people, and some have worked for the Park Service all their lives. The area is very stable, with little in- or out-migration. Unemployment has never exceeded four percent. Although many fought in World War II or have had work that took them away, most dancers still live within a few miles of their home places and would rather commute two hours to work than move away.

Old-Time Dancing History

Born in 1917, caller Roncie Bunn remembers that when he was a youngster, his uncle called all the same old-time square patterns that appear today. Back in his youth, however, the patterns had different names. Another difference was that only one couple moved around the circle, dancing the pattern with each other couple in turn. After the first couple had danced the pattern with all the other couples, then the next couple took a turn traveling around the circle. His uncle had been calling dances all his life, so Bunn's recollections mean that these patterns and the general form of the old-time square date back at least to the beginning of this century.[36]

Dancing occurred on a regular basis in homes, barns, or unused houses in the Blue Ridge until the early 1950s.[37] Dances—weekly in some communities, less frequently in others—were accompanied by fiddle, banjo, and guitar. Caller Verlyn

Brady recounts "all night frolics" in the 1940s that lasted for two days and nights in homes at Christmas time. Everyone from teenagers to middle-aged persons attended these dances.[38] The first public dances occurred around that time.

In the 1960s, wagon trains, which always included dancing in the evenings, became a popular recreation. Friends gathered to drive their old farm wagons and horses, no longer needed for farm work. By 1970, wagon training had become a week-long event involving as many as two hundred people during the Fourth of July holiday. Each night, the group arrived at a different school, where the Parent Teacher Association (PTA) provided a supper for sale and a band for dancing. The journey concluded on Friday night at Fancy Gap School. The dances at Fancy Gap were so popular, they became a year-round event. Old-time dancing, through its connection with the wagon train, is associated with the former rural lifestyle and grows out of an already existing community.

The Dance Event

The Fancy Gap Elementary School's PTA has organized the dance at Fancy Gap every Friday night since approximately 1971, making it the longest running dance in this study. Held in the school cafeteria, it is an ongoing fund-raising project of the PTA. Dancers agree that good old-time music is the most important ingredient for good dancing. For many years, the regular band has been Whit Sizemore and the Southern Ramblers, who play old-time music exclusively. The idea of taking dance lessons is comical to Fancy Gap dancers. As one dancer said, "How *would* you teach this?" Musician and dancer Calvin Cole says, "Just watch the lady in front of you. If she falls down, you fall down too."[39]

Old-time dancers are mostly middle-aged people and retirees who have been dancing all their lives, although each Friday the group of two- to three-hundred dancers also includes twenty or so children and teens who attend with their parents or on their own. In some cases, three generations of dancers in one family attend together.

In Fancy Gap, several consultants placed emphasis on the importance of having a big crowd in order to have a good time. Their only complaint on viewing the video-taped footage of their dance was that because we filmed on the night of a flood, and only about one hundred people attended, the tape did not show the characteristic "room bursting with people." Dancing has remained a constant in community life rather than waning and waxing and continues to be part of a varied fabric of community-based recreation that includes ball games, fairs, wagon training, and family get-togethers. Square dancing predominates at Fancy Gap in terms of time spent and numbers of people participating. Each Friday evening includes eight square dances of approximately fifteen minutes, occupying a total of two out of the three hours. In between the square dances, the band plays a ballad or a flatfoot or two-step tune to allow the dancers and musicians to rest. Sometimes two- to three-hundred dancers join the circle for a square dance, but never more than fifty to a hundred take the floor for the other dances. Interaction with the large community group is the most important part of the evening. (Figure 1–2.)

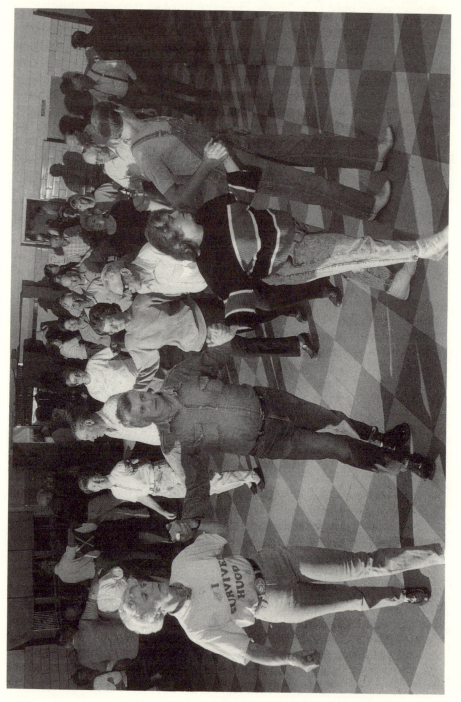

Figure 1-2. *Old-time dancers at Fancy Gap, Virginia. Photograph by Kenneth Murray.*

Structure and Style

Similar in structure to those at Chilhowie, each Fancy Gap square dance begins with "circle left and right," "swing the partner," "promenade," and another pattern for the whole group. The promenade has a more informal appearance here than in Chilhowie. The partners' arms are casually draped on each other, the woman's left hand on the man's right shoulder and his right hand on her waist.

The center portion of the dance consists of only one two-couple pattern, which caller Verlyn Brady terms the "main dance," rather than several different patterns, as was the case in Chilhowie. In it, couples join with others nearby or across the circle, not just on the periphery. They repeatedly do the same pattern, determining their own pacing for each interaction. The effect is a cheerful, rhythmic free-for-all in which the shape of the circle completely dissolves. This process takes about ten minutes, during which time the caller does not speak at all. Mr. Brady says he thinks that the dancers want him to say as little as possible so they can enjoy the dancing and the music.[40] When he calls "swing your partner and promenade," couples complete the entire pattern they are doing, even though they may have just begun it, before swinging and then filtering into the promenade circle. As the term "main dance" implies, this opportunity to interact with other couples and individuals at a pace mutually established within each group of four is clearly the most important part of the evening's most popular dance.

Various whole group patterns conclude each dance. Examples are a bridge pattern performed around the periphery of the circle, with couples passing under the upraised arms of the oncoming line of other couples, and a snake-like pattern in which lines of four dancers are successively joined until all form one long line. This long line is led eventually into a tight spiral. For some of these large group patterns, Mr. Brady leaves the stage and directs the group with gestures and words rather than using a call, a technique reminiscent of an older style in which the caller directs while he dances.

In the characteristic four-person patterns in the Blue Ridge, the dancers rarely hold hands with each other; instead they dance circular patterns around each other. An example is "lady round the lady" in which one woman dances around the other woman and then around the other man, while her partner dances around the other man and then around the other woman. Like every two-couple pattern, it ends with swinging the other person's partner and then one's own partner.

On completion of each pattern, the two couples separate and flatfoot while looking for other free couples with whom to dance. They often cross the room to find another couple and never dance with the same pair twice. The goal of the evening is to dance with as many different people as possible. Socializing with neighbors and longtime friends is an important part of the entertainment of the evening. As dancer and musician Calvin Cole says, "I like to go, like to dance, like the music, like the people . . . like to ask and be asked . . . like to grab first one and then the other" to dance with.[41]

Flatfooting is the name given in Fancy Gap to the "dance of rhythm-making with the feet." Those identified as good dancers barely lift their feet off the floor, keeping them directly under the body and letting the forearms hang close to their sides. A certain reserve is important. Arm and leg gestures that are too flamboyant or swinging someone too hard are considered unacceptable, "more acting [showing off] than dancing."[42]

Torsos are tilted very slightly forward, even less than at Chilhowie. With their postures creating an air of introspection, the dancers gaze forward and down. They listen to the music and, with the balls of their feet, make small patting gestures that correspond to what they hear. Cole says that good dancers will just "pat a tune with [their] feet . . . tick, tap, tap, hitting the tune right along."[43] No one here has the notion of producing certain steps. Everyone on the dance floor forms a network within arm's reach of the next dancer and turns right and left on every phrase or two as if to be available to the other dancers. In flatfooting and in square dancing, the whole group establishes a beat together by slightly lowering the center of gravity on each beat and then letting it rebound to normal on the "and," with a fluid and resilient rocking motion. Even in the solo dance of flatfooting, then, the individual is in relation with all others and with the music.

SUMMARY AND CONCLUSIONS

"Rhythm-making with the feet" varies among the three communities to such an extent that I have begun to believe that the different names represent not just different styles, but different dances. To summarize: the footwork of the Coalfields emphasizes the heel. In the Valley, dancers use the whole foot, while in the Blue Ridge, they pat the toe or ball of the foot on the floor. The Coalfields dancers swivel the turned-in leg out to the side, the Valley dancers pick their feet up behind, and the Blue Ridge dancers keep their feet directly beneath them and very close to the floor. The Coalfields dancing feels emphatic, the Valley dancing accented, and the Blue Ridge style is resilient. The forward tilt of the torso is most extreme in the Coalfields, less so in the Valley, and least in the Blue Ridge. Group size increases progressively from only two people in the Coalfields to groups of from two to six dancers in the Valley to the entire room full of dancers in the Blue Ridge. As group size increases, eye contact decreases, ranging from almost constant contact with the partner in the Coalfields, to fleeting contact among the small group in the Valley, to almost no contact at all in the Blue Ridge. Only Coalfields dancers raise their arms above shoulder level. Valley dancers keep them bent at the elbow at waist level, and Blue Ridge dancers let them hang by their sides.

Square dance also varies from site to site in the two locations—the Valley and the Blue Ridge—where such dancing takes place. While keeping many of the style characteristics of the clogging/flatfooting in each area, the square dancing also varies structurally. For example, each Valley square dance features six to eight two-couple patterns, or "circle fours," and the emphasis is on variety and skill. The caller's patter style keeps all the dancers moving in unison at a fast pace. In the Blue Ridge, the caller calls only one two-couple pattern—the "main dance"—in each dance. In addition he speaks very little, allowing the dancers' primary focus of attention to be dancing to the music and dancing with as many other couples as possible. In the Valley, all four dancers usually hold onto each other's hands all during the "circle-four" pattern; in the Blue Ridge, the dancers are usually unattached while executing the two-couple "main dance" patterns.

These differences undoubtedly reflect the experiences of the dancers during this century. Coalfields dancing reflects its heritage, a heritage that consists of many specific flatfoot, buck dance, and Charleston steps and the general cultural diversity that characterized the coal camps. In particular, a strong African American influence is evident in the Coalfields dancing. With its extreme forcefulness and large movements, the dancing also gives people the opportunity for individual expression in a stressful environment. Finally, old-time dancing is associated with cultural pride.

Since the time of the first settlers from the Eastern seacoast, Valley residents have been exposed to a multitude of diverse influences due to living in a travel corridor. In addition, the residents' location has resulted in a mobility that has in turn produced a faster-paced lifestyle. Their clogging style, which emphasizes variety, and their fast-moving and varied square dance structure reflect these factors. For the Valley residents, old-time dancing is a novel form of recreation and a way of connecting with their history.

More than the other regions, the Blue Ridge communities continued in the nineteenth century model of rural Appalachian settlements outlined by historian Ronald Eller, with politics and religion organized along kinship lines and with personal freedom being valued within a closely knit framework.[44] The square dance provides a clear structure within which individuals, attending with their families, are free to interact according to their own sense of time.

Today, the differences in old-time dancing among the three areas also reflect the varying place of dance in the community and in the lives of the individuals, resulting in equally varied attitudes toward dance. In the Coalfields, old-time dancing is used as a form of personal expression and as a way of getting to know other individuals. In fact, people often choose their partners in order to flirt with them. Dance solidifies the larger community group by supporting the miners' strike and providing funds for the fire department.

In the Valley, old-time dancing is a hobby and a form of exercise, pursued for its own sake by individuals and couples. As a result of seeing each other at several dance events each week, the dancers have developed a sense of community among themselves, but it is limited in that they rarely get together except for dances or dance classes. They have also come to value the performance skill that develops as a result of practice. In the Valley, dancers choose their partners either because they are among the best dancers, or in order to give everyone a chance to dance.

Finally, in the Blue Ridge, old-time dancing grows out of an existing community and serves to perpetuate and reinforce that community. It is viewed as one of several ways of socializing among area residents who have known each other all their lives. The goal of dancing in the Blue Ridge, then, is to mix and connect with as many people as possible.

There is certainly no such phenomenon as a single old-time Appalachian dance style for either "rhythm-making with the feet" or square dance. Economic, political, social, and demographic factors have influenced old-time dancing. In each geographical area, these factors laid the groundwork for particular responses to popular dance styles as they appeared. New stylistic elements have been incorporated into the dancing according to each community's specific expectations and attitudes.

In the Coalfields and in the Valley, where old-time dancing was frowned on, this form of dance has re-emerged as an expression of pride in one's heritage. In the Blue Ridge, where it has always been a part of the life of the community, it continues to reinforce that community even as it incorporates change. Dancers and dance communities make choices in style and repertoire according to their distinct aesthetics and values. The results of these choices, in turn, further shape the attitudes of the dancers, either reinforcing or altering the structure and style of the dancing and its place in the life of the community.

NOTES

1. Jerry Duke, *Clog Dance in the Appalachian Mountains* (San Francisco: Duke Publishing Co., 1984).

2. Richard Nevell, *A Time to Dance: American Country Dancing from Hornpipes to Hot Hash* (New York: St. Martin's Press, 1977).

3. Burt Feintuch, "Dancing to the Music: Domestic Square Dances and Community in Southcentral Kentucky 1880-1940," *Journal of the Folklore Institute* 18, no. 1 (January-April 1981): 49-68.

4. Gail Matthews, "Cutting a Dido: A Dancer's Eye View of Mountain Dance in Haywood County, North Carolina" (M.A. thesis, Indiana University, 1983), and Gail Matthews-DeNatale, "Kinesic Conversations: Statements about Identity and Worldview in Appalachian Dance," in *Of, By, and For the People: How Dance Proclaims Political Ideals, Ethnicity, Social Class, and Regional Pride* (Riverside, California: Society of Dance History Scholars/Congress on Research in Dance, 1993).

5. Thomas A. Burns with Doris Mack, "Social Symbolism in a Rural Square Dance Event," *Southern Folklore Quarterly* 42, no. 4 (1978): 295-327.

6. Paul L. Tyler, "Square Dancing in the Rural Midwest: Dance Events and the Location of Community," in this volume.

7. Colin Quigley, *Close to the Floor: Folk Dance in Newfoundland* (St. John's: Memorial University of Newfoundland Folklore & Language Publications, 1985).

8. Frank Hall, "Improvisation and Fixed Composition in Clogging," *Journal for the Anthropological Study of Human Movement* 3 (1984-1985): 200-17.

9. Veronica Miller, conversation with the author, 20 July 1988.

10. I use the term *consultant* in order to recognize the expertise of local individuals who provided the information for this study.

11. Hall, "Improvisation and Fixed Composition in Clogging."

12. I use the term *pattern* rather than *figure* because figure is not a local term for the units of the square dance. Although pattern is also not a local term, I use it as a more neutral term.

13. Although these patterns bear a resemblance to commonly known folk and Western club square dance figures, I am deliberately avoiding using the names from those other forms;

I want to make clear the distinction between indigenous old-time square dancing and these other forms.

14. Louise Hamm Widner, interview with the author, 3 August 1989.

15. Calvin Cole, interview with the author, 30 June 1989. Originally appeared in Anne Johnson and Susan Spalding, *Step Back Cindy*, 30-min. VHS 1/2-inch video documentary (Whitesburg, Kentucky: Appalshop, 1990).

16. Nova Deel, interview with the author, 5 July 1989.

17. J. P. and T. M. Flett, *Traditional Dancing in Scotland* (London and Boston: Routledge & Kegan Paul, 1964).

18. Johnson and Spalding, *Step Back Cindy*.

19. Karl B. Raitz and Richard Ulack, *Appalachia, A Regional Geography* (Boulder, Colorado: Westview Press, 1984), 162–163.

20. Deel, interview.

21. The African and African American origins of the banjo are thoroughly documented by Dena J. Epstein in *Sinful Tunes and Spirituals: Black Folk Music to the Civil War* (Urbana: University of Illinois Press, 1977), 34–38. It is reasonable to assume that the predominance of the banjo in the Coalfields, and not in the other subregions, is due in part to the greater African American population in the Coalfields in the first half of this century.

22. A cakewalk is a raffle in which a homemade cake is the prize.

23. For definitions of various styles of music, see Bill Malone, *Country Music, U.S.A.: A Fifty Year History* (Austin: University of Texas Press, 1968).

24. Clifford Steffey, interview with Anne Johnson, 30 August 1989.

25. Steffey, interview.

26. Widner, interview.

27. Bill McCall, interview with the author, 5 July 1989.

28. Evelyn Sturgill, interview with the author, 3 August 1989.

29. Gene and Jane Salyers, conversation with the author, 21 March 1989.

30. In a Paul Jones, couples change partners at a signal from the leader.

31. In Western club square dance, there are two types of calls: patter or hash calls, and singing calls. Patter or hash calls are chanted rhymed couplets which are essentially faster-paced versions of those found in old-time square dance. Unlike old-time calls, singing calls are actually sung along with the music.

32. Kirby Smith, interview with the author, 21 August 1989.

33. McCall, interview.

34. McCall, interview.

35. Smith, interview.

36. Roncie Bunn, interview with the author, 18 July 1989.

37. Charlotte Bevil, interview with the author, 18 July 1989.

38. Verlyn Brady, interview with the author, 30 June 1989.

39. Cole, interview.

40. Brady, interview.

41. Cole, interview.

42. Cole, interview.

43. Cole, interview.

44. Ronald D. Eller, *Miners, Millhands and Mountaineers: The Modernization of the Appalachian South, 1880–1930* (Ann Arbor, Michigan: University Microfilms International, 1976), 45–46.

Chapter 2

"You Have to Watch Your People": Calling Old-Time Appalachian Square Dance

AN INTERVIEW WITH VERONIA MILLER

Susan Eike Spalding and Jane Harris Woodside

Veronia Miller calls old-time square dances weekly at the Beechwood Family Entertainment Center in Fall Branch, Tennessee. A native of northeast Tennessee,
Miller is retired from manufacturing work. In the mid-1970s, she began square
dancing with her husband, a caller and lifelong square dancer. After his death in
the early 1980s, she took over his calling duties. In 1984 and 1985, she participated in a Folk Arts in the Schools program sponsored jointly by the Country
Music Foundation in Nashville, Tennessee, and the Center for Appalachian Studies and Services (CASS) of East Tennessee State University in Johnson City, Tennessee. In 1990 and 1991, she conducted dance workshops for the Seminar on
Older Persons sponsored by Southwest Virginia Training Consortium in Abingdon, Virginia, called square dances at the 1992 Old Oaks Festival at Tusculum
College in Greeneville, Tennessee, and has taught old-time square dance at Milligan College in Milligan, Tennessee. These excerpts are from an interview conducted by Susan Eike Spalding and Jane Harris Woodside in August, 1987.

It was probably 1976 or 1977 that my husband and I started going to dance at Slagle's Pasture in Elizabethton, Tennessee. My husband had to stop dancing when he
had a heart attack so he started calling the square dances. Slagle's Pasture originally
started as just a group of people listening to the music. Then they wanted to get
into square dancing, so they asked him to come call and get the square dances
started.

I guess we had gone over there on Saturday nights about five years before he died.
I had a partner from Sugar Grove, North Carolina, and he and I led the square danc-

ing. And then one Saturday night—my husband always had lodge meetings once a month on Saturday nights—he was late getting there, and someone asked me to call a square dance. I said, "I don't know how." They said, "Yes you do." Well, I figured if I can dance it, I ought to be able to call it, so I got up and called it. After that, every time he was absent, I called the square dances. And then after he passed away, I decided just to call. And that's how I got into square dance calling.

I've been calling at the Beechwood here in Fall Branch since about 1985. You meet so many nice people in square dancing. I think many years ago there was a lot of drinking at square dances, but all the places I go, they don't allow drinking. And you get to where you're just one big family. You know everybody, and you know their children and their children's children.

We're a lot of middle-aged people. Of course, there are a few younger ones, but I guess you feel more relaxed if you're with people more your own age. And being a widow myself, I know that there's so many things that a widow doesn't fit in without a partner. But you know, you can go down there and flatfoot. And we have a lot of men that maybe their wife doesn't dance, and they will ask someone else to dance so that the widows and the single women do get to dance.

Of course, a lot of my husband's calls, I use. I've added a few, and there's a few more I'd like to add if I can get my people together enough to do it. I got some calls out of a library book. It was a history of dance, I think, all types of dance, that I found at a school library. Of course, you know, you have to change the wording a little bit to go with the music. Usually your square dance calls are little snappy words that rhyme. And some of these words, you just have to change the meaning, put a different word in that will more or less rhyme with what you're using. I think it just sounds better. For example: "Make your feet go wickety-whack." Well, that sounds more like something you'd use for a child.

When you're calling a dance, you think about what you're going to use before you use it. I mean, your mind, the little cogs up there, have to be going around so you can think of what your next call is going to be, even though you've got a general idea of what you're going to use. Sometimes you know, that figure with the "right hand cross and the left one back" or "right hand cross and both hands back?" Well, sometimes you get started and you think, "Now which one am I using?" Sometimes, I guess, I'm so repetitious that I've noticed that if I say "right hand cross," sometimes you'll see the dancers put that left one back. And when I see somebody doing that, I'll automatically say "and both hands back" to catch them off guard. You just have to switch them around. You don't want to be too predictable.

What makes a good caller? Well, I always thought a person had to have a loud enough voice to come out over the music. And the square dance caller has to speak very plain. You have to go slow enough for the dancers to hear you. I have called square dances sometimes where the PA system wasn't very good. You can tell very shortly that you aren't being heard because they'll start sticking their hand up behind their ears to let you know they can't hear you.

I still think I sound terrible on a tape. One night, the band didn't show up down at Beechwood, and someone had recorded an entire program so I got to hear myself call a square dance. I was hysterical. I said, "I don't believe I *sound* like that." I think men make much better square dance callers because they have a more bassy voice. You know, it echoes above the music. If you get a high-pitched instrument and a lady with a high-pitched voice, you just don't hear her well. Her pronunciation of the words doesn't come out right.

Back in the old days, it just wasn't a woman's place to call a square dance. It wasn't very feminine, I don't think. I think women thought it was a man's place to call. Of course, we're getting women ministers now, and you know, it used to be you never heard of a lady that was a minister. I think it kind of follows the trends.

You have to watch your people. That's the main thing because you could just get out there and look out in the audience and start calling square dance calls, and you'd really have a holocaust on the floor. In your Western club square dances, they sing their calls. It is a much faster dance. In Appalachian square dancing, you wait for the person to do what you called. What I do, I pick out my slowest couple, and I watch them. When I call something, and they have done it one time, I know everybody else has done it twice. If you get up there and you just start calling and calling and calling, well, your people haven't done what you called the first time by the time you've gotten to your third call. So you have to watch your people.

Now, it's very easy to go completely blank when you're calling square dances. You just let them keep promenading around until something comes to you. You get distracted, you get to listening to the music. If it's a real good fiddle tune, you've got your mind on that music. And if there's someone out there that's a clown on the floor, you get to watching them. I get so interested in what's going on, I have wondered sometimes how long it's been since I called a call. But that's the fun of it. You have to just put yourself in there like you were going around with them. That's the way I do it. In fact, I'd *love* to be down there dancing. I never get a chance because if there's ever anyone down at the Beechwood that calls square dances, and I'm there, usually they won't call. Every once in a while, somebody will try to call, but then nobody can dance to them.

For example, they might more or less sing their calls; usually their calls are more on the Western club type. And people that are used to dancing just plain old circle Appalachian square dance calls cannot get in there and pick up their calls and dance their dances. I've been there, and I've told these callers, "Be my guest." And I know what will happen as soon as they get up there. They start calling calls, and it's worded different to the way I call, and it's much faster. And the dancers can't get it. And this couple'd sit down, and that couple'd sit down, and these guest callers wind up with four people on the floor.

I would never go into a place and ask to call a square dance. I think that's too pushy. I mean, that's like, "Well, I'm pretty good," like I had that ego, "I think I do as good as you're doing, and I'd like to call myself. I'd like these people to hear me." That would be my idea of the way I would see people looking at me. "Oh, she thinks she's so good, she wants to call." And even if someone asked me to call, I wouldn't dare walk into a place that I had never been before and call a square dance until I'd heard their square dance caller because you don't know what they're used to danc-

ing. I know from dancing myself, you'd be lost if someone came in and started calling something they'd never heard before.

I learn a lot from going to other areas of Appalachia, especially North Carolina.
I just love to hear somebody else call. But I always take a pencil and a piece of paper.
I'm ready to jot down a few calls. I'm open to suggestions.

Chapter 3

Square Dancing in the Rural Midwest: Dance Events and the Location of Community

Paul L. Tyler

In an article in a "big city" newspaper,[1] the small town of Hoagland, Indiana, was portrayed as possessing a community spirit as sure a thing as death and taxes.[2] In *The Search for Order*, historian Robert Wiebe argued that around the turn of the century, "the personal informal ways of the community" gave way to a new regulative, hierarchical order.[3] If Wiebe's assertion is correct, then Hoagland must be a warm and spirited anomaly in an impersonal, bureaucratized society, just the sort of sequestered folk society that would send folklorists scampering for their tape recorders and cameras.

Indeed, Hoagland could furnish a thrill to any folklorist who happened by. The newspaper article referred to above marked the occurrence of the town's annual Oktoberfest in which the community venerates its German heritage with three days of polkas and waltzes. The energy of the dancers reaches a peak, however, when the band leader calls out, "It's English square dance time!" Nearly two hundred couples rush onto the floor to join in a four-couple square dance that will be directed by calls sung in English by the band.

While the polka and waltz, dances in which couples course independently around the floor, have been gaining in favor since the mid-1970s, the square dance retains greater popularity among Hoaglanders. In the square dance, each couple joins with three others to claim a small segment of floor space in which they will proceed through at least two separate dances, each a series of simultaneous and complementary interactions involving individuals, couples, or all dancers designated by gender. Each square dance begins with the formula of "allemande left," followed by a "grand right and left" and "promenade home" in which all circulate around the square interacting briefly with each dancer of the opposite gender before reuniting with their partner. This oft-repeated chorus alternates with a simple figure led in turn by each couple or by one of its members.

If imagined from a bird's eye view, the figures—each distinctively identifying a separate dance—trace intricate designs on the floor. But from the point of view of the active dancer or dancers, a figure is primarily movements around, amid, and alongside other members of the set, with or without tactile contact. The basic figure types employed in Hoagland draw on a few simple movement plans that, with striking exceptions, respect the boundary established by the four-couple formation: these include circles, movements along a segment of the circumference, crossing patterns, interplay between the center and the outside, symmetrical shapes, and the common theme of visiting each of the other couples in the set.

The movements required for a square dance involve little more than a rhythmic walk. Even the couple swing, which usually culminates a figure or marks the transition from one segment of the dance to another, is danced in Hoagland as a vigorous walking pivot step. The end of a square dance is reached when each couple or equivalent unit of the set has led the figure, and the final chorus has brought each couple back to its home place in the set (Figure 3-1).

The fact that square dancing is a key element of the Oktoberfest marks the Hoagland area's long-standing love affair with this traditional dance form; it also emphasizes the rural identity of the community. More than being an expression of community spirit, square dancing defines the Hoagland community. It helps bring the community into being.

Hoagland is not an isolated backwater of tradition. As a small town at the edge of a metropolitan area, it has been continually threatened with suburbanization as scores of new residents have fled Fort Wayne, Indiana's second largest city, to build new homes along the county roads. Since most people from Hoagland work and shop in Fort Wayne, the town has long relinquished what little economic autonomy it had. And as an unincorporated town, Hoagland is politically a nonentity.

So, from whence comes the ubiquitous community spirit observed by the big city journalist? Taking a cue from *Habits of the Heart* by sociologist Robert Bellah, we could call Hoagland a "community of memory," a community that has not forgotten its past.[4] I will focus on square dancing as a "practice of commitment"[5] that helps the community remember its past. In Bellah's words, such practices of commitment "define the patterns of loyalty that keep the community alive"; they "define the community as a way of life."[6] Or, in the words of one of Hoagland's residents, a retired teacher quoted in the newspaper, "People's relationships don't change; it's a close-knit place."[7]

Set in the flatlands of northeastern Indiana, Hoagland is centered in a region of small towns and farms where square dancing has been extremely popular for at least the last eighty years. The magnitude of dance activity has ebbed and flowed during this time, hitting a peak during the nationwide square dance revival of the 1940s

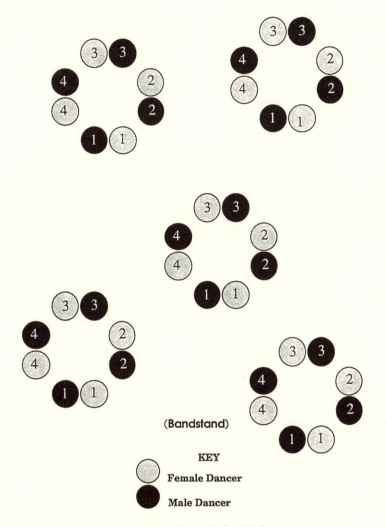

(Bandstand)

KEY

Female Dancer

Male Dancer

Figure 3-1. *Four-couple sets on the dance floor, Hoagland, Indiana.*

and 1950s. A heightened interest in square dancing arose again in the late seventies and eighties among certain segments of the population. But while the form or structure of the dancing itself has not changed appreciably during the last seven decades, the customary contexts for dance events have altered radically. I will outline four relatively distinct historical settings for square dances in the Hoagland community: domestic dances, public dances, dance halls, and dance clubs.

DOMESTIC DANCES

In rural Indiana, as elsewhere in the United States, house parties and barn dances were at one time a common context for square dance events. In the Hoagland area, house dances were a frequent occurrence, at least into the 1920s. They were either family affairs or neighborhood events held on a Saturday or Sunday night in someone's home: "We'd roll up the rug, and they would dance in the living room."[8]

There are few Hoagland residents left from the generation for whom square dancing in someone's home was a common activity. Those living today who remember these events are mostly from extended families of musicians. Their parents, aunts, uncles, and grandparents would gather regularly—in some cases, weekly—for a session of singing and playing. Square dancing was often a part of such family affairs. Sometimes a few neighbors were invited "so there wouldn't be too many, you know. And maybe they'd have two squares that would dance."

Dance music at these family-centered house parties was supplied by a fiddler or two—such as the family patriarch and one of his sons—accompanied by concertina, guitar, banjo, or piano (the latter often played by the fiddler's wife, sister, or daughter). One of the dancers, usually a man who was not a musician, would call out the figures. Neither musicians nor callers received any remuneration for performing: "But we had a lot of fun. Those were the good old days."

Another domestic setting for square dancing that was common in the Hoagland area into the 1930s was the neighborhood-centered dance, held either in the house or, more frequently it seems, outside in the barn. These affairs reached beyond the family circle to bring together neighbors who lived within a few miles of the host's home. A number of families took turns each summer, cleaning out their barns for a "big dance" held on a Saturday night. Men had to pay twenty-five or thirty-five cents admission, while the women got in free. One family, with three daughters of marrying age, held a free barn dance each summer to repay the young men who had, through the year, escorted their daughters to dances. Sunday nights often found a smaller number of friends and neighbors gathering to dance in a farmhouse. But even at these smaller house parties, the men paid a fee that went to the musicians.

The musicians at house dances, usually an informal ensemble led by a fiddle, lived in the area but were not necessarily a part of the immediate circle that held the dance. The hosts of a big dance often engaged musicians from an adjacent neighborhood, from up to ten miles away. While musicians were regarded and compensated as specialists, the square dance caller had not yet emerged as a separate profession. One or more of the dancers present provided the calling. Commonly the caller stood to one side to prompt the dance figures, though occasionally he called from the floor while he danced.

Because there are few people still living who can tell of firsthand experiences with domestic events in Hoagland in the first decades of this century, I am left to puzzle over how inclusive these events were. Many of the barn dances and some of the house parties were held only for the young people, both single young adults and young married couples with no children. Other events were attended by whole families, though some in the community felt it was not proper for a couple with children to go out dancing. Perhaps the most inclusive dance events were the wedding dances held in the barn at the bride's family home.

The extent to which dances were by invitation only is also something of an enigma. While some barn dances were open to all, others were supposedly limited to "an invited crowd" because, as one informant told me, "they kind of invited according to the room they had to dance." Still, "if the people heard about it, why they'd come anyhow, and oh, there'd be such a barnful, you couldn't hardly get through."[9] House dances, of course, were more restricted. But were they open to all within the immediate neighborhood, or did they serve a narrower social network that took in only a segment of the community?

PUBLIC DANCES

These puzzles disappear when we enter the period of public dances. Starting in the early thirties, public barn dances became very common in northeastern Indiana. There is no doubt that these events were open to all comers. And come they did, some from quite a distance. It became fairly common for people to journey up to twenty miles to or from Hoagland to attend a Friday or Saturday night barn dance.

As early as the twenties, people from Hoagland attended public dances in a barn connected to a tavern at the crossroads community of Zulu, about ten miles northeast of Hoagland. By the end of the thirties, a circuit of weekly dances was in full swing. On Friday and Saturday nights, when the young folks from Hoagland weren't dancing in local resident Hi Sorg's barn just north of town, they traveled south to the Sunset Hall in Decatur, a roller rink where the young men paid a dime per dance admission onto the floor, or to Coomer's barn, across the state line in Ohio.

These intercommunity public barn dances were mostly for young people, and they helped the young expand the boundaries of their experience beyond that of their parents. Still, members of their own immediate community served as a first point of reference. "We went every week, and we would go to every dance . . . a couple times a week. And a lot of the kids from Walther League [a church youth group], we all went together. Nobody was with anybody; we all just went together . . . as a group, and we really had fun. . . . There was just a whole group of us." Yet there were also opportunities for forging new connections between communities. Social dancing, of course, has always been closely connected with courtship. As this informant remembers, "I guess there probably was [courting]. We didn't pay much attention; we just danced. . . . There was a lot of them that did meet at the dances and then got married."[10]

The line between domestic and public dance events is nearly imperceptible. We have seen that the barn dances of the thirties became bigger, more public affairs that encompassed several different communities. As fewer dances were held in a living room with the rug rolled back and as the dances held in a barn cleaned out for the occasion drew a larger crowd from a broader territory, the events changed qualitatively. The roles of musician and caller became more specialized and professionalized, though some dances still relied on volunteer callers who were not paid. And the dancers became more attuned to fashions of the day. Some informants have suggested that during the thirties, square dances were less popular than couple dances like the fox-trot. Yet by the time of World War II, when a square dance revival was blossoming all across America, young people in Hoagland were quite crazy about square dancing. Those who hosted barn dances did so in part because there was a little money to be made. One shining exception to the profit motive were the dances at Sorg's barn. The Sorgs were an older couple with no children of their own who apparently held dances because they enjoyed having young folks around.

If barn dances, then, became intercommunity affairs for only a segment of the population, how do these events relate to the notion of community? For one answer to this question, let us detour to Kentucky and the work of folklorist Burt Feintuch, who pondered the meaning of such changes in a similar tradition. Feintuch found that domestic dances, up until World War II, were open to all in the neighborhood. And though he admitted the existence of religious opposition to dancing, he equated the community with the dancing throng. In domestic dances, "the neighborhood participants gathered for a social evening, and in the dances themselves they symbolically acted out their norms of community in which couples were the basic unit, and their social networks—their neighborhoods—were represented as a bound unit, the square."[11]

This is familiar territory for folklorists: an airtight functionalist explication of how a traditional expressive form reinforced social cohesion. Here, the dancing folk of south central Kentucky are portrayed as a bound community, an inclusive and integrated whole.

But then came change, drastic change that in Feintuch's view led to the breakdown of community and the devolution of the square dance. With increased mobility, people's social networks began to stretch beyond the neighborhood. Then around World War II, square dancing in Kentucky found a new context, the commercial dance hall. Feintuch interprets these changes as evidence of growing social instability: "Rather than symbolizing a closed and stable network, as did the squares of domestic dances, the public dances reflect a social structure in which all do not know each other."[12]

This kind of analysis, founded on a devolutionary premise, is as familiar to historians as it is to folklorists. Historian Thomas Bender in *Community and Social Change in America*, points out that the "community breakdown thesis," the motif of "decay and dissolution," is a common rhetorical device in historiography. Historians conventionally treat development in their own specialized areas of study as "the great change in which the scales were decisively tipped in favor of modernity."[13] For example, Robert Wiebe pinpointed the late nineteenth century as the historical moment in which America's island communities fell victim to social change.[14] Other historians, enumerated by Bender, located the eclipse of community in the 1650s, the 1690s, the 1740s, the 1780s, the 1820s, the 1880s, and the 1920s.

Where does community come from, and where does it go? Community doesn't break down just because of social and cultural change. It goes with people as they interact in new settings, conserving old relationships while dealing with changes that affect their daily lives. The case of Hoagland and the square dance shows that community can be redefined and reconfigured.

DANCE HALLS

As the nationwide square dance revival of the post-depression days grew, square dancing around Hoagland entered a new commercial phase. The rural area south and east of Fort Wayne got its first commercial dance hall in 1941 when Amos Kline, a young farmer who lived about ten miles north of Hoagland, remodeled his barn into a dance hall with a new floor, bandstand, and refreshment counter. Everyone, or so it seems, went to Kline's barn for Saturday night dances from 1941 to 1948. Young people from Hoagland were prominent. According to Amos Kline, of the four hundred people who came to his place every week, most were from the German Lutheran neighborhoods around Hoagland and Decatur to the south and the German Catholic community of Hessen Cassel west of Hoagland.

Amos Kline hired professional bands from Fort Wayne and from the greater rural district. Each band supplied its own caller, a nonmusician who was given a cut of the band's fee. By demonstrating an ability to deal with large, noisy crowds, thanks in part to the benefits of sound amplification technology, the square dance caller emerged as a respected professional. Still, the bands were accorded greater prominence. Amos Kline frequently booked the Blackhawk Valley Boys, an accordion- and guitar-led quartet from Illinois and stars on WOWO in Fort Wayne where they appeared weekly on the Hoosier Hop, a coast-to-coast radio "barn dance" show. Because of their mass-mediated fame, they always drew a huge crowd.

Soon several other farmers in the Fort Wayne area followed suit and converted their barns into full-time dance halls. The best-known, by far, was the Hoagland Hayloft, located about a half-mile west of town on the Hoagland Road. It is from this point on that the name *Hoagland* can be applied to a larger community than the town itself, for it was the popularity of the Hayloft that identified the town as the square dance center for an area of isolated farmsteads grouped around rural churches and parochial schools. With several weekly dances featuring all the name bands in the area, the Hayloft's fame put Hoagland on the cognitive maps of people from the big city of Fort Wayne, from Decatur and Bluffton (county seats of adjacent counties to the south), and from numerous crossroads communities and rural neighborhoods in a six- or seven-county area, including parts of northwestern Ohio.

In the midfifties as the square dance revival reached its zenith, nationally as well as in Hoagland, the caller began to be more important than the band. Though a few callers remained independent, to be hired out by various bands as needed, the most successful callers were attached to a specific band. The familiarity nurtured by the regular alliance between caller and band allowed for the development of personal styles of calling, as the caller was sure the band could follow him. Carl

"Tuffy" Schaper, still highly revered for more than ten years after his death by both dancers and other callers, got his start at the Hoagland Hayloft. Tuffy's band, The Mudslingers from near Decatur, were a new generation of dance band. Even though they were still led by a fiddler—and they were one of the last to feature a fiddle—the concertina had been replaced with a piano accordion, and the guitars were electrified.

On the national scene, electronic amplification had a devastating effect on old-time square dancing and fiddling. Many callers across the country, building on their newly gained professional recognition, began using portable record players. They could make more money if they did not have to split the take with a four- or five-piece band. In Hoagland, to the contrary, amplification was adapted to the prevailing system, allowing callers and bands to be heard by the growing crowds.

As the euphoria of the square dance revival began to wane by the late fifties and early sixties, two things began to happen in the context of commercial dances. First, in most places in the country, callers were in control. Through national organizations, they standardized and regulated the square dance scene, creating the "modern Western" or "club" dance movement—but not in Hoagland. Callers there continued with the style the locals know as "hoedown." To the few old-time fiddlers left in the area, a "hoedown" signifies a straight fiddle tune, any number of which will fit any patter call; that is, calls that are chanted without a recognizable melody line. Most callers and dancers in the Hoagland area use "hoedown" differently. In this less specialized usage, it refers to simple dance figures that require no formal learning, danced to a caller and live music. The prevailing notion among Hoaglanders is that people in Hoagland today are still doing the old "hoedown" figures that have always been done. In fact, callers in the area gradually forsook the older patter calls and began to do only singing calls, where the calls are sung to the melody of popular songs, mostly from previous generations.

Secondly, with the rise of rock 'n' roll, a new generation of youth, and the growing family responsibilities of the young couples who had been the lifeblood of weekly square dances, regular commercial dances began to disappear. By the sixties, the Hayloft's big regular dance was a Thursday teen dance with a rock band. The hall continued to thrive, however, as a reception hall. Already in the early fifties, a few families broke with custom and rented the Hayloft instead of holding their daughters' wedding dances in the barns at home. Big weddings at the Hayloft, with lots of square dancing, became frequent, eagerly anticipated community events. Such wedding dances in a sense represented a return to family- and neighborhood-centered domestic dances, but on a much grander scale. On the one hand, the dancing included all ages and generations; on the other hand, the events were ostensibly exclusive in that guests might have to show their invitation to a county sheriff's deputy to gain admittance to the Hayloft parking lot. Still, "crashing" the gate was something of a game for uninvited young people, and even for some of the invited who became conspirators. The sudden presence on the dance floor of people not on the guest list was nearly always tolerated to some degree.

As community events, commercial dance hall dances and big wedding receptions reflected a much wider community than had the domestic and public dances of previous generations. The Hoagland community had grown considerably, even though the town itself saw relatively little increase. Weddings continue to be important social events, as well as dance events, in Hoagland. Even though there are no more regular square dances, some people dance almost weekly at wedding receptions and anniversary parties at the Hayloft and other area barns converted into reception halls.

CLUB DANCES

Opportunities to dance have proliferated in the last fifteen to twenty years as a number of new contexts have developed. Because of the diversity of contexts, it is a bit difficult to find a single term to characterize the typical contemporary setting for a square dance event. I choose to refer to the present as the period of club dances, with these two caveats: (1) the term has nothing to do with modern Western square dance clubs, and (2) the idea of "club" covers a variety of formal organizations and informal voluntary associations.

The wide range of such dance clubs in the area signifies both the segmentation of Hoagland's dancing population and the expansion of the community's boundaries once again. All of these dance clubs, and I'll describe them shortly, draw participants from the town of Hoagland and its immediate rural vicinity. And even for many of those dancers whose place of residence is not strictly Hoagland, there is a sense of identification with Hoagland as a community of memory.

The oldest dance club in the area is the Hoagland Country Club. "Country Club" is rural, populist, and tongue-in-cheek. It was initially formed in 1957 by the owners of the Hayloft in cooperation with several volunteer leaders from the community but has since become totally independent. The club now holds its dances at the United Auto Workers union hall south of Fort Wayne on the highway toward Hoagland. The modest dues, around forty dollars per year per couple, entitles one to attend three dances per year, where a meal of ham sandwiches, potato chips, carrot sticks, and a few other traditional foods is served and where the main event is square dancing. Membership is limited because of space, so there is a waiting list. At present, it is mostly younger couples in their twenties and thirties who are lining up to join.

The newest dance club, the Hoagland Polka Boosters, represents the growing popularity of a dance form that was new to Hoagland when a local entrepreneur sponsored the first Oktoberfest in 1974, sparking a revival of interest in the community's German heritage. The club holds monthly dances, except in the summer, on Sunday afternoons at Quixote Hills, a new reception hall just across the Hoagland Road and down a little ways from the Hayloft. Members pay annual dues of fifty cents, giving them the privilege of supporting the organization by working at dances to which all comers, even the workers, pay an admission fee. As with the Hoagland Country Club, the Hoagland Polka Boosters have members who live as far as fifty miles away.

The membership of the Polka Boosters is comprised mostly of older couples, many retired, who have recently taken polka and ballroom dance lessons at a studio in Decatur.

Why are the Polka Boosters included in this discussion of square dancing? The reason is that those who promoted polka dancing in Hoagland discovered at the outset that their new venture would not succeed if they did not offer a few square dances at each event. The inclusion of square dances on the program at polka events is now standard in Hoagland.[15] At many of these events, square dancing calls forth the greatest proportion of active participants and, at times, the highest level of overt enthusiasm. Polkas do not have a complementary role or impact at square dance events in Hoagland.

Two other important clublike dance events in the area are not formal organizations at all but regular, open, public barn dances. Each has a bit of commercial motivation behind it, though neither does any advertising but relies on word-of-mouth. These two dances run in alternate seasons. The winter dance is a monthly fund-raiser for the Catholic Church in Besancon, just north and east of Amos Kline's farm. The other is a barn dance near Roanoke in Huntington County to the west, where Dale Alles, the caller, hosts a dance featuring an accordion- and saxophone-led band made up of eight of his children. He has had to build additions to his barn, not once but twice, to hold the two hundred plus dancers, mostly teenagers and young adults, who travel from as far as seventy miles away to attend. These dances are fairly distant from the town of Hoagland, but they draw participants from the Hoagland area, especially from the Catholic segments of the community. Alles's barn dance, in particular, was begun as a conscious effort by Dale and some of his friends to recreate "the good times we used to have at the Hayloft" in the fifties.[16]

CONCLUSION

Much more could be said about these contemporary dance events or about the other places where Hoaglanders go to square dance and, increasingly, polka. Here my remarks will be limited to the relation between these dances and the notion of community. Despite the segmentation brought about by the variety of dance contexts in the present, and despite the continual stretching of the community's boundaries through changing contexts in the past, square dancing in Hoagland is still a community activity. Released from territorial limitations by the mobility of the automobile and freed from social constraints by the liberalizing of traditional networks, people in rural America have greater potential today than ever before to form their own webs of association. In Hoagland and its surrounding area, traditional dance forms thrive as dynamic centers that anchor these webs and nourish the relationships from which they are constructed. In truth, square dancing is a community-building activity for Hoaglanders and many others.

From whence comes community? It comes from shared memories and from practices that reenact those memories and reinforce people's commitment to their shared identity and common past. Hoagland's community spirit is not pure; it does not manifest an ideal community as a stable, bound whole. But as Hoagland's sense of identity is tied up with square dancing—and today with polka dancing and the Oktoberfest as well—I am more and more persuaded that here community can be reconfigured in the face of social change. And remember the retired teacher's observation that "people's relationships don't change," no matter how much other things in life do.

NOTES

All information about Hoagland contained here came from a series of approximately twenty-five interviews conducted from 1976 to 1988. The interviewees include callers, musicians, dance organizers, and long-time dancers either from Hoagland or connected with the dance scene in Hoagland. I am very grateful for their gracious and able participation.

1. Nancy Vendrely, "Hoagland Shines During Oktoberfest," *Fort Wayne Journal-Gazette* (15 September 1988), 14–15.

2. An earlier version of this chapter was read at a panel presented by the Dance & Movement Analysis Section of the American Folklore Society's 1988 meeting in Cambridge, Massachusetts.

3. Robert Wiebe, *The Search for Order: 1877-1920*, a book in the series *The Making of America*, ed. David Herbert Donald (New York: Hill & Wang, 1967), xiv.

4. Robert Bellah, et. al., *Habits of the Heart: Individualism and Commitment in American Life* (New York: Harper & Row, 1985), 153. In the glossary to *Habits of the Heart*, the authors define *community* as a "group of people who are socially interdependent, who participate together in discussion and decision making, and who share certain *practices* . . . that both define the community and are nurtured by it. Such a community is not quickly formed. It almost always has a history and so is also a *community of memory*, defined in part by its past and its memory of its past." (p. 333.)

5. In *Habits of the Heart*, the authors define *practices* as "shared activities that are not undertaken as means to an end but are ethically good in themselves (thus close to *praxis* in Aristotle's sense). A genuine community—whether a marriage, a university, or a whole society—is constituted by such practices. Genuine practices are almost always practices of commitment, since they involve activities that are ethically good" (p. 335).

6. Bellah, et. al., *Habits*, 153–154.

7. Vendrely, "Hoagland Shines," 15.

8. The following quotes about house dances are from Estina Veit, interview with the author, 18 June 1988.

9. Clara Franke, interview with the author, 27 December 1976.

10. Estina Veit, interview with the author, 18 June 1988.

11. Burt Feintuch, "Dancing to the Music: Domestic Square Dances and Community in Southcentral Kentucky (1880-1940)," *Journal of the Folklore Institute* 18, no. 1 (January–April 1981): 49–68. This quote is from p. 65.

12. Feintuch, "Dancing," 65.

13. Thomas Bender, *Community and Social Change in America* (Baltimore: Johns Hopkins University Press, 1978), 43–53.

14. Wiebe, 44.

15. This practice is also common at polka events in communities along the Maumee River in northwestern Ohio. This area, with a rich German heritage, is the cradle of the polka revival that spread to Hoagland in the mid-seventies. Big city bands from Detroit and Toledo rarely are able to do "English" square dances, and even if they can, they report that there is little call for it apart from this region of Ohio and Indiana.

16. Dale Alles, interview with the author, 18 September 1979.

Chapter 4

"There's a Lot of Pride Wrapped Up in What We Do": Reminiscences of a Fraternity Stepper

AN INTERVIEW WITH CHARLES COLLIER

Jane Harris Woodside

During the 1980s Charles Collier was a stepper while a member of Alpha Phi Alpha fraternity chapters at both Mercer University in Georgia, where he earned a B.A. in Sociology, and at Emporia State University in Kansas, where he earned an M.S. degree in Counseling and Student Personnel. Today, he is the Coordinator of the Pre-Medical Reinforcement and Enrichment Program of the James H. Quillen College of Medicine at East Tennessee State University. He also serves as the advisor for the Sigma Beta undergraduate chapter of Alpha Phi Alpha fraternity at East Tennessee State University. Performed by African American fraternity and sorority members throughout the country, stepping is a complex performance event, involving combinations of singing, speaking, chanting, and synchronized movement. Contemporary step shows incorporate not only African American folk elements, but also advertising jingles, television theme songs, and the latest musical hits.

In a taped interview during the spring of 1990 with Jane Harris Woodside, he offered his recollections of what it meant to be an African American fraternity stepper.

Step shows are generally held around campus homecomings, during the probate periods for incoming members; sometimes they take place around a particular fraternity's Founder's Day. During these special times, several step shows go on. Some fraternities use them as fund-raisers throughout the year. Sometimes, steppers are asked to perform for a certain function. For example, earlier this year we had a step show in the University's eating facility during orientation. We had a very large turnout; the audience seemed to enjoy it, and all the participants were pleased with the outcome.

I learned to step as a pledge. As part of the pledging process we were taught the steps by a "big brother," an older member of the fraternity. We would practice, and on becoming full-fledged members we had a step show. Stepping was quite different from any other type of movement I'd done.

There are certain unique basic steps to each fraternity and sorority. Alpha Phi Alpha would have some of the same steps in Georgia or Kansas as they do here in Johnson City. In each geographical area you will find some steps or variations to a particular step, but basically it's the same type of movement.

Most routines are preplanned and rehearsed. They start out with the basic steps and just creatively come up with variations on them. They call the person who's responsible for leading this "the Step Master." He or she is usually the one who comes up with the steps and relays them to the rest of the members. The Step Master is either chosen by vote, or there are one or two really good steppers in the group that just stand above the other members, and they usually allow that person to lead and come up with the steps.

Generally a step show will begin with an entrance. The group comes into the area doing some modern-type dance like you would do at a party, but they all do it together. Once they're up on stage, they go into their stepping routine. Usually it is accompanied by some boasting about their organization or some jeering at another fraternity or sorority. So that's basically the format: the entrance, the stepping, which makes up the middle part of the show, and the exit. The exit will probably be either a very simple step, or they'd go back to a modern dance. Usually you find that they start off slow, reach a very high peak, and then taper off toward the end. For the entrance and exit, top-forty music might be used. Today, a lot of rap is used.

There are chants, and there are also steps that just rely upon the sound, either made by mouth, by handclapping, by stepping of the feet, or by use of props such as canes. Each group sets the atmosphere with the type of chants and steps that they begin their performance with. Stereotypically speaking, the Omega Psi Phis are thought to be very robust: real loud and stomping. The Kappa Alpha Psi brothers are known to be the glamour boys: very laid back, very suave, and debonair. The Alpha Phi Alphas are all of these characteristics and more. Sorority stepping is—not to be chauvinistic—more ladylike, very dainty, more on the light side.

The outfits that the groups come up with for stepping are in the group colors. Alpha Phi Alpha would be either in old gold, black-and-old-gold or just black, and their attire might consist of khaki pants, a nice dress shirt and tie sometimes, and very hard patent leather shoes that will sound off—not a tennis shoe because, of course, that won't sound off as much.

This is not a participatory type of show. It's an exhibition with a great deal of competition. Depending upon the sponsor and how they want to construct the program, there are step competitions where you have judges and different groups competing against each other. It's usually done by a tally sheet. But competition is very high among the Greeks, even if it's informal. A lot depends on the crowd reaction at the end of your performance. You just hope that you've rehearsed and practiced enough before going on because you're so caught up in the emotion of it once you're up there that you can't stop to look around.

A "good" stepper is a member of an ensemble versus just being an individual. All members are together. They're very precise in their movements, and an audience member could easily scan the stage while the performance is going on without ever missing something. That's when you know it's a good step. It becomes even better when there's a lot of speed along with that precision. That really gets the audience going. They're really amazed at how the group can keep in step with one another and at the same time maintain speed.

Being in a step show is a very exhilarating experience. There's a lot of pride wrapped up in what we do—pride in the origins of stepping in African culture. I think stepping maintains a link with our culture, our ancestral background—even if the steppers don't know it, even if the audience isn't aware of it. I don't think that's well known to the general audiences, and I personally think it's important that before each step show there should be a narration that talks about this.

It's also pride in the brotherhood or sisterhood, in doing a complete project unique to your group, working together because you've been practicing for several weeks before you perform. You go through a lot of emotions: people get mad and disagreements erupt, but they come together in the end. Having a final product makes it worthwhile. We take pride in the work that has been accomplished. And in the process, I think, bonds are strengthened.

Chapter 5

Stepping, Saluting, Cracking, and Freaking: The Cultural Politics of African American Step Shows

Elizabeth Fine

Spotlights rake over the dark auditorium as the opening music of *2001 (A Space Odyssey)* blares through the loudspeakers. The audience searches for the performers as the music suddenly shifts to a hard, driving beat and a recorded voice calls out, "Ladies and Gentlemen." Now the spotlights illuminate the white tuxedos of the Delta sisters as they dance down the aisles toward the stage. In their white suits and gloves, their red cummerbunds, boutonnieres, bow ties, and high heel shoes, and with red masks over their eyes, the thirteen performers make a dramatic and well-rehearsed entrance to the Overton R. Johnson Endowed Scholarship Step Competition.

Step shows are an exhibition form of dance practiced by African American fraternity and sorority members at college campuses throughout the country. This chapter explores the cultural politics of step shows as they have developed at Virginia Polytechnic Institute and State University (VPI&SU) in Blacksburg from 1984 through 1989. The term *cultural politics* refers to the social and political forces that influence what elements of a culture are featured or suppressed, promoted or ignored, sanctioned or censored.[1]

The Overton R. Johnson Step Competition was organized in 1983. Named in memory of a popular African American professor on campus, the Competition's

An earlier version of this chapter was published in *The Drama Review*, 35 no. 2 (Summer 1991). Reprinted by permission of MIT Press. © 1991 New York University and The Massachusetts Institute of Technology.

goal was to raise scholarship funds for African American students. The Overton R. Johnson Step Competition has given stepping a much higher profile on the VPI&SU campus, with attendance growing more than sixfold since its inception. In 1984, I first began videotaping and studying step shows at VPI&SU, where I observed the more recent phenomenon of competition stepping as well as the older style, informal shows. As the Competition helped to foster the dance form's popularity over the years, a real shift took place in the types of steps performed before the increasingly large and broad-based audience. This chapter examines the ramifications of this new institutionalized setting on the style and cultural politics of stepping at VPI&SU.

DEFINING STEPPING

While the term *stepping* suggests only physical movement, stepping or blocking is a complex performance event and ritual that involves various combinations of singing, speaking, and chanting, as well as synchronized movement and percussive footwork. This form of folk dance draws on African American folk traditions and communication patterns, as well as material from popular culture, such as advertising jingles, television theme songs, and top-40 hits.

Students at VPI&SU use both *stepping* and *blocking* to describe this activity, but stepping appears to be the more widespread term. The term blocking originates from the block or yard where members of a fraternity or sorority might gather to talk, sing, or put on a show.[2] Fundamentally, stepping is a ritual performance of group identity. It expresses an organization's spirit, style, icons, and unity.

Stepping is a dynamic and popular performance tradition among African American fraternities and sororities. Approximately five thousand individual chapters of the eight national black Greek organizations, with half a million members throughout the United States, participate in stepping.[3] No doubt the widest national exposure to stepping resulted from Spike Lee's 1988 movie, *School Daze*, which contains a step show that embodies interfraternity tensions similar to those described in this chapter.[4] Still, despite its popularity on American college campuses, few people other than African American fraternity and sorority members and their friends have ever seen a step show. Scholars too have largely overlooked this dynamic and popular tradition. Stepping deserves attention, however, because it is a rich tradition that involves great creativity, intelligence, wit, and physical skill.

Stepping has changed rapidly in the last thirty years. In 1940, according to an alumnus of Kappa Alpha Psi at West Virginia State College, the fraternities participated in group singing, often while they were holding hands or moving in a circle, but they did not step.[5] Another Kappa said in a 1987 newspaper interview that his fraternity began stepping in the 1940s and developed stepping from marching in line while pledging to the group: "Through the years brothers added singing and dancing, and in recent years we started using canes when we step."[6] This information corroborates a *Wall Street Journal* article that claims that stepping's "synchronized and syncopated moves date back to the 1940s, when lines of fraternity pledges

marched in lockstep around campus in a rite of initiation."[7] Civil Rights activist
Julian Bond reports that he could remember stepping contests when he was a student at Atlanta's Morehouse College in the late fifties.[8] In the fifties, according to
informants at VPI&SU, blocking or stepping was mainly a singing event with some
movement, usually in a circle.[9]

One cannot hope to comprehend the complexity and richness of the stepping tradition by surveying only a few groups or routines. The fraternity Kappa Alpha Psi, for
example, is noted for their dexterous use of canes (Figure 5-1), whereas the brothers
of Alpha Phi Alpha pride themselves on the vigor of their stepping. All of the eight
organizations draw on such African American folk traditions and communication
patterns as call-response, rapping, the dozens, signifying, marking, spirituals, handclap games, and military jodies.[10] The following descriptions of step shows that took
place in front of a student dining hall illustrate four different steps based on these
folk traditions. The first is based on a military jody, the second uses rapping, the
third uses call-response, and the fourth is based on children's handclap games.

Due to space considerations, as well as to the difficulty of completely notating
both the verbal and nonverbal dimensions of each routine, I have chosen in most
cases to transcribe the words and some paralinguistic features only and to provide
general descriptions of the movement. But in order to provide at least one full example of a step routine, I transcribed both the words and movements for the synchronized handclap routine.

Figure 5-1. *Kappa Alpha Psi fraternity members and sweethearts performing at a step show at
East Tennessee State University, Johnson City, October 1990. Photograph by Pat Arnow.*

In the first example, "Do It On Two," performed in 1984, eight Alpha brothers line up in a file, one behind the other, and begin an iambic step and clap, punctuated by a loud, grunted "Huah." The leader in the front calls out, "Do it—huah!" and moves to one side of the group like a drill sergeant. He then yells out calls, accompanied by a step, which the group in file imitates. This routine looks and sounds like a military jody, or marching chant:

LEADER: We're gonna roll it on out!

　　GROUP: We're gonna roll it on out!

LEADER: We're gonna roll it on out!

　　GROUP: We're gonna roll it on out!

LEADER: We're gonna do it on two!

　　GROUP: We're gonna do it on two!

LEADER: We're gonna do it on two!

　　GROUP: We're gonna do it on two!

LEADER: I say one!

　　GROUP: One!

LEADER: I say two!

　　GROUP: Two!

The second example, "Clutch Me, Baby," from the same step show, employs rapping to extol the sexual virtuosity of the Alphas.[11] The group again stands in a single file, one behind the other, and after the opening refrain each member takes a turn standing to one side of the group and rapping out a boast:

　　ALL: Oh clutch me, baby.
　　You doing okay
　　For A Phi A.
　　You're doing all right.
　　You do it all night.

LEADER [*standing to one side*]: Clutch me, baby.
Marcus is my name.
Sex is my fame.
Cause when my luck is right,
I do it every night,
Cause it's a smooth roman rocket
That always hits your pocket.

　　ALL: *Refrain.*

SECOND IN LINE: Double clutch me, baby.
My name is Rodney P.
Just bear with me a moment,
I got a story, you see.
You said, "I like my women sweet,"
And I like them plump
Cause all I want to do is the
A Phi Hump.

[*The step continues until each of the eight brothers has performed a rap.*]

A very common type of step routine is built on a call-response pattern, a prevalent African American communication pattern illustrated by "Clutch Me, Baby."[12]
In the 1986 Alpha Kappa Alpha (AKA) show, the sisters stand facing the audience
in two rows with the show's director and choreographer, called the stepmaster, in
the center of the front row. The stepmaster begins a sultry hip-swinging step and
calls out a series of questions, to which the sisters respond. This step is called the
"Marcita step," named after the woman who created it:

LEADER: Sorors.
    ALL: Ye-ah.
LEADER: I said, my sorors.
    ALL: Ye-ah.
LEADER: Can we break it.
    ALL: Ye-ah.
LEADER: On down now.
    ALL: Yeah.

At the end of this last response, the group breaks into a fast and complex step
with intricate footwork, which contrasts with the slow, sultry hip-swinging step.
They then return to the slow hip-swing for another call-response verse.

Still another type of step imitates children's handclap games. During the same
1986 step show, ten AKA sisters begin in two rows and look out over the audience.
Then they turn to face each other and advance while doing a handclap routine.
When the two rows meet, they clap with each other with an exaggerated African
American hand slap of greeting known as *giving skin*.[13] As they give skin, they call
out greetings in unison, such as "How you doing?" and "Sorors." To demonstrate
unity, each member rotates down the row and around to the other side in a circle, so
that each has clapped with and greeted everyone (Figure 5–2).

In order to illustrate stepping's intricate footwork and handwork, a detailed text
of another AKA routine from that same 1986 performance follows, with musical

Figure 5-2. *The sisters of Alpha Kappa Alpha sorority "giving skin" in a synchronized handclap routine at VPI&SU, Blacksburg, Virginia, 1986. Photograph and video by Robert Walker.*

notation representing the rhythm of the hands and feet. The basic rhythm for all three steps is a 4/4 measure.

SYNCHRONIZED HANDCLAP ROUTINE

This routine begins with the eleven sisters in a row facing the audience, with their hands clasped in front of their chests. Every other woman performs Step I twice, while the others perform Step II twice (Figure 5-3). Then the women switch steps—those who performed Step I now perform Step II twice and vice versa. The entire group then performs Step I nine times while moving backward and splitting into two parallel lines that are perpendicular to the audience. These two lines then move close together and face each other, with the leader located behind and between the two rows and facing the audience. When they are in this position, the entire group performs Step III twelve times; the whole group (including the leader) rotates counterclockwise with each repetition so that each sister has given skin to each other. By the time the step has been executed twelve times, the leader once again is standing between the two rows, but at this point, she has moved to the front of the formation (Figure 5-4). The routine ends with the sisters facing the audience, frozen in the stance in which they began the number with their hands clasped in front of their chests.

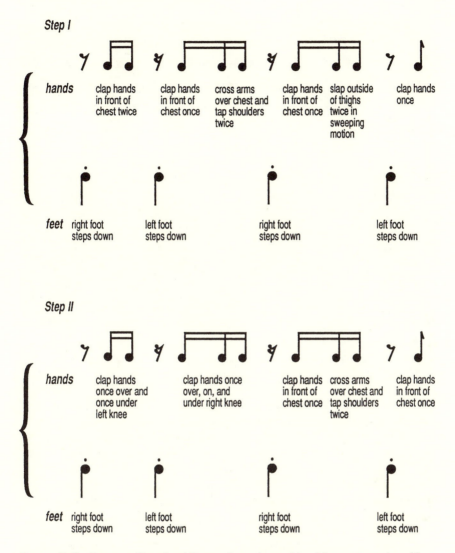

Figure 5-3. *Diagram of Steps I and II, part of a synchronized handclap routine performed by the sisters of Alpha Kappa Alpha Sorority, VPI&SU, Blacksburg, Virginia, 1986.*

The black Greek organizations step for a number of reasons. The president of AKA sorority says, "It gives good publicity for the organization. It shows unity."[14] Groups also step to raise money. The success of the annual Overton R. Johnson Endowed Scholarship Fund Step Competition at VPI&SU attests to the ability of blocking to draw a crowd.

Like other Greek organizations, African American fraternities and sororities are intensely competitive. One of the most important functions of stepping is to express

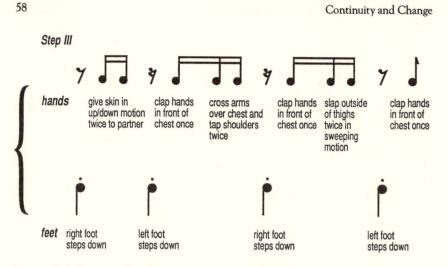

Figure 5–4. *Diagram of Step III, part of a synchronized handclap routine performed by the sisters of Alpha Kappa Alpha Sorority, VPI&SU, Blacksburg, Virginia, 1986.*

that competitive spirit. This rivalry greatly influences the content and style of stepping that is further shaped by the kinds of African American folklore that students draw on to create routines.

Like any other kind of folklore, step routines are transmitted orally. They are also transmitted by videotape and copied texts. Chapters of Greek organizations from nearby schools frequently visit each other and exchange steps, and national meetings provide the opportunity for steps to circulate widely.

Since each fraternity and sorority has the same national organizational history and symbols, each group has a core of common material. For example, each fraternity and sorority has *trade steps* by which each group is known. Kappa Alpha Psi performs a trade step called "Yo Baby Yo." The oldest African American fraternity, Alpha Phi Alpha, founded in 1906, has a trade step called "The Granddaddy." And the oldest African American sorority, Alpha Kappa Alpha, founded in 1908, performs a trade step known as "It's a Serious Matter."

Each of these trade steps has a recognizable rhythm, set phrases, and set movements that remain fairly constant, yet each can also be varied in innovative ways. The following text of "The Granddaddy" step, recorded by Florence Jackson,[15] illustrates one of the earliest steps and one that is still performed today. The circular form of the step is typical of early step routines, which may have some roots in the African American traditions of ring shouts and juba, dances which were performed in a circle.[16] To symbolize the fraternity's age, the brothers mime an old man's walk, leaning on an imaginary cane and moving with shaking knees:

We're the Alpha brothers, for heaven's sake,
We're the granddaddies, making no mistake.

We're the first, the first, and we're never late,
From us all the others originate.
We're gonna break it down for our grandsons' Que.
We're gonna break it down for Omega Psi Phi.

[*Depending on the chapter, the group would continue to* break it down *for selected organizations. When the dancers talk about breaking it down or* mocking, *they mean that they imitate them.*]

While steps such as "The Granddaddy" are clearly a long-established fraternity tradition, some students trace the dance's lineage back even further and believe that stepping itself is directly linked to African dance traditions. When I asked the president of AKA at VPI&SU about the history of stepping, she said:

It goes all the way back to African culture. And in the African cultures, they had tribes, and you know, they were just small little centralized, localized groups of people. And what they would do to show rivalry between the kings and different tribes and then to show that they do compete, they would have something similar—they would step, they would block, they would dance. I mean except that it would be more of a tribal type of affair. But it was basically the same thing to show how much better one tribe is than another. So that's something that may have an influence on how come we do it here.

Apparently this belief about African roots is widespread. Students at the University of Southern Florida also proudly stated that stepping originated in African dance traditions.[17]

FREAKING, SALUTING, AND CRACKING

Stepping is a form of ritual communication that employs at least three distinct types of acts: *freaking, saluting,* and *cracking or cutting*. In freaking, a member breaks the norm of synchronization and unity in an attempt to get greater audience response. The "freaker," or "show dog"[18] as he or she is sometimes called, is a crowd pleaser. In saluting, a fraternity or sorority ritually greets another Greek organization by imitating the steps, style, or symbols of the organization.

Competition and rivalry come to the fore in cracking or cutting. In the crack or cut, one group makes fun of another group, either verbally, nonverbally, or both. Many of the verbal cracks are based on the very strong African American tradition of verbal dueling, expressed in such well-known folklore genres as rapping, the dozens, sounding, and signifying.[19] Cracking can be done nonverbally as well by parodying the steps or style of another group. Students at VPI&SU call such nonverbal cracks *mocking* and *breaking it down*. The competitive spirit that characterizes the relationship between organizations comes to the fore in the crack or cut.

The first example of cracking, performed by Alpha Phi Alpha, was again performed outside a student dining hall in the spring of 1984 (see Figure 5–5). This is a popular crack theme called, "We're Laughing at You." This step employs the folk tradition of signifying, which criticizes through indirection and innuendo. It also uses marking or mocking to make fun of the Kappas. One student steps forward from the group and says:

I once [*Points index finger*]
Knew some Kappas
That went to this school.
They were sloooow walking,
[*Exaggerated slow walk, as in slow motion*]
Sweeeeet talking, [*Rubs hand over his hair*]
Oh, oh,
So very very cool. [*Closes eyes and clenches fists in front of chest on the word* cool]

As if to underscore the message, another brother doubles over in an exaggerated belly laugh—"ho-ho-ho." The success of this crack depends not only on the audience's knowing that Kappa Alpha Psi cultivates a cool, playboy image, but also on the performer's ability to imitate this style in a comic way.

Figure 5-5. *An Alpha Phi Alpha brother cracks on the Kappas' suave, sweet-talking image through "marking," or "mocking," a nonverbal imitation. In this frame from video, the performer is saying, "Sweeeeeet talking." VPI&SU, 1984. Photograph and video by Robert Walker.*

The next example of a crack step also draws on marking. In addition, however, the step echoes the dozens or sounding. In the following example, Alpha Phi Alpha members crack on the style of the Sigmas and salute their own step by first performing their own step, called "Yo Mama Didn't Tell You 'Bout A Phi A," in a lame, uncoordinated fashion, which they say is the way the Sigmas step, and then performing the same step again with the hard-stepping vigor that is a nationally recognized hallmark of Alpha Phi Alpha stepping:

[This routine was performed outside of a student dining hall. One of the brothers goes to the audience and brings back a white, blond coed (a friend) to the center of the performing area. The other brothers form a large circle around her, and the brother asks:]

BROTHER: Who was the first person to tell you about A Phi A?

[The coed smiles, shakes her head, and holds her palms up, as if to say, "I don't know."]

BROTHER: You mean to tell me your

   ALL: Mama didn't tell you 'bout A Phi A.
   She didn't tell you 'bout the brothers and their sexy ways.
   She didn't tell you how they slide to the side so sweet.

[The group performs above verse with faint voices and uncoordinated, weak movements, circling around the girl.]

STEPMASTER: [Interrupting verse] Hold on. Stop, stop.

   BROTHER: What's wrong, man?

STEPMASTER: Cats, if we're gonna do this step,
We can't look like a bunch of Sigmas.
If you're gonna do this step,
You have to put your heart in it, like this:
[Loudly] I said, Your
Mama didn't tell you 'bout A Phi A.
She didn't tell you 'bout the brothers and their sexy ways.
She didn't tell you 'bout how they slide to the side so sweet.
She didn't tell you 'bout the first of all black Greeks.
She didn't put you on her knee and break it on down.
Uh! Uh!
Uh! Uh! A Phi A!

[The group performs this verse loudly while skipping in a counter-clockwise circle, with exaggerated and emphatic swinging of arms and hard-hitting feet. The step continues with a series of cracks on the other fraternities, repeats the verse above, and ends with the two brothers escorting the coed back to the audience.]

Here we see a remarkable example of performance criticism embodied in a performance. Step shows are full of metaperformances that focus attention and comment on either other performances or on themselves.[20] While the saluting steps imitate other performances in a positive way, the cracking steps imitate them in a more critical way. Both steps exhibit what anthropologist Victor Turner terms "performative reflexivity," a condition in which "a sociocultural group, or its most perceptive members acting representatively, turn, bend, or reflect back upon themselves, upon the relations, actions, symbols, meanings, codes, roles, statuses, social structures, ethical and legal rules, and other sociocultural components which make up their public 'selves.' "[21]

What are the functions of cracking, and what impact does it have politically among the competing Greek organizations? First and foremost, cracking creates what Richard Bauman calls "differential identity."[22] In other words, cracking defines a group's identity by contrasting it with other groups. Second, cracking is entertaining—it elicits laughter and howls of appreciation from the audience.

If there is a little competition between groups, cracking is taken lightly. But if there is intense competition for members, then cracking can create great tensions. Since the mid-eighties, there has been enormous rivalry at VPI&SU between two sororities, Alpha Kappa Alpha and Delta Sigma Theta.

In 1986, a member of AKA explained that because of the political atmosphere, her sorority could no longer crack freely:

I mean, you know, it's funny. People like to listen to those [cracks] and everything, but . . . like our sorority, you can't do it without being cut up left and right. . . . It wouldn't be to our benefit to do it. For example, if you wanted to sponsor parties or sponsor other events with other fraternities and sororities, they're less apt to do it if we have—I don't know—splattered blood on another fraternity's or sorority's face, they're less apt to do things with us. So I mean, you know, it's all important to keep good relations with other fraternities and sororities without, you know, hurting somebody's feelings. So you know, it's best for the time being that we don't say anything. But others, like the fraternities, oh, they just have a good time cutting up.

CRACKING AND THE INSTITUTIONALIZED STEP SHOW

The Overton R. Johnson Step Competition represented a new arena for block shows, the first institutionalized setting for stepping on the campus. With the Competition, new forces began to influence the form of stepping. These forces include:

1. A change of place from the yard, block, or small auditorium to the largest public auditorium on campus.
2. A change in audience from a small, almost exclusively African American audience to one that includes members of all the black Greek organizations, African American professors, visiting African American Greeks from other schools, judges (both African American and white), members of the general public, and university administrators.
3. Formalized standards for judging the stepping competition. These standards emphasize appearance, crowd appeal, precision and synchronization, level of difficulty, vocalization, originality, and personality.

In the new setting of the institutionalized step show, the impact of the free-spirited and sometimes ragged and offensive crack steps seemed to be magnified. The first serious problem with cracking occurred in the 1985 Overton R. Johnson Step Competition with a series of hard-hitting cracks by AKA on their chief rival, Delta Sigma Theta Sorority:

> I was walking cross the yard just as happy as can be
> When a confused little pyramid approached me.
> I said, "Are you all right? Can I give you a hand?"
> She said, "Stop DST." I said, "Don't understand."
> I said, "Let me tell you something 'bout my sorority."
> She said, "Is it anything like DST?"
> I said, "Me, a D a S a T?"

> _____

> She even had the nerve to call us names.
> "We're all kind of animals is what they claim.
> The Sacred pyramid and elephant too."
> _____ or to the zoo.

> I said, "You steal too much.
> Oh, Sigma Gamma Alpha,
> You know, it's hard for you to do that
> Because you're nothing but a copy cat.
> But what can we expect from D. S. Thieves?"

> The Delta story has now been told
> That your new colors are red and gold.

> They even had to go and change their name.
> I said, "We're laughing at you."
> This is a serious matter.

As in many cracks, the sisters of AKA play off the icons of the Deltas: the pyramid and their red and gold colors. The lines about the colors and name refer to an event in the history of DST in which they had to change their name and colors because they had already been claimed by a white fraternity. But the crack that was most offensive to the Deltas, and elicited the biggest audience reaction, was the following:

> I said, "You steal too much. . . .
> Because you're nothing but a copy cat.
> But what can we expect from D. S. Thieves?"

As the president of AKA explained, the reference to stealing refers to the Deltas' copying other sororities' routines. But the Deltas took the crack more literally to refer to an embarrassing incident a few days before the Competition in which a couple of the Delta sisters had been arrested in a local store for alleged shoplifting.

These hard-hitting cracks created tensions between the two sororities that have persisted. In the weeks following the 1985 Competition, the president of the Deltas complained at a presidents' meeting of the African American fraternities and sororities that AKA didn't show them any respect. In response to this complaint, AKA picked up the respect issue and turned it into a crack performed in a block show outside a dining hall in the spring of 1986. The crack was performed to "It's a Serious Matter."

> Oh Delta Sigma Theta
> (Oh DST)
> You want respect,
> (You want respect)
> But it has to be earned,
> (But it has to be earned)
> Or you're gonna get burned.
> So don't flick my Bic.
> A ha, ha, ha, ha, ha.
> This is a serious matter.
> This is a serious matter.

This crack only intensified the tension between the two largest sororities, and the bad feelings between the groups were felt by many in the relatively small number of African American students (about 800) at the University. So the delegates from the eight Greek organizations charged with planning the 1986 Overton R. Johnson Step Competition drew up rules which prohibited cracking that year. Any fraternity or sorority that cracked would be eliminated from the Competition.

In the 1986 show, one can see the adaptive form of trade steps as AKA performs a non-crack version of "It's a Serious Matter." This routine recounts the history of the sorority as well as that of some of their favorite steps. The leader stands in the middle of the stage with a group of sisters standing to the left and right of her:

LEADER: Question.

STAGE RIGHT GROUP: Question, we have a question for you.

STAGE LEFT GROUP: Question, we have a question for you.

LEADER: I said, "What, what? It's a serious matter."

ALL: What, what? It's a serious matter.

ALL: What, what? It's a serious matter.

ALL: In 1908 was our founding date.

ALL: In '74, we did it once more.

LEADER: Tell me.

ALL: What, what? It's a serious matter.

LEADER: Tell me.

ALL: What, what? It's a serious matter.

[*Group does a nonverbal step-and-clap routine and repeats the "Serious Matter" refrain.*]

    ALL: Nine fine founders at Howard's Minor Hall,
    Twelve charter members, and that's not all.

Refrain.

When it was the Deltas' turn to perform, they showed every sign of winning the Competition until they came out with a none-too-subtly disguised crack that responded to the "respect crack" that AKA had launched in front of the dining hall. During the crack, an AKA audience member shouted in a high-pitched voice, "Skee Wee," right after the word, "respect" (Figure 5–6). This cry, which is the identifying call of AKA, was used to signal the judges that the caller had interpreted the step as a crack, according to an AKA informant.

    Oh, Delta Sigma Theta Incorporated
    From VPI.
    We're here to march, and we're here to step. I said, "S.O.I."
    Because you know that we know that you know who you are,
    Because you're walking round the yard just a-thinking you're a star.
    Respect?
    [*Audience member: Skee wee!*]

Figure 5–6. *Delta Sigma Theta cracks on Alpha Kappa Alpha by saying "Respect?" while undercutting the word with poses of contempt. VPI&SU, 1986. Photograph and video by Robert Walker.*

And we're laughing at you, and you know why.
You wanted the best, but you settled for less.
I said, "We're laughing at you, and you know why.
Cause Delta's gonna run it till the day we die."

CONCLUSION

Each year the Overton R. Johnson Step Competition grows in popularity. In 1983, it raised $400; in 1989, it raised over $2,500. Calvin Jamison refers to it as the "superbowl of blockshows" and compares it to a "fine art" and a "Broadway musical."[23]

Since the inception of the Competition, then, stepping has certainly become more institutionalized. Judges, drawn from faculty and staff, utilize criteria for judging, and those criteria do not include skillful cracking. In fact the rule against cracking in the Competition still holds. How has this institutionalization affected the style of stepping?

First, students say there is a greater emphasis on exclusively nonverbal steps, or what some term *hard stepping*. In hard stepping, groups strive for intricate, rhythmic steps. Second, since cracking is forbidden, students have changed their traditional crack steps to express non-cracks, as when AKA recited sorority history rather than cracks to their trade step, "It's a Serious Matter." Third, the groups use nonverbal and nonderogatory mocking as salutations. Finally, the groups include more skits and singing which make their performances look more like variety shows rather than straight stepping. As one student told me, "Once you can't crack, it will have to be more of a show with dancing and singing. Otherwise, it will be too boring." In general, then, much of the spontaneity and freaking found outside on the block is disappearing.

Clearly, some of the danger, tension, and political impact has been taken out of stepping in its institutional setting. These changes parallel the changes David Chaney has found in his study of the shift from folk to popular culture. In his book *Fictions and Ceremonies*, Chaney discusses four modes of incorporation or types of pressure that structure cultural politics in the transition from folk to popular culture. These four pressures are:

1. Commercialization—supplanting amateur production of performance by commercially inspired professionals;

2. Suppression—deliberate attempts to stamp out or control what were felt to be illegitimate performances;

3. Bourgeoisification—a process in which a concern for respectability came to supplant the value of vitality;

4. Alienation—transforming of work so that for the majority, it becomes alienating, with consequential implications for leisure.[24] [In other words, as work becomes more alienating, more emphasis is placed on leisure.]

Of these four pressures, suppression and bourgeoisification seem to be most evident in the institutionalized step competition at VPI&SU. Chaney's term *bourgeoisification* is not only an awkward sounding word, but the term is objectionable to many African Americans who are sensitive to charges of becoming bourgeois.[25] We might replace it with the term *respectability*.

Fortunately for the vitality of stepping at VPI&SU, the institutional pressures of suppression and respectability are resisted by breaking rules, as the Deltas did with their cracks in the 1986 show, and by continuing to perform in traditional arenas where such rules are not imposed. The African American tradition of verbal dueling is so strong that it is hard to leave a verbal attack unanswered. The AKAs refused to let the Deltas have the last word with their "respect" crack in the 1986 Step Competition. At the Black Alumni Weekend, held the following fall, AKA answered the Delta crack with a new crack sung to *The Beverly Hillbillies* theme and performed in their trade step, "It's a Serious Matter." The crack, which they copied from their sorors at Virginia State, went like this:

> The first thing you know, there's DST,
> The white man said, "This is my fraternity."
> He said, "I'm going to sue you, and that's the way it be."
> He took them to court, and what do we see?
> Red-gold, Red-white,
> Why the heck can't you get it right?

This analysis of the cultural politics of step shows at VPI&SU provides a microcosmic view of the phenomenon of step shows in general. Although more case studies are needed, this analysis leads us to some tentative conclusions about the performative genre of step shows within the subculture of black Greek organizations.

First, step shows provide an excellent example of anthropologist Victor Turner's thesis about the interaction of cultural performances with the social drama. Turner argues that "the major genres of cultural performance not only originate in the social drama but continue to draw meaning and force from the social drama. . . . Such genres partly 'imitate' (by mimesis) the processual form of the social drama, and they partly, through reflection, assign 'meaning' to it."[26] For Turner, a social drama is a "disharmonic social process, arising in a conflict situation."[27] Richard Schechner explains the crisis situations of social dramas: "These situations—arguments, combats, rites of passage—are inherently dramatic because participants not only do things they try *to show others what they are doing or have done*; actions take on a 'performed for an audience aspect.' "[28]

In the social drama provided by black Greek organizations, individuals who pledge a fraternity or sorority participate in a major ritual of status transformation and elevation. Membership represents access to a network of fellow brothers or sisters that can play a vital social role not only in the college years but throughout life. To establish and maintain a unique Greek identity, each fraternity and sorority must define itself with symbols and styles that distinguish it from any other group. Indeed, members first learn to step as part of their initiation process and are expected to perform publicly as a sign of their new status. Stepping performances have become a key way for displaying and asserting group identity, as well as for negotiating the status of each group within the social order.

The two basic types of steps, saluting and cracking, imitate two fundamental poles within the social drama of black Greek organizations. The first pole is a tendency toward identification and unity with all black Greeks since certain fraternities and sororities tend to date members from each other's groups. All such fraternal organizations share common experiences. The act of saluting by imitating the steps or style of another group embodies this friendly impulse toward unity. The second pole is a tendency toward competition and difference, since organizations must compete against each other for membership. The act of cracking, or making fun of another group, dramatizes the competitive tendency. A well-executed crack simultaneously elevates the status of the performers and lowers the status of the target group.

The third type of step, freaking or show dogging, exercises the need for individual identity within the group. While the main emphasis of stepping is to illustrate group solidarity and unity, the occasional deviations from group synchronization assert the freedom and power of the individual to vary, in creative ways, from the group norm.

As stepping moves from the esoteric arena of the intergroup shows to public displays at institutionalized stepping competitions and conferences with heterogeneous audiences, we can expect that groups will tend to suppress the competitive tendency embodied in cracking. For example, when the Kappa Alpha Psi Fraternity at East Tennessee State University (ETSU) did a step show for a Center for Appalachian Studies and Services dance program in 1990, they chose not to perform any crack steps. When I asked the fraternity president why they would not do crack steps, he told me that they would be inappropriate for a non-Greek audience. He said that such a diverse audience would not appreciate the meaning of the cracks and that they might foster the wrong impression. In the public discussion following the step show, after a few rival black Greeks in the audience had hooted at some of the Kappa steps, one of the Kappa brothers said, "I want to make it clear that while we do step and while we talk about other fraternities and they talk about us, I want to make it clear that we do get along with the other black Greeks, that there is unity on this campus."

While suppressing cracking may blunt the potential for stepping to create a breach or crisis in the social drama of black Greek life or comment on an existing one,[29] even without cracking, stepping remains a fundamentally competitive performance tradition. As one Kappa brother from ETSU said, "We mainly step to show the other fraternities that we are the best." This agonistic nature of step shows makes them a performance tradition charged with high energy and life.

NOTES

As a white folklorist who has never been affiliated with either black or white fraternities or sororities, I could only begin to understand stepping through the cooperation and help of the members of African American Greek organizations who agreed to be interviewed and who took time to explain the many codes in stepping. While there are many nuances of this tradition that only a group member could fully appreciate, I have tried to bring the insights of an outside observer who has recorded step shows and participants for several years. This chapter is dedicated to those students who have so generously shared their insights with me.

1. My definition of cultural politics has been influenced by David E. Whisnant, *All That Is Native and Fine: The Politics of Culture in an American Region* (Chapel Hill: University of North Carolina Press, 1983).

2. Calvin Jamison, interview with the author, Blacksburg, Virginia, 1986. In 1986, Jamison was assistant to the president of Virginia Polytechnic Institute and State University (VPI&SU). Jamison is a VPI&SU graduate and an alumnus of an African American fraternity founded in the 1960s, Groove Phi Groove. He participated in stepping as a student and in 1983 organized the Overton R. Johnson Endowed Scholarship Stepping Competition at the University.

3. The four national African American Greek fraternities include: Alpha Phi Alpha, Omega Psi Phi, Phi Beta Sigma, and Kappa Alpha Psi. The four national African American Greek sororities include Alpha Kappa Alpha, Delta Sigma Theta, Zeta Phi Beta, and Sigma Gamma Rho.

4. Spike Lee (producer, director, and screenwriter), *School Daze*, distributed by Columbia Pictures, New York, 1988. In *School Daze*, the step show replicates in a performative genre the major tensions among African American students that are the subject of Lee's film. Significantly, cracking precipitates and escalates the rivalry between the Gamma fraternity and the non-Greek faction led by Dap and their corresponding female counterparts, the Gamma Rays and the Jigaboos. The Gamma Rays, or little sisters of the Gamma's, are light skinned and espouse "white" standards of judging beauty, while the Jigaboos reject Greek organizations, are dark skinned, and espouse African standards of beauty. The women begin the cracking from the audience, and the non-Greek male group, "Da Fellas," escalates the tensions by performing a step routine centered on insulting the Gammas. After calling them poor and fags, "Da Fellas" conclude their crack with "get back, or we'll kick your Gamma ass." As "Da Fellas" exit from the stage, a fight breaks out between them and the insulted Gammas.

The conflict between the dark-skinned and light-skinned women is similar to the perceived conflict between Alpha Kappa Alpha and Delta Sigma Theta at VPI&SU, which some students believe involves skin color. One aspiring AKA member said that some people say that one has to have the color of a brown paper bag to be a member of AKA, while the girls of DST are darker. While this stereotype has a slight national consensus, women of all shades of complexions are found in both sororities. For more on the rivalry between sororities, see Yvette Jenkins, "Greek and Elite, *Essence* (August 1988): 124.

5. Thomas Harville, interview with the author, Johnson City, Tennessee, 3 March 1990. This former member of Kappa Alpha Psi fraternity now lives in Johnson City, Tennessee. He joined the Kappas in 1940 at West Virginia State College in Institute, West Virginia.

6. Melinda J. Payne, "Stepping Out on Campus," *Roanoke Times and World News* (15 October 1987), A8.

7. Asra Q. Nomani, "Steeped in Tradition, 'Step Dance' Unites Blacks on Campus," *Wall Street Journal* (10 July 1989), A4.

8. Marilyn Freeman and Tina Witcher, "Stepping into Black Power," *Rolling Stone* (24 March 1988): 48.

9. Florence Jackson, "Blocking: A General Overview" (unpublished manuscript, VPI&SU, 1984). Florence Jackson is a member of Alpha Kappa Alpha who interviewed several former fraternity members on campus who were familiar with stepping in the fifties. More research from other campuses is necessary to extend this claim to stepping nationally.

10. Military jodies are call-and-response chants that often accompany marching during military drills. The drill sergeant serves as the leader and initiates the song or "call"; and the troops provide the chorus or "response." The chants perform a practical function by establishing a tempo for the marching soldiers. In addition, as folklorist Jan Harold Brunvand points out, they also provide an ample opportunity for commentary on military life. See Jan Harold Brunvand, *The Study of American Folklore: An Introduction*, 2d ed. (New York: W. W. Norton & Co., 1978), 88–89.

11. See Thomas Kochman, "Toward an Ethnography of Black American Speech Behavior," in *Rappin' and Stylin' Out: Communication in Urban Black America*, ed. Thomas Kochman (Urbana: University of Illinois Press, 1972), 243.

12. For more on call and response, see Jack L. Daniel and Geneva Smitherman, "How I Got Over: Communication Dynamics in the Black Community," *Quarterly Journal of Speech* 62 (1976): 26–39.

13. See Benjamin G. Cooke, "Nonverbal Communication Among Afro-Americans: An Initial Classification," in Kochman, *Rappin' and Stylin' Out*.

14. Unless otherwise noted, all interviews are from fieldwork conducted at VPI&SU during the years 1984–1990. I have omitted names of informants to protect their privacy.

15. Jackson, "Blocking: A General Overview."

16. See Letitia Coburn, "Juba and Ring Shout: African American Dances of the Antebellum South" (Paper delivered at the Southern Dance Traditions Conference, East Tennessee State University, 2 March 1990), 5–15. Coburn cites descriptions of juba dances from Eileen Southern, *The Music of Black Americans, A History* (New York: W. W. Norton & Co., 1971), 100, and from Solomon Northup, *Twelve Years a Slave* (Auburn, New York: Derby & Miller, 1853), 94–102, quoted in Eileen Southern, ed. *Readings in Black American Music* (New York: W. W. Norton & Co., 1971), 100, that are remarkably similar to the hand and feet movements found in stepping.

17. AKA sorority members, interviews with the author, University of South Florida, Tampa, 9 February 1990.

18. Members of African American sororities at the University of Southern Florida in Tampa were not familiar with the term *freaking*. They use the term *show dog* instead.

19. See William Labov, "Rules for Ritual Insults," in Kochman, *Rappin' and Stylin' Out*, 265–314, and Lawrence W. Levine, *Black Culture and Black Consciousness: Afro-American Folk Thought from Slavery to Freedom* (Oxford and New York: Oxford University Press, 1977), 346–358. The *dozens, sounding,* and *signifying* are among the most frequently heard terms for the African American verbal duels, which employ ritual insults as their main weapons. As often happens in the very fluid, sometimes confusing world of folk culture, different terms can be applied to slightly different activities as one travels from place to place. For example, as Levine points out, in Baton Rouge, Louisiana, the dozens was limited to the exchange of insults that were disparaging remarks about one another's mothers, whereas in Chicago, the dozens referred to contests in which the opponent's entire family tree was open to attack.

As Levine observes: "Wherever they existed and whatever they were called, these verbal contests . . . involved symmetrical joking relationships in which two or more people were free to insult each other and each other's ancestors and relatives either directly or indirectly. The mother was a favorite though not invariable target. A group of onlookers was generally present, audibly commenting upon the performances of each player, judging their relative abilities, inciting them, and urging them on . . ." (p. 347). For a discussion of marking, see Claudia Mitchell-Kernan, "Signifying, Loudtalking, and Marking," in Kochman, *Rappin' and Stylin' Out*, 332–35. For an in-depth examination of signifying, see Henry Louis Gates, Jr., *The Signifying Monkey: A Theory of Afro-American Literary Criticism* (Oxford and New York: Oxford University Press, 1988).

20. For more on metacommunication see Gregory Bateson, "A Theory of Play and Fantasy," in *Steps to an Ecology of Mind*, ed. Gregory Bateson (New York: Ballentine, 1972), 177–93; Roman Jakobson, "Closing Statement: Linguistics and Poetics," in *Style in Language*, ed. T. A. Sebeok (New York: John Wiley & Sons, 1960), 350–77; Barbara A. Babcock, "The Story in the Story: Metanarration in Folk Narrative," in *Verbal Art as Performance*, ed. Richard Bauman (Rowley, Massachusetts: Newbury House, 1977), 61–80; and Victor Turner, *The Anthropology of Performance* (New York: PAJ Publications, 1986), 102–103.

21. Turner, *The Anthropology of Performance*, 24.

22. Richard Bauman, "Differential Identity and the Social Base of Folklore," in *Toward New Perspectives in Folklore*, eds. Americo Paredes and Richard Bauman (Austin: University of Texas Press, 1972), 31–41.

23. Calvin Jamison, interview with the author, Blacksburg, Virginia, 1986.

24. David Chaney, *Fictions and Ceremonies: Representations of Popular Experience* (London: Edward Arnold, 1979), 42.

25. See E. Franklin Frazier, *Black Bourgeoisie: The Rise of a New Middle Class in the United States* (New York: The Free Press, 1962), 83–84. Frazier is critical of African American Greek letter societies. He holds that they "foster all the middle-class values" and "tend to divert the students from a serious interest in education" (p. 83).

26. Turner, 94–95.

27. Turner, 74.

28. Richard Schechner, "Towards a Poetics of Performance," *Essays on Performance Theory, 1970–1976* (New York: Drama Book Specialists, 1977), 108–139. This quote is from p. 120.

29. Turner, 74. Here Turner identifies four phases to social dramas: breach, crisis, redressive action, and reintegration. The dueling sequence of cracks between DST and AKA described in this paper can be understood as redressive action that "furnishes a distanced replication and critique of the events leading up to and composing the 'crisis.' This replication may be in the rational idiom of the judicial process, or in the metaphorical and symbolic idiom of a ritual process" (p. 75).

Chapter 6

Anglo-American Dance in Appalachia and Newfoundland: Toward a Comparative Framework

Colin Quigley

How are we to understand the relationships of local Anglo-American dance traditions to one another and to the complex whole of traditional vernacular dance of the British Isles and America? What do these relationships tell us about the nature of such dance and the best ways that we as dance scholars can study these rich, dynamic, and complex traditions?

In order to begin to answer these questions, I will focus on two widely separated, quite different North American regions peopled by British immigrants who have continued to practice their dance traditions in an uninterrupted manner, adapting them to the ever-changing cultural and social contexts. Newfoundland and the central Appalachian Mountains represent only two of the many far-flung manifestations of a widespread and diverse body of dance traditions that have emanated from British sources and spread throughout North America and, indeed, much of the colonial world.[1] Two of the dances, the Running Set and the Big Circle Dance, both named by dance collectors, come from the Appalachian Mountains of the Eastern United States, which has long been seen as a regional enclave of Scots-Irish tradition in the New World. The other two dances, the Reel and the Goat, are from the lesser known traditions of Newfoundland, the easternmost maritime province of Canada, which was settled by English and Irish immigrants during the eighteenth and, especially, early nineteenth centuries.

This chapter will not simply compare dance traditions found in these two regions but will go on to ask larger theoretical questions toward the establishment of a comparative framework. To aid in developing a broader view, researchers must work together to develop shared concepts and approaches concerning relevant categories of observation and analysis such as ethnographic description, historical research, stylistic comparison, and social and cultural analyses.

RESEARCH PARADIGMS

In the past, investigation conducted with preservation and promotion of tradition as its goal has often consisted primarily of the collection of examples of a few dance genres selected according to the investigator's standards of tradition, aesthetic preference, and appropriateness for contemporary recreation. Scholars inherited this research model from pioneer English folk song and dance collectors Cecil Sharp and Maud Karpeles. Karpeles, for example, never published descriptions of some of the dances she saw during her 1929 and 1930 trips to Newfoundland, despite the "very wonderful stepping,"[2] because she did not think them suitable for use in the revival movement. There is no record of their musical accompaniment because, in her view, "the tunes were of no special value."[3] Sharp apparently felt no compunction about substituting one dance music tradition for another:

The tunes we heard at Hindman, Hyden, and elsewhere were not very good ones, far inferior, for instance, to those of the English peasant-fiddlers; though the players in Kentucky generally managed, notwithstanding the melodic poverty of the tunes, to play them with such force and abandonment that they made excellent accompaniment to the dance.

It seems possible to find other airs which, while equally satisfying the requirements of the dance, shall be superior to the Kentucky tunes in melodic interest. An attempt in this direction has been made in the collection of airs . . . published in connection with this volume.[4]

I shall be very surprised if within a few months of its publication, the members of the English Folk Dance Society here and in England are not dancing it [i.e., the Running Set] merrily in every one of the Society's Branches and Centres.[5]

Investigation of Anglo-American dance traditions long continued to be hampered by these earlier research paradigms reflecting the investigator's personal preferences. Contemporary dance researchers are, however, interested in augmenting our knowledge of traditional dancing as it is actually practiced rather than as we might reconstruct it, perhaps in the process re-envisioning the dance according to our own tastes as Sharp and Karpeles did.

Currently, there are a number of research paradigms in this area. One important development has been a movement toward in-depth study of dance events, focusing on only a few at a time within a limited locality. It is essential that we continue in this direction and not fall into the older pattern described above. Conducting ethnographically well-documented case studies is crucial for furthering the goals I am espousing. More complete ethnographies of movement would permit the integration of movement description with analysis of its immediate performance contexts and broader cultural issues, an especially laudable direction taken in some recent work.

Nevertheless, use of consistent and systematic movement description lags behind in this new thrust, and it is crucial that we not lose touch with the movement elements of the dance events. How to integrate apparently opposing approaches is a central challenge. For example, ethnographic dance analysis has been characterized frequently as either structural or contextual, dealing with either the movement or its surrounding factors.[6] The dance event concept provides one model for this integration that has been widely adopted,[7] but this framework can be somewhat self-contained. Ethnomusicologist Alan Merriam warns of the dangers of "micro-ethnography,"[8] while Bruno Nettl encourages his fellow ethnomusicologists not to forget the importance of the overview toward which the much criticized "armchair" scholars strove.[9] How can we move to comparative generalizations while avoiding the pitfalls of earlier efforts by Sharp and others, to which the event model has been our response? The following sorties into the territory of comparative study are meant to suggest the kinds of research questions and analytic models that can address the big picture as well as the small.

A RUNNING SET IN NEWFOUNDLAND?

The focus of the first of these sorties is the question: "Is there a Running Set in Newfoundland?" In order to begin to answer that question, I engaged in a comparison of dance structure, formation, and the "figures," or paths followed by dancers in both Appalachia and Newfoundland. The figures are the most fully and explicitly articulated category of native dance description as well as the most widely documented by dance collectors. Newfoundland and Appalachia share movement repertoires in all three dimensions of structure, formation, and figures, and the two traditions are strikingly similar. Comparing the two raises problems and possibilities in application of historical method to the study of traditional vernacular dance and again brings attention to the legacy of Cecil Sharp.

Sharp first named and described the Running Set of Kentucky in 1917; it has become one of the dominant images of Appalachian traditional dance. Based on the recollections of older people in Kentucky, recollections that stretch back to the early part of the century, folklorist LeeEllen Friedland has reconstructed the salient features of the Running Set: a circle formation of as many couples as could dance together at one time, from four to eight depending on the size of the room; a structural pattern of group figures, followed by the progressive lead of a "minor set" figure (in counterclockwise direction) by each couple in turn, with a group figure between each successive lead.[10]

The Running Set's status is due partly to its perceived antiquity. Sharp believed the Running Set to be a survival[11] of an early and otherwise undocumented phase in the development of English Country Dance.[12] Sharp argued that he was led to view the dance as of an earlier period than those in Playford's *English Dancing Master* of 1651 because of the Running Set's "forceful emotional character," its lack of "courtesy movements," its speed, and "the way the dancers comport themselves."[13] Because Sharp held that in all cases, ruder dances lacking "courtesy movements" evolved into more refined versions, he believe that the Running Set had to be an older dance form. In my judgment, however, such "drawing room" manners as those to which Sharp refers might be deleted from a dance as easily as they may have been added to more rustic originals, as Sharp presumes they were added during the time period of the Dancing Master collection. In short, style is not necessarily proof of age.

Sharp finds one structural parallel to the Running Set in the Playford collection, a "round for as many as will" with successive parts led by each couple in turn, but lacking the interpolated promenade which he observed in Kentucky. He views the Playford round as a late example of an earlier type, not an unreasonable interpretation and one supported by Margaret Dean-Smith,[14] who dealt with the historical sources in more detail than Sharp. However, this Playford round is not necessarily a "corrupt" version of the hypothetical historical source of his Running Set. Sharp's view of it as such derives from his romantically inspired evolutionary premise.

While Sharp's conclusion might seem reasonable, it is seriously flawed. He writes:

Although we may be unable to ascribe to the Running Set a definite date we may with some assurance claim: that it is the sole survival of a type of Country-dance which, in order of development, preceded the Playford dance, that it flourished in other parts of England and Scotland a long while after it had fallen into desuetude in the South; and that some time in the eighteenth century it was brought by emigrants from the Border counties to America where it has since been traditionally preserved.

Subsequent investigations have indeed led "to the discovery of more examples of this particular type of Country dance . . . [making] it necessary to modify the theory above enunciated," as Sharp went on to suggest.[15] Debate continues about the historical background of the Running Set and related dances.

One such related dance, which has become emblematic of Appalachian Mountain tradition, is the Big Circle dance, so named by dance collectors. Many more couples are involved in it than in the Running Set, all progressing simultaneously as they perform the "minor set" figures, again the collectors' term. Its relationship to Sharp's Running Set and the place of both within the tradition and the revival movement have sparked some debate. Folklorist Burt Feintuch in particular sees a shift from the smaller set with its successive leads by individual couples to the simultaneous progression of the big circle form as parallel to changing patterns of community socializing.[16] Friedland has questioned this interpretation, arguing that the circular formation was the original,[17] although it was usually composed of only four to six couples.

As this debate demonstrates, how one explains the meaning, significance, and historical relationships of these similar dance forms turns in part on an interpretation of whether and to what extent dance enacts the dancers' more general socialization patterns. Our understanding of these forms is enhanced if we do not view the Appalachian tradition in isolation, but rather see its dances as one manifestation of a very widespread dance culture. This dance culture has emanated primarily from various parts of the British Isles at different time periods and undergone adaptation and modification in response to local conditions. By comparing the movement resources available throughout the breadth of the tradition and the principles of coordination as they are understood by the dancers themselves, we can more productively investigate questions concerning how people manipulate these expressive forms. Dancers of the past and of isolated rural areas have been no less active and creative in devising movement responses to their particular experience than have been the urbanites generally represented by surviving dancing masters' collections or today's revivalists. As researchers, we must try to understand all dancers' responses in terms of the available resources that constitute their tradition in order to gain insight into their expressive needs and aesthetic preference.

THE GOAT: TRADITIONAL DANCE IN NEWFOUNDLAND

By way of illustration, the course of development of dance followed in Newfoundland provides contrasts and parallels to the Kentucky experience. The examples I use for comparison are drawn from the extensive resources of the Memorial University of Newfoundland Folklore and Language Archive (MUNFLA), which include both my own fieldwork material, gathered throughout the entire province since 1978, and many student collections, some of which were made with my guidance.

As in the Appalachian Mountains, traditional dance forms in Newfoundland include individual percussive dancing, known as step dancing; mixed-sex couple dancing such as waltzes and polkas, which were known traditionally but were performed rarely and were never viewed as distinctively Newfoundland in character; and, most importantly, group dances of several types. The so-called Square Dance, consisting of local variations of the Plain Quadrille, was most widely reported and performed at the time of my research.[18] The Lancers Quadrille was also widely known, while very few longways dances were reported.

Recalled at least by name in many areas but performed now only in a few places is a dance known variously as the Reel, Cotillion, or Old Eight.[19] This dance type is significant for our understanding of the dynamics of the dance tradition in that it is reported from older contexts and from contemporary settings most like those of the past. The dance events at which it was performed most often were "house times," when dancing was performed in homes by small family and neighborhood groups. The dances were generally informal in organization. Most sources recall that this form was replaced by the Square Dance, which is more typical of the "hall times" held in public buildings, such as parish halls or schools, and attended by a larger number of participants drawn from several nearby communities within a region, thus comprising a bigger and less close-knit group.

Despite the many references I found to this dance form in Newfoundland, I was unable to discover the details of its performance until I came across the dance called the Goat from Harbour Deep,[20] filmed in 1980 by Memorial University Extension Media. I correlated it with notes in Maud Karpeles' journal describing a Reel she saw in Stock Cove, Newfoundland, in 1929.[21] These dances are clearly the same structural type as the Appalachian circle dance, although far removed in their historic and geographic genealogy. The Goat, like the Kentucky dance, is performed by four couples; Karpeles' Reel features six couples. In both Newfoundland and Kentucky, the dancers are arranged in circular formation. Each couple in turn leads a "set" by dancing one of several figures with each of the other couples in turn, thus progressing around the ring. Between the sets, group figures are interpolated. Couples in the Goat and Reel, however, are numbered clockwise, not counterclockwise as is generally the case in Kentucky, and lead to the left, not to the right.

To understand the context in which the Goat is performed, one must know that the community of Harbour Deep is one of the more remote communities in Newfoundland today. Situated on the east coast of the Northern Peninsula, it is not linked to other communities by road. During the summer months, a coastal boat stops there twice a week, while in the winter, when ice often blocks the harbors, snowmobiles make overland travel easier than in the summer months. The self-contained character of social life in such circumstances, which was more typical of many outport communities before World War II, has contributed to the perpetuation of older patterns of socializing within this community. Significantly for traditional dance, Christmas remains an important seasonal period of intensive socializing, lasting a full twelve days. This twelve-day period is highlighted by the dancing of the Goat, which might take place several times. The dance would also be performed occasionally at weddings and other less formal gatherings during the year.

A thorough description of such a dance event made by a student in 1972 will assist in the historical placement of the Goat relative to similar Appalachian dances.[22] The Anglican Church Women's Association of Harbour Deep organized this dance, which was held during a "women's time" at Christmas and took place in the "lodge." A supper was held around 7 P.M., lasting until 9 or 10 P.M. In an observation significant for placing this occasion within the spectrum of Newfoundland dance event types, the collector noted:

Although everybody knows that the dance will take place, nobody has made provision for an accordion player. Usually someone is sent to collect an accordion player and an accordion. One of the many children present is appointed this task. I never was sure the reason for this; the accordion player was never paid [for] his services and rarely volunteered his talents. It was usually only after a search that he would be prodded to play. But once he started, "he let her go!"[23]

This comment clearly places this event toward the more informal, close-knit, fewer-participant gathering end of the spectrum. The hall in which the dance is held, while public, is smaller than those in larger communities, and people recalled that until its construction some twenty years earlier dancing was done in kitchens, in which environment this dance form took shape. Thus the Goat has its roots in "house times" and therefore can be inferred to be an older dance form.

The student collector's informants explained that the name "the Goat" referred to the fact that the dance was "wild like a goat." Others spoke of "running the goat,"[24] suggesting a reference to that exhausting experience and presenting a parallel to Sharp's use of the phrase to "run" a set.[25] Two informants said its true name was "cotillion."

The Goat is the earliest dance form recalled by Harbour Deep residents. The possible English sources of this Newfoundland dance are of a more recent vintage than related Appalachian forms. While Europeans had arrived in Appalachia by the late eighteenth century, Harbour Deep was not settled until the late nineteenth century, most likely by people from older Newfoundland communities. Harbour Deep's predominant family names and Anglican religion suggest that the settlers' old-country origin was West Country England, the source area for much of Newfoundland's immigration after 1830. Communities of a size and makeup sufficient to support dance traditions of this kind, except for St. John's and a few other major centers, are unlikely to predate this period by much. On the other hand, Stock Cove, where Maud Karpeles recorded the Reel, is an older community of primarily Irish descent. Other archival sources indicate that this structural type, resembling the historical cotillion with its series of "change" figures and a repeated interpolated "chorus" figure, was widespread in Newfoundland well into the first decades of the twentieth century.

It is thus not possible to ascribe the Newfoundland versions to either an English or Irish old-world source at this time. The form may have been familiar to both groups or disseminated from one or the other source within Newfoundland. A similar situation exists in the Appalachian region, where some communities evidence Scots-Irish background, whereas others are predominantly English in ancestry. Dance forms today are similar in both kinds of communities, with some overlap in forms and styles.

THE GOAT AND THE RUNNING SET

The film of the Goat[26] shows clearly its structural similarity to the Running Set, as well as the existence of several common figures in both. There is a group figure, sometimes called "dance around," like that noted as typical in Kentucky by Friedland.[27] This group figure is repeated between the subsequent minor set figures and consists of circling in a ring to the left and right while step dancing. Next comes the "through the middle" figure, which is reminiscent of many American square dance figures during which one couple dances across the set to pass between the opposite couple, separates, and travels around the outside of the set back to place; it seems to correspond to Sharp's "going down town."[28] Finally, there is the "men's turn off," which is similar to Sharp's "box the gnat,"[29] in which the leading man and his partner go into the center of the set. The leading man turns a woman in the set by his right hand, then turns his partner by this left hand. He continues this sequence until he has turned every woman in the set. He then repeats the pattern, giving right hand to each man but step dancing with them rather than turning. The women also perform this figure but turn both men and women without step dancing. One of the figures of the Goat, "on the Labrador," in which one couple dances a path through and around the others, seems specifically designed for a four-couple set and is not found in Karpeles' Stock Cove reel. It seems most similar in conception to the "waltz swing," in which groups of three dancers dance around one another.[30] The group figures that conclude the dance are also among those recorded by Sharp in the Appalachian region. A Newfoundland "through the bushes" is an American "right and left,"[31] and "thread the needle" parallels Sharp's "wind up the ball of yarn" figure.[32]

Anyone familiar with this dance genre will realize that there are many names for variants of these figure "types." A more thorough comparison would require the kind of index essayed by J. Olcutt Sanders in his 1942 "Finding List."[33] Such a classification system could be used to facilitate comparison, without necessarily applying an outmoded diffusionist model.

Many differences between the Goat and the Running Set are also apparent. Most immediately noticeable is the sound and rhythmic feeling of the accordion accompaniment used for the Goat. Differences in the qualities of dance movement are also apparent and perhaps related to the contrastive rhythmic character of the music. In the Goat, more emphasis is placed on men's competitive stepping, for which opportunities are provided within the framework of figures. Footwork in the swing is executed a little differently in the Goat as well, the woman almost backing up as a couple rotates around their axis. A more thorough movement analysis would yield many more comparisons.

If we acknowledge the close relationship of these dances, despite the contrasts, we can see them as offshoots of the same family tree with a variety of historical precedents. Early nineteenth century cotillions, as suggested by some informants' use of this name, would seem to provide the most immediate structural model for Newfoundland versions. Whether these might be a source for the Running Set as well, rather than a hypothesized pre-Playford English Round, is one question raised by this comparison. On the other hand, the wide separation of these two manifestations of a similar form suggests that these dances may represent the persistence or even the re-emergence of a structural scheme that is inherent within their common dance tradition. Comparison of the Goat and the Reel with other Newfoundland group dances suggests that dance elements are rather freely interchangeable, and that distinctions, even among dances of different structural patterns, are not unbridgeable. The same may be said about group dances of different localities within the Appalachian region.

In Newfoundland, this circular progressing-couple dance structure did not survive the transition from house to hall time. It was generally replaced by quadrille forms, which emphasize facing-couple interactions, making them more square than circular. The figures in the newer form, rather than repeating themselves, follow a progressive discursive structure with each interaction being different than the last. These quadrille forms were better suited to the participation of larger numbers of people in larger spaces. Dancers became progressively integrated into a coordinated dancing group through a standard sequence of increasingly coordinated group movements, while drawing on some of the same repertoire of figures.[34]

In the Appalachian region we may see a similar shift in the character of dance contexts and adaptation to larger numbers of dancers in larger groups, but Appalachian dancers draw on slightly different movement resources. Quadrille forms were not integrated into a distinctively Appalachian dance style. They are found, rather, in the later square dance repertoire that seems to have been developed during the late nineteenth and early twentieth centuries by people from a variety of regions with slightly different dance repertoires who mingled in their move westward.[35]

Investigation of the history of these dances cannot, I think, be a search for the origins of a dance as a "diffusible entity" to be found at a particular time and place: neither a stage of cultural evolution, as Sharp posited, nor a dance form such as the French cotillion of 1798 or the English country dance of the border counties of 1700. In fact, the more widely one gathers examples, and the more closely one examines them, the more variation one finds and the more mutable the tradition appears to be.

I would argue that these dances have no single historical source, nor even a single immediate predecessor. Rather, the history of these dance forms, as suggested by this comparison, would seem to be one of a continual reordering of dance movement elements including structural schemes, group formations, and figures drawn from throughout the available dance repertoire and resources provided by tradition. Comparison of many versions of the Newfoundland square dance and the Lancers reveals substitutions and reshufflings of structural units including the minor elements such as individual step dance, partner swing, and "ladies chain" across the set sequences, as well as among the major figural components.[36] Such a view more explicitly acknowledges and emphasizes the active participation of dancers in the creation of tradition than does the search for historical origins.

In addition to the study of figure dancing, a second area receiving scholarly attention is percussive dancing, known in Newfoundland as step dancing and in the Appalachian region variously as buckdancing, clogging, or flatfooting. Perhaps because it has been less well documented than aspects of group formation—structure and figure—research within this genre has not been primarily historical but has focused on characterization of style. All too easily an emphasis on identification and description of stylistic distinctions can lead to stereotyping. This seems especially true when essaying regional generalizations. There is a common tendency among dance collectors and presenters to speak rather glibly in terms of style, be it by type, such as buckdancing or clogging, or by region, such as Appalachian, the Cumberland Plateau, or in my case, Newfoundland and its various bays and vernacular regions. Stereotypical images of Appalachian percussive dancing have been promulgated by performing clogging teams across the United States. The most revealing aspect of Mike Seeger and Ruth Pershing's 1988 video documentary, *Talking Feet*, is the great diversity of dance movement it presents from within the Appalachian region, effectively debunking this stereotype.[37] There is a danger that we bring such distinctions unexamined to our investigations, rather than waiting to discover within the material what the significant identifications may be. Clearly, a broadly comparative framework is needed.

DEVELOPING A FRAMEWORK FOR RESEARCH

Systematic recording, analysis, and comparison of all movement dimensions is needed, and this process has been hampered by the continuing use of idiosyncratic description and notation systems. Dance ethnologist Frank Hall's morphological and structural analysis of clogging is one of our best models for this to date, using Labanotation to illustrate fundamental movement units and letter symbols to illustrate their combination.[38] His approach is informed by concepts drawn from Kaeppler's investigations of Tongan dance, which are among the most uncompromisingly directed toward discovery of native categorization, structural principles, and understanding.[39] By this means, he is able to analyze buckdancing and precision clogging performances, not only to clarify their generic characteristics, but also ultimately to suggest differences between improvisational and compositional processes within this expressive system. The approach, more than the specific graphic technique, is crucial here, although Labanotation does have certain well-recognized advantages as a movement notation system because of its comprehensive and systematic design and widespread readability. Our investigations must move beyond the use of notation as memory aid and teaching tool. The approach taken to recording movement description needs to serve analysis as well as teaching.

In developing a framework for research we need to move beyond the limitations of genre study. Dancers are always moving their bodies, even when attention is on the movement dimensions of formation, path, and dancer interactions. Clogging or stepping are defined in terms of the individual dancer's footwork, but they need to be seen in relation to the totality of dance movement. How dancers do or do not incorporate stepping with figure dancing is a crucial difference between Newfoundland and Appalachia, for example, and may be an important variable in more wideranging comparisons. Dance movement analysis, in turn, is only one part of an ethnography of movement that should take account of the entire dance event, as well as the movement components of the culture at large.

The social and cultural factors of the dance must also be taken into account. An important indication of the need for a comparative approach that can include these factors was provided for me at the 1989 Center for Appalachian Studies and Services traditional dance conference. As I showed the video footage of the Goat, it became more and more clear that the Newfoundland women were remarkably inactive compared with the Appalachian dancers we had seen. Audience members asked, "Why? What does this difference mean about Newfoundland society?" I might now rephrase this as two questions: what does the difference between men's and women's dance movement indicate about gender identity and expression in Newfoundland, and what does its contrast to Appalachian dancing indicate about these two societies? In other words, how might one account for such an observed difference in movement behavior?

Even a preliminary attempt to account for these observed patterns of gender differentiation in dance must integrate many levels of cultural context. Outport Newfoundland society is dependent on a fishing economy based on market capitalism operating in a very harsh environment.[40] This combination, together with historical circumstances during the latter nineteenth and early twentieth centuries, has led to a rather insular community social life in which group dance has been used as a medium to express an ideal of social integration at certain community-wide events.[41] In some contexts, primarily hall times it seems to me, the women provide a framework within which the step-dancing men have the freedom to express their individuality and competitive relationships without threatening to break their community ties. In other settings and occasions, such as the house party, at which the expression of individual vitality takes precedence over making the lineaments of community visible, women seem free to express themselves through step dance in less structured relational formats, although they do not compete directly with men. Perhaps the strictures on the expression of role relations are stronger in the more public contexts, particularly the symbolically intensified wedding occasion.

Relating these patterns to the larger distinctions between gender roles in other spheres of life would be another step in such an investigation, one which I have yet to take. Nor have I begun to answer the comparative question: if so in Newfoundland, why not in the Appalachian region or, for that matter, elsewhere? Peter Cooke's films of dancing from the Shetland Islands, in which the women's stepping is much more restrained than that of the men, reflect some similarities to Newfoundland.[42] The many women shown dancing in Mike Seeger and Ruth Pershing's film, *Talking Feet*, suggest there is less gender-based movement differentiation in the Appalachians. More information from many expressions of the Anglo-American tradition is needed before questions can be profitably asked or answered at this scale in an attempt to relate differences in movement to differences in other aspects of social and cultural context. This is the kind of comparative investigation from which we are the farthest. It is a level at which it is hardest to control the many variables at work but one that suggests the possibility of more fundamental generalizations about the workings of this expressive medium. Further application of integrative models of ethnographic description and shared frameworks of movement description and analysis are needed, along with continuing dialogue, to discover threads that tie together the manifold varieties of these dance traditions.

Our comparative framework needs to extend well beyond the immediate communities in which we collect if we hope to discover and come to understand the range of transformations our dance movement resources have undergone. Within this analytical frame, our primary research questions ought to be: What are the movement resources available? What are the principles that dancers use when they put those movement resources together into new combinations? And finally, what are the factors affecting their use? Such a descriptive analysis of dance movement needs to be understood in native terms: What significant movement features do the dancers recognize? What significant distinctions do the dancers make? Do they recognize style distinctions, and if so, how are these constituted? And how might one account for native perception of these significant differences? A general project might consist of documenting the full range of available movement throughout a tradition and asking: What components are used to make distinctions? How and by whom are they made? And how and why does such differentiation happen?

Juxtaposing the clearly related, yet widely separated, dance traditions of Newfoundland and the Appalachian region reveals surprising consistencies, as well as differences, that highlight pervasive shared components and shed new light on possible historical origins. Given the complex possibilities revealed by such a wide comparison, however, I believe that the identification of historical forms that have been disseminated and modified by dancers in different regions is only part of a larger project. Examination of the common repertoire throughout this dance tradition, its form, structure, and style, when integrated with thorough ethnographies of movement, will permit investigation of the processes that generate differentiation and innovation as well as the more usually emphasized conservation and perpetuation. The focus will shift from mere description of dance forms to the processes by which dance becomes a personally and culturally expressive medium.

NOTES

1. For example, see John F. Szwed and Morton Marks, "The Afro-American Transformation of European Set Dances and Dance Suites," *Dance Research Journal* 20, no. 1 (Summer 1988): 29–36.

2. Maud Karpeles, Field notes, Memorial University of Newfoundland Folklore and Language Archive (MUNFLA), St. John's. Ms. 78–0003/folder 2, 4690.

3. Karpeles, Field notes, Ms. 78–0003/folder 7, 6.

4. Cecil J. Sharp and Maud Karpeles, *The Country Dance Book* (1918; Rpt., East Ardsley, England: EP Publishing, 1976), 18.

5. Sharp and Karpeles, 15.

6. Anya Peterson Royce, *The Anthropology of Dance* (Bloomington: Indiana University Press, 1977), 64–85.

7. For example, see Lisbet Torp, ed., *The Dance Event: A Complex Cultural Phenomenon* (Copenhagen: ICTM Study Group on Ethnochoreology, 1989).

8. Alan Merriam, "On Objections to Comparison in Ethnomusicology," in *Cross Cultural Perspectives in Music*, eds. Robert Falck and Timothy Rice (Toronto: University of Toronto Press, 1983), 174–189. This quote is from p. 174.

9. Bruno Nettl, *The Study of Ethnomusicology: Twenty-nine Issues and Concepts* (Urbana: University of Illinois Press, 1983), 52–64.

10. LeeEllen Friedland, "Traditional Folk Dance in Kentucky," *Country Dance and Song* 10 (1979): 5–19.

11. See Jan Harold Brunvand, *The Study of American Folklore: An Introduction*, 2d ed. (New York: W. W. Norton & Co., 1978). The "survivals theory" is one of the basic theories that attempts to account for the origin of folklore. As folklorist Brunvand explains in *The Study of American Folklore* (p. 27), "The survivals theory pushes the origins of folklore back to a 'savage stage' of civilization and maintains that modern folklore is an inheritance or 'survival' from the past."

12. Sharp's historical theories are cast within a framework of unilinear cultural evolution unconvincing today. Theresa Buckland criticizes the theoretical and methodological under-

pinnings of this perspective, which provided a rationale for considering circular dance formations to be survivals of hypothesized pagan worship around a sacred object. See Theresa Buckland, "English Folk Dance Scholarship: A Review," in *Traditional Dance, Volume I*, ed. Theresa
Buckland (Crewe, England: Crewe and Alsageer College, 1982), 3–18.

13. Sharp and Karpeles, 9–13.

14. John Playford, *Playford's English Dancing Master 1651: A Facsimile Reprint with an Introduction, Bibliography and Notes*, ed. Margaret Dean-Smith (London: Schott & Co., 1957),
xvi–xix, 20, 30.

15. Sharp and Karpeles, 13.

16. Burt Feintuch, "Dancing to the Music: Domestic Square Dances and Community in
Southcentral Kentucky (1880–1940)," *Journal of the Folklore Institute* 18, No. 1 (January–April
1981): 49–68.

17. See Friedland, 5–19.

18. Quadrilles were four-couple square formation dances composed of a sequence of figures, usually five, which first appeared at the end of the eighteenth century, becoming more
popular after the first decade of the nineteenth century. While found in many variations, the
"first set" or "plain" quadrille demonstrates a fair degree of stability in its figure patterns and
became very widespread in popular practice. The Lancers is another quadrille sequence that
likewise achieved widespread currency. See Phillip Richardson, *The Social Dances of the Nineteenth Century in England* (London: Herbert Jenkins, 1960), and Roy Dommet, "The Kitchen
Lancers," *English Dance and Song* 41 no. 3 (1979): 7.

19. The cotillion, a four-couple square formation, came to England at the end of the eighteenth century from France, where it had derived from the *contredanse*, a French version of the
English country dance. It is distinguished by the alternation of standard "changes," patterns
that were the same for all cotillions, and a distinctive "figure." See Elizabeth Aldrich, *From
the Ballroom to Hell: Grace and Folly in Nineteenth-Century Dance* (Evanston, Illinois: Northwestern University Press, 1991).

20. Memorial University of Newfoundland Educational Technology, *Running the Goat
in Harbour Deep*, 30-minute 1/2-inch VHS, #C18 (St. John's: Memorial University, 1980).

21. MUNFLA, Ms. 78-0003/folder 2, 4694–4696.

22. MUNFLA, Ms. 72-155.

23. MUNFLA, Ms. 72-155, 7.

24. MUNFLA, Ms. 72-155, 11.

25. Sharp and Karpeles, 8.

26. MUNFLA, *Running the Goat in Harbour Deep*.

27. Friedland, "Traditional Folk Dance in Kentucky."

28. Sharp and Karpeles, 29–30.

29. Sharp and Karpeles, 29–30.

30. Sharp and Karpeles, 41.

31. Sharp and Karpeles, 31.

32. Sharp and Karpeles, 34.

33. J. Olcutt Sanders, "Finding List of Southeastern Square Dance Figures," *Southern Folklore Quarterly*, 6, no. 4 (December 1942): 263–275.

34. I have discussed this process of change in more detail in Colin Quigley, *Close to the
Floor: Folk Dance in Newfoundland* (St. John's: MUNFL Publications, 1985): 93–94.

35. Friedland, "Traditional Folk Dance in Kentucky."

36. Quigley, 28–43; 93–95.

37. Mike Seeger and Ruth Pershing, *Talking Feet: Solo Southern Dance: Flatfoot, Buck, and Tap*, 87-min., color, VHS and Beta 1/2 inch video (El Cerrito, California: Flower Films, 1988).

38. Frank Hall, "Improvisation and Fixed Composition in Clogging," *Journal for the Anthropological Study of Human Movement* 3 (1984–1985): 200–17.

39. Adrienne L. Kaeppler, "Method and Theory in Analyzing Dance Structure with an Analysis of Tongan Dance," *Ethnomusicology* 16, no. 2 (May 1972): 173–217.

40. Gerald Sider, *Culture and Class in Anthropology and History* (Cambridge: Cambridge University Press, 1986).

41. Quigley, 60–64.

42. See Peter Cooke, *The Bride's Reel in Cullivoe, Shetland*. The film is on deposit in the Video Archives of the School of Scottish Studies, University of Edinburgh.

Part 2

Conserving Tradition

"Conserving Tradition" focuses on the conscious efforts on the part of people from within a community to preserve or, in the case of the Eastern Band Cherokee, to revive their own indigenous vernacular dance.

In "Finding the Way Between the Old and the New," a title that could serve as the motto for most of the preservationists described in this section, scholar David Whisnant offers a "complex and instructive example of intentional intervention into traditional culture by a forceful entrepreneur."[1] It is his account of Bascom Lamar Lunsford and his founding of the Asheville Mountain Dance and Folk Festival in 1928. A lawyer, Lunsford came from the mountains near Asheville, North Carolina. Transplanting old-time square dance into the competitive and public setting of a festival gained mountain dance new audiences and new respect, just as Lunsford intended. But it also resulted in the evolution of what was once the informal social form of old-time Appalachian square dance into a well-rehearsed, polished team exhibition dance performed in matching costumes, resembling those of Western club square dancers. Just as with the African American steppers in "Continuity and Change," a change in context altered the nature of the dance.

In folklorist Gail Matthews-DeNatale's study of freestyle clogging, we leave Asheville and move one county to the south to Canton, North Carolina, and approximately fifty years later. Freestyle clogging teams, the descendants of the performance form that resulted from Lunsford's creation of a new context, now see themselves as the ones upholding the standard of authentic mountain dance. Bob Phillips, a team director and freestyle clogger from Canton, articulates this view, even as the very existence of freestyle clogging is challenged by yet another innovation, precision clogging, which took many competitions by storm in the 1950s. In freestyle clogging, dancers use percussive footwork while executing old-time square dance figures. No two dancers do precisely the same footwork at any given moment.

Barbara Bogart of Kingsport, Tennessee, speaks about precision clogging. As precision team leader Bogart explains, the distinguishing characteristic of precision clogging (in contrast to freestyle clogging) is that all dancers strive to synchronize their steps. Precision teams are also far less likely to employ old-time square dance patterns, points out Bogart. In an interview excerpt, she also asserts her claim to being a rightful heir of old-time Appalachian dance.

Finally, folklorist Jane Harris Woodside travels roughly another twenty miles south of Canton, North Carolina, to the Qualla Boundary Reservation, home of the first Appalachians. She traces the periodic attempts of the Eastern Band Cherokee over almost two centuries to resurrect their tribal dance. These are mostly animal dances, originally religious in nature. As the dancers imitate a bear searching for food or the sacred eagle soaring on outspread wings, they express their sense of kinship with these animals. Walker Calhoun, an elder who is one of the leaders of the current attempts to preserve Cherokee dance, gives a vivid picture of the role that such dance still played in community life during his youth as a result of an earlier revival effort.

All of these studies deal with performance forms of vernacular dance, and all occur over a relatively contained geographic area. Taken together, however, they span most of the twentieth century.

DISCUSSION

At least among some members of the communities in "Conserving Tradition," vernacular dance serves as an expression of cultural identity. These are, for the most part, dancers with a sense of mission. For the mountaineer and the Native American, as for the striking mine worker and the African American steppers in "Continuity and Change," these assertions of cultural identity and pride are in part intended to counteract popular (and negative) misconceptions about their culture. One of Lunsford's avowed purposes in staging the Asheville Mountain Dance and Folk Festival, for example, was "to draw attention to the fine cultural value of our traditional music and our dancing, and the fine honor of our people."[2] A 1976 *Cherokee One Feather* article on the introduction of traditional dance programs in the schools sounds a similar note when it expresses the hope that "if we continue to teach our Indian children the true history and culture [through dance], they will learn that we were not the dirty, animal-like, less than human beings as some textbooks, television and movies portray us."[3]

In each case, the attempts of preservationists from within the community are sparked by larger social and economic factors, such as industrialization or the change from agriculture to tourism as an economic base. Tourism is one of the major industries in the western part of North Carolina covered by all three studies. Conse quently, performing for audiences of outsiders has been a factor in both the preservation and adaptation of dances. On the one hand, the demand of tourists for entertainment with a distinctive regional flavor is one of the reasons that dance forms such as freestyle clogging are still being performed. However, in order to play to these visitors, the dancers become more concerned with presentation, with how the dance looks to "outside eyes." As a result, what were once social forms become increasingly performance oriented.

Some individuals fear that mainstream culture will obliterate their own distinctive cultures. They are afraid that they will lose their cultural identities. Cherokee traditional dancer and director of Cherokee Tribal Child Care Services Gilliam Jackson stated his belief about the importance of maintaining distinctively Cherokee traditions in general: "When these things are gone, I think we're going to be in a state of confusion: we're not going to know who we are."[4] Vernacular dance, then, is one way that these groups maintain their sense of identity. They highlight their differences from mainstream culture; as with the African American steppers, they use dance to establish their "differential identity."

Change presents people in these communities with new options. As Matthews-DeNatale points out, dancers today have a variety of vernacular styles from which to choose. Their stylistic choices reveal much about the degree to which they are willing to abandon the old and adopt the new; they say a great deal about where individuals stand regarding issues of continuity and change.

In the process of making choices about styles, vernacular dancers formulate their own notions of what is traditional and what is not traditional. Again, as Matthews-DeNatale observes, confrontation with change results in vernacular dancers' consciously labeling certain elements such as old-time square figures as "traditional." Previously, they may have just thought of such elements as "dancing." They find themselves clarifying the meaning and importance of the old ways in their lives. The relative stability in communities such as Fancy Gap in Virginia's Blue Ridge Mountains, therefore, might partially explain why the whole issue of tradition never comes up among many of the old-time square dancers described by dance ethnologist Susan Spalding in "Continuity and Change."

These emic, or insider, definitions of tradition vary from group to group, and it is not impossible for one group's tradition to be cited by another group as an upstart innovation. In fact, the pattern that frequently emerges from these chapters is that people within a given culture often consider the dance form immediately preceding the currently popular style as "traditional" because it represents an earlier lifestyle. For example, one way that both freestyle clogger Bob Phillips and Cherokee dancer Walker Calhoun connect their traditional dance forms firmly to the past in a personal way is to use the performance style of their mothers and grandmothers as a defining aesthetic criterion. Phillips considers freestyle clogging traditional because it precedes precision clogging in his area of western North Carolina, while Barbara Bogart, a precision clogging team director from Kingsport, Tennessee, considers her precision style to be traditional because it still uses some old-time square dance configurations and does not incorporate the more progressive jazz moves used by other teams. In each case, dancers choose certain elements that they see as representing a connection with the past and call those elements "traditional."

While the impetus behind these preservation efforts is certainly conservative, conservation does not preclude adaptation and change. The very festival that Lunsford hoped would help preserve mountain dance effected important changes in that vernacular dance style. The Festival's competitive context, not to mention the increasing proportion of tourists in the audience, helped produce freestyle clogging teams that were crisp, unified, and decked out in matching costumes. When Calhoun's troupe performs at festivals for outsiders, they too are careful to wear colorful costumes representing turn-of-the-century, European-influenced dress and to explain the meaning of their tribal dances to the uninitiated. In addition, the Cherokee reconstruct their interrupted tradition out of individuals' memories and draw on anthropologists' field recordings and published accounts. The preservationists are bound to fill in the gaps with personal interpretations and contemporary influences, such as costumes decorated by ribbons associated with a 1970s-era Native American protest march. Both mountain square dance, a social form, and the often highly religious Cherokee tribal dance ultimately evolved into a performance form.

In each of these articles and interviews, then, we hear individuals from within the dance community making judgments concerning what is traditional and what is aesthetically pleasing.

NOTES

1. See Whisnant, "Finding the Way Between the Old and the New," in this volume.
2. Quoted in Whisnant.
3. "Traditional Dances Taught in School," *Cherokee One Feather* (11 February 1976): 3.
4. Quoted in Woodside, "Everybody Needs Identity," in this volume.

Chapter 7

Finding the Way between the Old and the New: The Mountain Dance and Folk Festival and Bascom Lamar Lunsford's Work as a Citizen

David E. Whisnant

Time and a new way of life, a force stronger than Bascom is at work on all folk activities. Bascom is struggling to find the way between the old and the new.
Sarah Gertrude Knott[1]

He always said the festival would be "along about sundown." Bascom Lamar Lunsford, whom they called the "minstrel of the Appalachians," would signal the fiddler to play "Grey Eagle," and Asheville's Mountain Dance and Folk Festival would commence. For nearly fifty years it was a ritual: Bascom would emcee, Aunt Samantha would play her banjo, Sam Queen would dance, and the string bands and dance teams would compete. Bascom and Samantha and Sam are gone now, but the festival is into its second half-century, and its longevity raises a host of questions about the dynamics of culture in the Appalachian region. This chapter addresses some of those questions by examining the festival's beginnings in 1928 as part of Asheville, North Carolina's Rhododendron Festival.

It constituted an important transitional cultural form between "the old and the new"—between the old, rural, traditional, community, and family-based culture, and the emerging urban, industrial, media-dominated mass culture that swept through the mountains as it did through the rest of the country. It furnishes a complex and instructive example of intentional intervention into traditional culture by a forceful entrepreneur who did what he did partly because, as he said, he "just liked mountain people," but who viewed those people from his special perspective as a member of the small but important local, intellectual, effectively bicultural elite whose role in mountain life has never been adequately comprehended. And finally, Lunsford's festival demands serious attention because it is a precocious and important example of cultural work by one who understood the emerging politics of culture in the United States and consciously chose to do that work as his primary civic responsibility.

Lunsford always said he lived "on South Turkey Creek," as indeed he did, but anyone familiar with local geography knows that South Turkey Creek is hard by Asheville, which was already in 1928 the major metropolitan center within more than a hundred miles in any direction. Thus, what Lunsford did, and the festival he created around the Vance Monument on Pack Square in June of 1928, must be understood within the context of the subtle but profound conflict of style and values between 1920s Asheville and the outlying communities of Beaverdam and Candler, Soco Gap and Avery's Creek, Spook's Branch and Dunn's Rock, whose pickers, singers, and dancers gathered once a year with Bascom.

ASHEVILLE'S 1920s BOOM AND THE RHODODENDRON FESTIVAL

> And yet, there was surging into those chosen hills the strong thrust of the world. . . . The streets, ten years before raw clay, were being paved: [W. O.] Gant went into frenzies over the paving assessments, cursed the land, the day of his birth, the machinations of Satan's children. But Eugene followed the wheeled casks of boiling tar; watched the great roller . . . felt, as he saw the odorous pressed tongue of pavement lengthen out, a swelling ecstasy.
>
> Thomas Wolfe, *Look Homeward Angel* (1929), 142–43

In 1883, Julia Wolfe bought a lot for $1,000 on Pack Square in Asheville. For years her husband ran a shop nearby, where he carved stone grave markers. Her son Tom turned one of his father's stone angels into a symbol of the relentless cultural, social, and philosophical changes that were coming to the mountains—and to America—and that made it impossible for anyone ever to go home again. In 1921, Julia sold her lot for $30,000, and Asheville's first skyscraper, the fifteen-story Jackson Building, was erected on the site.[2] The dramatic transition is emblematic of the "force stronger than Bascom" that Sarah Gertrude Knott spoke of, that W. O. Gant saw as the "machinations of Satan's children," that brought his son a "swelling ecstasy," and that made it so compelling and so difficult for Lunsford to find a way between the old and the new in 1928.

Asheville was a rather sleepy town until the railroad reached it in 1886, but for the next half century it boomed. George Vanderbilt arrived in 1889, bought 130,000 acres of mountain land and spent five years building a 250-room French Renaissance chateau just outside town. St. Louis entrepreneur E. W. Grove (who had made his money hawking "Grove's Tasteless Chill Tonic") came in 1900, built the massive stone Grove Park Inn, decapitated Battery Park Hill to build a tourist hotel, and dumped the dirt into a ravine to create business property on what became Coxe Avenue. The population rose dramatically—from only 2,600 in 1880 to 15,000 at the turn of the century, by which time the city had already had electricity and streetcars for more than a decade. By 1928, Asheville's attractions as a tourist center had long been established, the population was nearly 50,000, and the Chamber of Commerce was sending "goodwill ambassadors" across the United States to promote the "Land of the Sky."[3] Real estate speculation, overexpansion, and boosterism were the rule of the day. Lunsford's festival came just at the crest of the wave that finally broke in 1929 amid a scandal over fraud in the sale of water works bonds that left the city and county bonds on the ineligible list of the New York Stock Exchange for thirty years. A state-imposed limit on indebtedness hampered further speculative development.[4]

But in 1928, the scandals and the bust were still in the future. Taking its cues from the Florida land and tourism boom, the Asheville Chamber of Commerce hired Fred L. Weede,[5] former Secretary of the Chamber in Miami, a city that had been described in a joint proclamation by local mayors as "the most Richly Blessed Community of the most Bountifully Endowed State of the most Highly Enterprising People of the Universe." In the early 1920s Miami was, historian Frederick Lewis Allen concluded, "one frenzied real-estate exchange," where to prevent traffic congestion "the city fathers had been forced to pass an ordinance forbidding the sale of property in the street."[6]

To celebrate the boom, the Miami mayor's proclamation designated three days at the end of 1925 as "The Fiesta of the American Tropics." They projected vast balls and dances, and promised, according to Allen, " 'that through our Streets and Avenues shall wind a glorious Pageantry of Sublime Beauty Depicting in Floral loveliness the Blessing Bestowed upon us by Friendly Sun, Gracious Rain, and Soothing Tropic Wind.' " But by mid-1926, the Florida economic boom had turned to bust, and soothing tropic winds spawned a September hurricane that wiped out entire new towns.

Asheville had no hurricanes and appeared to be still on the rising side of the speculative curve, ripe for the manipulations of various boosters. Every year in June, early in the tourist season, the mountainsides around Asheville bloom riotously with the colorful rhododendron. The Chamber of Commerce had apparently contemplated holding a tourist-oriented public celebration as early as 1923, when it adopted a five-year development plan.[7] The idea of a Rhododendron Festival was formally presented in November 1927, and the first festival was scheduled for June 1928. Intense promotion included invitations to prominent people throughout the country, special rates by the railroads, and local campaigns to engage the efforts of clubs and civic groups.[8] Fifteen Southern states sent young women to represent them at the various balls and to ride on the elaborate parade floats. The Rhododendron Pageant, a central feature of the Festival, consisted of "seven dramatic episodes set in lands in which the rhododendron grows." There was an "Indian episode" and a "Chinese episode" with a hundred-foot-long dragon. The Festival prospered for a dozen years.

In 1935, portions of the pageant were broadcast over network radio from a "Castle of the Mountain King" erected in the municipal stadium at McCormick Field. Later Festivals included Cherokee participants, and at the final one in 1940 there was a Negro Festival Parade.

CULTURAL COGNITIVE DISSONANCE: LUNSFORD'S FIRST FESTIVAL

For all its spectacular success as a promotional scheme, the Rhododendron Festival must at last be seen as a product of the peculiar social and economic pathology of the late 1920s, imported like a gaudy souvenir shawl and thrown around a mountain version of Miami madness. Asheville was on the make, and speculative subdivisions were springing up almost daily. Fantasies of instant wealth were the dominant preoccupation; pretension was the dominant style.

An editorial in the Asheville *Citizen* a year before Lunsford grafted a presentation of mountain music and dance onto the Rhododendron Festival revealed poignantly some of the cultural implications of what was happening in Asheville and its outlying districts. Asheville's major cultural news in August 1927 (the year that Bascom's festival is sometimes erroneously said to have begun) was "opera week."[9] Sponsored by the Asheville Music Festival Association, opera week imported the San Carlo Opera Company for performances of European grand opera (*Tosca, Aida, Faust*). On August 13, the *Citizen's* editorial was entitled "Opera and a Fiddler." Opening with a sketch of well-dressed opera goers passing by "an itinerant fiddler, who leans against a wall beside the street tuning his instrument," it explored the cultural irony of a week of grand opera in a mountain city:

He will play for whatever they give, but if no one will wait to listen, he begins anyhow to play a tune that he alone can distinguish amid the din of passing feet. Inside, skilled musicians trained at high cost prepare to present an opera. Outside, one untrained but doubtless talented attracts only an occasional alms giver. Why had the begger-musician [sic] chosen a place so near the opera door? . . . No one stops to ask the fiddler's story. . . . Opera goers inside enjoy a colorful presentation of make believe tragedy set to music. Outside, another music-lover ekes a meager living, from a society in which he has become a misfit, by playing a soft accompaniment to the unsung story of his life.[10]

In 1928, Bascom Lamar Lunsford was in his mid-forties. He had spent most of those years coming to understand the tragedy implied by the editorialist's image and seeking a broad and sympathetic audience for the "unsung story" of mountain musicians. How he viewed either Opera Week or the Rhododendron Festival is not recorded, but it seems reasonable to infer that he saw them as an opportunity to seek at least a position of parity for the fiddler by the opera door, and thereby to inject a note of cultural realism and authenticity to the imported booster fantasy.[11]

The first festival, called variously by the newspapers a "folk frolic," a program of "folk songs and dances," a "big dance festival," and a "folk festival," was held on Tuesday evening, June 6, on Pack Square. It was sponsored by the Elks Lodge, the Monarchs Club, and the Central Labor Union. Although it was nominally directed by a committee of which Lunsford was merely one member, it clearly was Lunsford's show.[12] There were to be five or six groups of dancers (the newspapers called them "clubs," although they had not previously been organized as such) from Buncombe, Henderson, Haywood, and Swain counties, each with its own band of musicians. Dance groups were limited to eight couples and were given twenty-five minutes each to perform. Performances were to be competitive, and prizes of $35, $25, $15, and $10 were to be awarded to the winning dance groups and musicians. The music was to be "confined strictly to mountain tunes" such as "Sourwood Mountain," "Sally Ann," "Cumberland Gap," and "Kidder Cole." It would be, the *Citizen* promised somewhat condescendingly, "one of the quaintest attractions of the Rhododendron Festival."[13]

The morning after the festival on the Square, however, the *Citizen* was more enthusiastic. Five thousand people had attended, sitting as far up on the Vance monument as possible and leaning from second and third story windows around the Square. "Pack Square never presented a more colorful sight in all its history," the *Citizen* reported. "The iron fence around the . . . monument was not exactly broken down but at least offered no bar to those who wanted grandstand seats to witness a throwback from the modern jazz mad world."[14] Significantly, the *Citizen's* writer seemed to grasp intuitively the cultural clash between Lunsford's festival and its Rhododendron Festival context and reached back for older and more appropriate (if finally somewhat romantic) analogues: "The scene suggested a permanent thing," the writer observed. "Something that might be continued from year to year as a festival of Western North Carolina—on the order of the great festivals of older nations which have been handed down from generation to generation. Like the jousts of the early English and King Arthur and his mythical court." Although it was precisely the romanticism of "King Arthur and his mythical court" that lay behind the image system of the Rhododendron Festival, with its crowning of a King and Queen and its "Castle of the Mountain King," the message Lunsford wanted to convey—despite the improbable setting in which it was launched—apparently found its mark. His festival indeed became "a permanent thing," whereas the Rhododendron Festival expired in 1940.

As Lunsford's Mountain Dance and Folk Festival (as it came to be called after it separated from the Rhododendron Festival in 1930) enters its second half century, several questions thrust themselves forward: Where did Lunsford get the idea, and what, if any, antecedents or models were in his mind? To what extent did the Mountain Dance and Folk Festival reflect mountain culture itself, and to what extent did the festival reflect Lunsford's personality and his personal *view* of mountain culture? What long-term effect or impact has the Festival had on the dynamics of culture in western North Carolina? And what does it teach us about the perils and possibilities of presenting traditional culture to mass audiences?

THE FESTIVAL AND LUNSFORD'S "WORK AS A CITIZEN"

He maintained that if anyone ever had a calling, he had a calling.

Jerry Israel [15]

The Mountain Dance and Folk Festival, Loyal Jones says in his biography of Lunsford, "evolved out of and was supported and fed by the local village and rural community social gatherings that had performed their traditions and oral literature in America for two hundred years."[16] While that is true in a very broad sense, it is also true that there had previously been no such event—certainly not one that had become traditional—as that which Lunsford produced in 1928. Actually, there are two broad possibilities for antecedents: (1) the traditional work-related and social gatherings in mountain communities, and (2) Bascom's prior experience as a private folk entrepreneur and promoter. Available evidence suggests that the second was more important than the first in shaping the 1928 festival. Although Bascom recalled fondly the music he heard as a young man in tobacco barns at curing time, the "religious singings," the "parties and serenades," the "shoe-arounds" that were held at schoolhouses with music and dancing, and the music and dancing sometimes associated with quiltings, bean stringings, and corn shuckings, such events bear little resemblance to the 1928 festival.[17]

On the other hand, Lunsford had presented local musician Uncle Billy Hill as an entertainer at the Nebo school commencement as early as 1910, had himself lectured and performed widely, and by at least 1925 had begun staging public entertainments at schoolhouses in which he gave a money prize to the student who contributed the best ballad or story. He had, moreover, developed considerable sophistication in moving back and forth between the world of folklore scholars, who were interested in documenting authentic cultural traditions, and commercial recording companies, which in the early twenties began to exploit a national popular market for "hillbilly" music. Thus he had been recorded by folklore collectors Frank C. Brown (1922) and Robert W. Gordon (1925), and by the commercial companies OKeh (1924) and Brunswick (1928). He had also attended fiddlers' conventions, such as the nearby ones at Mountain City, Tennessee, in 1925, and Banner Elk, North Carolina, in 1926.[18]

Thus, it seems most reasonable neither to look for a direct "model" for his festival, nor to see it as a continuation of traditional cultural forms. It resulted instead from a delicate hybridization (as a sometime itinerant salesman of fruit trees, Bascom no doubt understood that mechanism) of all his prior experience as hill-born lad, traditional musician and dancer, public lecturer and performer, spectator and promoter of musical contests, newspaper writer and editor (he edited the Old Ford *Sentinel* and the McDowell *Sentinel* during and after World War I and wrote a column for the *Citizen*), lawyer and college-educated sophisticate. What he produced on Pack Square in 1928 lay somewhere between a traditional evening of music and dance among friends and neighbors and the commercial hype of the Rhododendron Festival directed to an audience of strangers. Its content was drawn exclusively from the former; its form was accommodated more than slightly to the latter.

Although during its first two years—while it was part of the Rhododendron Festival—Lunsford's festival was shaped partly by circumstances and the wishes of others, in the long run it became almost solely the product of his own consciousness, desires, and view of mountain culture. Thus Lunsford's personality, his role as an entrepreneur, and his public projection of himself are important to understand. Because the general outline of Lunsford's life is well-known and a full account of it is now available, only two aspects need concern us here: his status as a member of the mountain intellectual elite and his propensity for self-promotion.[19]

Lunsford's father, James Bassett Lunsford (b. 1842), was a self-educated man who reportedly had such a "divine thirst for knowledge" that he kept books with him throughout his service in the Civil War. He was teaching at a subscription school at Mars Hill near Asheville when his son Bascom was born, and he later taught at a similar school attached to Rutherford College. Bascom himself attended public schools, Camp Hill Academy, Rutherford College, and Trinity College (later Duke University) law school. He taught in the public schools for a year (1902–1903), was a professor of English and history at Rutherford College (1914–1916), practiced law, edited two small-town newspapers (1916–1917, 1919) and worked for a year (1918–1919) as an agent for the Justice Department.[20] Thus Lunsford—for all the colorful stories (which are also true) about his working as a beekeeper, itinerant fruit tree salesman and the like—was an educated and sophisticated man who knew and loved the traditional culture in which he had been raised, but who also viewed it in wider intellectual frames of reference supplied by his personal and family history. Conversely, his neighbors on South Turkey Creek knew the same tunes he did, but they sometimes judged his scholarly, conservatorial, and promotional work with local culture to be an elegant variety of shiftlessness that kept him from tending to his farm.

Thus, if it was Lunsford's knowledge of and love for mountain culture that provided his motive, it was his *doubleness of vision* that gave form to his work. He made a set of observations and judgments about the worth of authentic mountain culture vis-à-vis both the popular misconceptions of it and the mass culture that was rapidly supplanting it. He made some calculations about the "Your-culture-isn't-worth-anything/Yes-you're-right-our-culture-isn't-worth-anything" feedback loop that was so destructive to mountain people's dignity and consequently to their will to survive culturally. And like a Janus who could see both ways, he placed himself at the center of that cultural conflict.

From that position he functioned for mountain people, apparently, as a mirror of—and magnet for—their better, self-respecting selves; for the mass audience within and beyond the mountains he became a corrective symbol of mountain culture, a charismatic counter-example that did not fit their preconceptions, an item of data that forced a reconsideration of theory.

The role Bascom chose for himself called for him, however, to walk a fine line between projecting a new and dignified image of a self-respecting mountain man and merely self-interested self-promotion. Those both inside and outside the region who commented on his work sometimes had difficulty deciding which agenda was dominant. Long before he began the Asheville festival, Lunsford was promoting himself as a lecturer and performer of mountain music. Surviving handbills and posters show him posed elegantly in white tie and tails, flanked by fiddle and banjo. Early in his career, North Carolina folklorist Frank C. Brown referred to him as "the kind of man who likes to see his name in print."[21] In a *Saturday Evening Post* article, Harold Martin described him in mid-career as "a man who likes to sell himself for the high dollar." When he walks, Martin continued:

he walks all reared back . . . with his hat set mathematically fore and aft on his head, and with a solemn look on his face. . . . When he stands, he stands all reared back, like a man of substance, with his thumbs thrust in his vest and with his watermelon paunch protruding beneath his sober blue-serge suit. It is reasonable to assume that when he lies down to seek his rest, he reposes stiffly, and with dignity, as if he lay in state.[22]

At the end of Lunsford's life, Greensboro *Daily News* writer Terry Bledsoe commented again on his "flair for promotion."[23] The careful self-promotion extended from what Erving Goffman would call Bascom's immediate "presentation of self" to his sophisticated manipulation of his public image as the "minstrel of the Appalachians" and the "squire of South Turkey Creek." "I used [those phrases] for all they were worth," Lunsford said. "The proper use of words and expressions can take you a long way." He later commented that "I had to be my own press agent so much of the time—a disinterested third person standing by to see what I did and what place it ought to fill."[24]

The risks in such a posture were substantial. Lunsford could have become a mere self-publicist or an essentially entrepreneurial performer on the folk circuit. Even worse, he could have been neutralized by the media and the larger audience as a "character." That none of those scenarios materialized makes it seem reasonable to conclude that Lunsford must have had a good grasp on his (partially given and partially chosen) position in the public debate over cultural styles and values, and must have retained a sophisticated functional, *instrumental* concept of his work. "My business," he said, "was to draw attention to the fine cultural value of our traditional music and our dancing and *the fine honor of our people* [emphasis added]. I was trying to perpetuate the real, true cultural worth of the mountain people. Our section, you know, has been slandered."[25]

In 1928, Lunsford was one of a small number who insisted that there was a connection between the cultural riches of the Appalachian region and "the fine honor of our people." (A more usual approach was to view mountain music and dance as a miraculous survival among a cultural group who hardly understood its value and who were most unlikely custodians of it.) His insistence that the connection existed and that it be recognized was highly consistent. He treated mountain people "as ladies and gentlemen" when he went into their homes, refused to don stereotypic hillbilly garb or "talk country" in his public appearances, and (at least in the early years) insisted that his performers not adopt either the cowboy costumes currently being worn by popular musicians in the "country" idiom or the hillbilly garb urged upon mountain musicians by commercial recording companies and radio advertisers.[26] More than most collectors or entrepreneurs, Lunsford comprehended what Cecil Sharp had noted years earlier about the dignity of mountain people. They had, Sharp found, "an easy unaffected bearing and the unselfconscious manners of the well-bred. . . . Although uneducated, in the sense in which that term is usually understood, they possess that elemental wisdom, abundant knowledge, and intuitive understanding which only those who live in constant touch with Nature and face to face with reality seem to be able to acquire."[27]

From a similar perspective, Lunsford sought to bring mountain culture to a broad audience through his Mountain Dance and Folk Festival and other promotional activities. "It was like a honey flow," said Lunsford the former beekeeper. "The mountains were full of music and it was time for it to spill over into other parts of the country."[28] But to continue the metaphor, it is important to realize that the mountain honey that flowed, flowed after being strained through Lunsford's own consciousness, aesthetic, and values.

Lunsford has been criticized from many perspectives. Some of the criticisms pertain to his *selection* of certain aspects of mountain culture to present, others to the reflexive *impact* of that selectivity upon it. His selectivity itself is easy to document; impact is more difficult to assess. In his own collecting and presentation, for example, Lunsford made a clear separation between material culture, and music and dance. He never displayed any interest in the former, and his presentations of the latter were weighted heavily toward string music and its associated dance forms. His essentially Victorian mores—wholly typical of most segments of society at the time—prevented him from collecting ribald songs, although they turn up with some frequency in the collection of his Ozarks contemporary, Vance Randolph.[29]

Early in his public career, Lunsford was criticized by some as a loner who wouldn't work with other people doing similar work. Others criticized his personal showmanship. Settlement and mission school teachers in the mountains objected to his use of what they considered to be nonpure (i.e., non-British derived) cultural materials. Others said he should not have allowed clog dancing in the festival, or that he should not have given prizes, which made participants vie for attention. Although Lunsford's personal showmanship and his preference for working alone cannot be denied, it is not evident in retrospect that they were necessarily ill-advised, given the public relations problems he faced. And one may easily set aside the criticism of his "nonpure" presentations: at length his judgments of the authenticity of cultural forms in the mountains have proved more durable than that of those who romanticized the mountaineer's "100% Anglo-Saxon" past and taught them songs and dances they had not performed in 150 years, if indeed ever.[30]

In recent years, Lunsford has been criticized more seriously for neglecting entire areas of mountain culture, such as that of Appalachian blacks.[31] Although Loyal Jones reports that Lunsford "collected songs in the Negro schools and churches of the mountains" and "frequently spoke highly of black singers and speakers he had met on his collecting trips to black churches and schools," I have encountered no reports of blacks performing in his festival.[32]

If Lunsford's judgments based on racial categories, political persuasion, and personal mores are sometimes rather apparent, his personal aesthetic is somewhat obscure except as one may tentatively infer it from his actual choice of performers and repertoire. Few direct statements of his aesthetic survive. "In a festival you get as much good in as you can," he said, "and keep as much bad out as you can. We keep it as genuine as we can." His use of the Biblical image of separating the wheat from the chaff to explain how he decided what to present in the festival was dramatic, but ultimately no more helpful to the historian or cultural analyst than such terms as "good," "bad," and "genuine."[33]

Although a full explication of Lunsford's aesthetic and politics lies beyond the scope of this chapter, it is nevertheless clear that both profoundly influenced the shape of his festival and, therefore, determined the image of mountain culture he projected to the public. Of greatest significance, however, is that Lunsford understood what he was doing in essentially political terms: consciously he chose to do his "work as a citizen" within the realm of the politics of culture. Whatever else it may have been, it was a farsighted choice. How may one assess its consequences beyond the obvious creation (and longevity) of the Mountain Dance and Folk Festival itself? At least four areas of impact may be identified: that on festival performers, that on traditional culture in western North Carolina, that on festivals elsewhere, and that on the popular image of mountain culture.[34]

Attempting to assess the festival's impact on performers and local traditions requires that one turn somewhat from the broadly conceptual approach that has characterized my analysis thus far to consider some further bits of specific historical data. In early 1979, I located and interviewed some members of two dance teams (those from Candler and Hominy) that performed in Lunsford's first festival in 1928.[35] Interviews produced virtually complete consensus on pre-festival dance practices in these two contiguous areas of Buncombe County. There were few, if any, public dances in such places as schoolhouses or other community centers; the vast majority were held in private homes, were small (four-eight couples), and were attended by invitation only (usually friends, neighbors, or relatives). In the years immediately before Lunsford's festival, such dances were purely social occasions, not related to work gatherings such as corn shuckings and the like.[36] Music was usually provided by a fiddle and banjo, and musicians were paid by donations of a dollar or two from each of the male dancers. There were no dance "teams" (everyone reported emphatically, "we all danced together"), and there was no competition, except perhaps a friendly and informal buck dance endurance contest between two men between dance sets. The predominant dance was the "big circle" mountain dance, with infrequent excursions into waltz, two-step, or fox-trot. Dances used a "smooth" step; buck or clog dancing was reserved for individual "exhibition" purposes between sets. The figures recalled by informants were those still familiar in local mountain dancing: for example, promenade, "bird-in-a-cage," "garden gate," "four hands across," "thread-the-needle," "shoo-fly-swing." No informant reported having danced in public at a county fair or similar event before Lunsford's 1928 festival, or having seen anyone else do so.

The 1928 dancers generally agreed that they made few conscious or intentional changes in their dancing in order to appear at the festival, and those that occurred were slight. They practiced several times before the event, mainly, it seems, to "get the figures down to a certain time." One dancer recalled that the music "was probably better" and that couples may have been selected by the team's caller-manager. Another recalled "working on our steps." (The formation of the "team" itself was a major change which will be discussed subsequently.)

My overall impression from the interviews was that during its first several years the festival had a rather slight impact upon the local dance tradition, at least in this one county, and that the impact it had was probably more positive than negative. Dancers recalled no sense of being exploited or stereotyped, and several said they "enjoyed it [dancing] more" after becoming involved in the festival. Home dances seem to have continued in these two communities for some years beyond the advent of the festival, and their eventual demise seems to have resulted mainly from broad social and economic changes unrelated to the festival (e.g., increasing urbanization, industrialization, and nonfarm employment).

Longer-term effects on local culture are more difficult to assess. One dancer recalled that "they got to playing faster music" after the festival began, and there is some evidence of increasing self-consciousness and a heightened sense of theatricality (Figure 7-1). In a photograph of the 1930 Candler team, the men are dressed in

Figure 7-1. *The Soco Gap Juniors at the Mountain Dance and Folk Festival, Asheville City Auditorium, Asheville, North Carolina, 1940s. Photograph provided courtesy of the Lunsford Collection, Mars Hill College Archives.*

nonmatching business suits (one wears a sweater) with both bow and four-in-hand ties; the women are in dresses of a variety of styles and colors—light and dark, plain and print. In a 1933 picture, all of the men have on white open-necked shirts and light-colored trousers, and the women are attired in light-colored dresses rather more formal than those worn three years earlier. The caller has on a bow-tie.[37]

The long-term impact of the Lunsford festival on local culture, although beyond the scope of this present analysis, is implied by some of the festival's initial effects upon dress, the importance of competition, some aspects of form (especially smooth vs. clog steps), and the shaping of the public image of mountain dancing.

The subtle changes in the dress of the 1930 and 1933 Candler teams presaged a later tendency toward the highly stylized costumes worn by later teams; identical jeans, socks, shirts, and back-pocket handkerchiefs for the men, and identical shoes, ruffled print dresses, and multilayered slips for the women—the whole image borrowed more from Nashville and cowboy movies than from authentic local traditions.

There were also impacts on the form of the dance. My informants were nearly unanimous in reporting, for example, that in big circle dances in homes they had used only a "smooth" step that had a slight rhythmic bounce, but which was definitely not a clog step. In later years, this "combination" step seems to have split into the exaggerated, sliding, nonrhythmic smooth step used by some teams, and the highly rhythmic, noisy clog step used by others.[38]

It seems reasonable to infer that these changes in dress and the form of the step were strongly related to the increasing intensity of competition fostered by Lunsford's festival, which always took the form of a contest. Much has been written about the presumed absence of a sense of competition among mountain people. Apologists for the region have argued that a humane spirit of cooperation was more characteristic of them, a spirit healthier than destructive mainstream varieties of competition. Critics have charged, on the other hand, that lack of a competitive spirit has left mountain people unable to function successfully in a free-enterprise social and economic system.[39]

Evidence offered by the 1928 dancers is mixed on the matter of competition. On the one hand, no one recalled dancing competitively before 1928, and no one recalled ever witnessing a musical or dance competition (although fiddler's contests, for example, were by then rather common in other areas of the mountains). On the other hand, they said it had been "fun to win," and they had "tried hard to win again."[40] All agreed, however, that competition was nowhere as intense in the early years of the festival as it later became.

Some interview responses also suggested something of a generational progression in the social context of the dances, their form, the intensity of competition, and their relation to family and community structure. The oldest dancer (born about 1895) recalled that the earliest dances in her community were associated with work gatherings; competition was entirely absent, and dancing was done with the rhythmic "combination" step. The next generation (those born around 1910) spoke mainly of informal social dances in homes. But this generation also began to dance formally and competitively on organized teams in their late teens and twenties, still using the combination step exclusively. Their children (generally born in the thirties) danced almost exclusively on organized competitive teams, some of which were "smooth" teams and some clog teams. Their grandchildren (that is, the grandchildren of the 1928 festival dancers) are currently most likely to be dancing on clog teams.[41] Early dances were held among friends, neighbors, and relatives, and the composition of the first teams strongly reflects that history. On the Candler and Hominy teams in 1928 there were four Cathey siblings, Lee Howell and three of his children, a half-dozen husband and wife couples, two Hall brothers, a number of first and second cousins, and so on. As social structure changed and dance competition increased, however, such relationships were less frequent. Some later teams were organized not out of families and communities, but among coworkers in local major industries (such as the 1934 team from nearby American Enka Corporation, which had opened to produce synthetic rayon fibers in 1929).

Thus, there have been easily observable changes in those cultural forms Lunsford set out to present, and some of them appear to have resulted from the festival itself. Bascom's own difficulty in "finding a way between the old and new" was mirrored, in fact, in the public's confusion over what was old and where it had come from. On June 5, 1928, Asheville's morning paper (the *Citizen*) had announced that the music for the Pack Square event would consist of "old favorites of the hills," and the program committee chairman promised that "songs and dances which had their origin in England before Colonial days will be on the program . . . and the ancient customs and dance tunes which have been preserved in their pure form by the mountaineers, will be presented." Even as early as 1928, however, such notions of purity of origin and preservation were already little more than myths. Conversely, the afternoon paper noted that "contestants have agreed to wear the regular barn dance customary garb—no special dressing up for city folks."[42] But no informant I interviewed spoke of any such local event as a "barn dance." The barn dance was a phenomenon not of local culture, but of commercial radio stations such as WBAP (Fort Worth, 1923), WLS (Chicago, 1924), and WSM (Nashville, 1925).[43] Thus the *Citizen's* purist myth was romantic and backward-looking; the slightly patronizing myth of the *Times*, the city's afternoon paper, was directly from the popular media. Neither reflected the actually existing cultural situation, *even as it was embodied in the 1928 festival*, which already involved considerable selection, filtering, and translation.

If one were to follow the impact of the Lunsford festival in detail for a half century, one strand would lead in and out of the towns, villages, small cities, coves, and hollows of western North Carolina, and end on the stage of the Asheville city auditorium in 1978, where uniformly attired teams of young dancers clogged at a fast clip, a wearying line of bluegrass bands followed one another across the stage, and most of those in the audience raised their hands when asked if they were from outside the Asheville area.

Another strand would lead, however, to Sarah Gertrude Knott's National Folk Festival, founded in 1934 in St. Louis with considerable advice from Lunsford and a contingent of his western North Carolina dancers and musicians among the performers. "We couldn't have gotten a National Folk Festival started without Bascom," Miss Knott said. Miss Knott was generous in recognizing her debt to Lunsford, but she was no mere imitator. Her own innovation was to combine the music and dance exhibitions of Lunsford's festival with exhibits of folk arts and crafts. Curiously, the 1928 Rhododendron Festival had included at the Grove Arcade Building (a half-dozen blocks from Pack Square) "an exhibit of mountain arts and crafts" supplied by mountain craft shops and schools such as Crossnore, Penland, and Asheville's Allanstand. Children from Penland also reportedly demonstrated "Old English folk dances." There is no evidence that Lunsford had anything to do with this event or that there was any connection between it and the Pack Square event. It is clear that, from the full range of cultural forms in the mountains, he chose to focus on music and dance rather than crafts. But whether he dissociated himself from the Arcade crafts and the dance exhibition out of an understanding that the craft and settlement schools were for the most part fostering a romanticized version of mountain culture is not known.[44] In any event, Miss Knott's National Festival, a conceptually expanded version of Bascom's, became a model for third and fourth generations of festivals throughout the country, including one founded as recently as 1976 in St. Louis.[45]

How successful Lunsford was—at least in a short-term, comparative sense—may be glimpsed in an obscure confidential memo recently turned up in federal archives. During the summer of 1936, musicologist Charles Seeger was traveling through the mountains as an official of the Resettlement Administration. Along the way he attended three folk festivals: Lunsford's ninth annual festival, the Pennsylvania Folk Festival at Lewisburg, and the White Top Festival at White Top, Virginia. He concluded that Lunsford, whom he judged to be "clearly of the same class" as the contestants and audience, "puts on a good show and is proud of it."[46] The audience, composed "mainly . . . of friends and compatriots of the contestants," was "quick to express approval or disapproval with unimpeachable authority." The "rural element" predominated, Seeger said, "to such an extent that even the hardened urban visitor felt partly absorbed by it. . . . [It] is a very worthwhile affair."

But the elements Seeger found so attractive in Lunsford's festival—the cultural homogeneity of promoter, participants, and audience, its captivating authenticity, its lack of condescension, and the high quality of the performances (although he had found the dancing better than either the playing or the singing)—were lamentably absent from the other two festivals. He found the Pennsylvania festival to be "a kind of vaudeville show in which the traditional element was squeezed to the wall when it could not be made grotesque, sensational, or ludicrous." Traditional performers were sandwiched between "a Russian Orthodox choir singing Rimsky-Korsakoff and a Symphony Orchestra playing positively low-down stuff." Some "old miners who sang some really fine stuff were patted on the back by the master of ceremonies and shooed around the stage and off it." The square dancing was not "a living thing, but was done in 'quaint' costumes."[47]

Seeger's severest criticism was reserved for the White Top, Virginia, festival, which he called "a feast of paradox." It was run, he judged, by well-meaning but deeply confused city people who romanticized the folk, formally protested any attempt to meddle with their "real" culture while actually reshaping it in an outrageously high-handed manner, wondered why local people didn't cooperate more willingly, and angled for federal subsidies for their enterprise. The Pennsylvania and White Top festivals, Seeger concluded, "are both reactionary to the core—under the guise of antiquarianism the one destroys, even while it popularizes, while the other, under a smoke-screen of pseudo-scholarship, is really sinister."[48]

To separate the impact of The Mountain Dance and Folk Festival upon dance and music in western North Carolina from the impact of broader social changes that were happening at the same time is beyond the scope of this chapter. However, one can say with confidence that Bascom Lamar Lunsford, working from a native but nonetheless "double" perspective, substantially revised popular perception of the mountain music and dance of his native counties and enhanced the musicians' and dancers' respect for themselves; that in designing the festival as his major tool, he drew ideas and partial analogues from a wide variety of vernacular social and cultural forms; that the festival reflected many aspects of local culture with considerable dignity, integrity, and fidelity; and that his efforts, although placed initially in the midst of an inappropriate and alien structure (the Rhododendron Festival) and pitted against dominant social, economic, and demographic trends in the area, were in the main successful.

But successful within what bounds? It was a limited success, assuredly, limited by historical circumstance (the format of the Rhododendron Festival in the beginning, for example) and by Bascom's own vision and energy. Like the rest of us, even the most creative and independent, he was finally a product of his own time and place. As Bill Finger has pointed out, for example, Lunsford—in the years of his greatest public prominence as the mythicized "minstrel" arbiter and presenter of mountain culture—did not include within his public presentations explicit statements concerning the complex economic and social changes that were transforming the very culture he cherished: textile and paper mills, resort development, the National Park Service, and a host of other federal agencies.[49] That he was poignantly aware of them there can be no doubt; indeed most of his public career affirmed values, ways of life, and a structuring of the social order counter to those upon which the new order was based.

Lunsford did not say all that could have been said; he did not present all that could have been presented; the keeper of bees and culture strained both honey and culture before offering them to the public. But beyond that, the metaphor breaks down: in a period in which an army of profit-oriented shysters and hucksters from Nashville to New York and Hollywood were buying and selling the mountains and their culture, Lunsford kept his integrity, his eye and ear for the authentic, his respect for both performer and audience, his sense of stewardship, and his precocious intuition that one's "work as a citizen" could be carried out in the area of the politics of culture. The passing of the years makes it seem an ever more impressive accomplishment.

NOTES

Latter portions of the research for this chapter were supported by National Endowment for the Humanities Research Grant No. RS-29670-79-73. Arguments and conclusions presented here are of course my own, and do not necessarily reflect the views of NEH. In preparing this article for publication I have benefited from the comments and criticisms of Archie Green, Loyal Jones, Jim Wayne Miller, Gerry Parsons, and Joseph T. Wilson. In addition, I am indebted to Laurel Horton, Ralph Rinzler, the Pack Memorial Library, and the Asheville *Citizen-Times* for numerous suggestions, insights, and archival materials on which my analysis is based.

1. Quoted in Loyal Jones, *Minstrel of the Appalachians: The Story of Bascom Lamar Lunsford* (Boone, N.C.: Appalachian Consortium Press, 1984), 127.

2. Information on Asheville's development is drawn from Blackwell P. Robinson, ed., *The North Carolina Guide* (Chapel Hill: University of North Carolina Press, 1955), 134–143, and Joan and Wright Langley, *Yesterday's Asheville* (Miami, Florida: E. A. Seeman Publishing, Inc., 1975), 91.

3. Lunsford himself later functioned in such a role, and the image of mountain culture he fostered was viewed by the tourist industry as one of the region's major attractions. See "Music, Songs and Folklore of the South," an article on Lunsford, in the *Southern Tourist* (26 March 1926), 60, 62. I am grateful to Laurel Horton and Archie Green for calling this article to my attention.

4. See Richard L. Hoffman's sketch of Asheville's history in "Community in Action: Innovative and Coordinative Strategies in the War on Poverty" (Ph.D. dissertation, University of North Carolina, 1969), 65–76.

5. Fred Weede actually arrived in Asheville to join the Chamber of Commerce about June 23, 1928, shortly after the first Rhododendron Festival ended. He had spent the previous six summers in Asheville, however, and may have been partly responsible for the original idea. Weede's career—and his role in the development of Asheville and western North Carolina in the late 1920s and 1930s—deserves more extensive analysis than is possible here, since it reflects in a dramatic way some of the tensions and contradictions of progressivism as it operated in the mountains. Weede was born in Iowa in 1873 and was educated first in the classics. He later graduated from the University of Pennsylvania in economics and finance and became a reporter for the Philadelphia *Times*. As a political writer and staff correspondent, he exposed registration and electoral frauds in Philadelphia. In 1908 he became general manager of the Erie (Pa.) *Herald*. He moved to Miami in 1920 and joined the Chamber of Commerce, first as publicity director and later as manager. He left the Chamber managership in 1925 and joined a real estate firm. Both in Miami and in Asheville, his boosterish promotional work was paralleled by attention to the more basic concerns of economic development. In Miami he was instrumental in deepening the bay for shipping; in Asheville he was active in (besides the Rhododendron Festival) the building of the city's first airport and its civic auditorium, in routing the Blue Ridge Parkway through Asheville, in establishing the city's burley tobacco market, and in persuading Dutch investors to locate the American Enka Corporation near Asheville.

My remarks on Weede's career are based upon articles in the Asheville *Citizen* and *Times* for June 3, 1928, December 31, 1939, January 22, 1940, November 15, 1959, and February 4 and 9, 1961; the Miami *News*, February 6, 1961; and Kenneth Ballinger, *Miami Millions: The Dance of Dollars in the Great Miami Land Boom of 1925* (Miami: Franklin Press, 1936).

For assistance in locating this information, I am indebted to the Asheville and Miami Chambers of Commerce, the Florida Collection of the Miami Public Library, the Pack Memorial Library, the Historical Association of South Florida, and the librarian of the Asheville *Citizen-Times*.

6. See Frederick Lewis Allen, *Only Yesterday* (1931; rpt. New York: Bantam Books, 1959), 197-205.

7. Fred L. Weede, "Asheville Rhododendron Festival" (Undated typescript, Pack Memorial Library, Asheville, N.C.). Weede managed the Festival, 1929-39.

8. From undated (ca. 1940) mimeo document, Pack Memorial Public Library. The descriptions of the 1928 Festival are based on accounts published in the Asheville *Citizen* and *Times*, (April-June 1928).

9. My account of "opera week" is based on articles in the Asheville *Citizen* (August 7-14, 1927). Although Bascom's own letterhead says his festival was "established in the year 1927," and the date has subsequently been repeated in the article on Lunsford in L. G. Pine, ed., *Who's Who In Music* (London: I. B. Shaw Publishing Co., 1951), 282; Loyal Jones, "The Minstrel of the Appalachians: Bascom Lamar Lunsford at 91," *John Edwards Memorial Foundation Quarterly* 9 (Spring 1973): 3; John A. McLeod, "Minstrel of the Appalachians: An Interpretative Biography of Bascom Lamar Lunsford," (typescript, 1973), 27, and elsewhere, I have been able to discover no concrete evidence that there was any such event before the first Rhododendron Festival, which was indisputably in 1928.

10. Asheville *Citizen*, (13 August 1927), 4.

11. Since official records of the Rhododendron Festival apparently have not survived, it is not clear how or at whose initiative the connection with Lunsford was made. I suspect that the initiative may have been Lunsford's.

12. Other members were C. H. Bartlett (a city official), chairman; C. P. Brownell; E. R. Lineberger; and Harry W. Wilson. My efforts to locate these men or their descendents were not successful.

13. Undated Asheville *Citizen* clipping (Mars Hill, North Carolina: Mars Hill College Lunsford Collection, probably 5 June 1928).

14. Unfortunately, I have been unable to discover any contemporary accounts or photographs of the festival. Results of interviews with some of the participants will be presented.

15. Quoted in Jones, *Minstrel*, 93-94.

16. Jones, *Minstrel*, xii.

17. From "Memoirs of Bascom Lamar Lunsford" (Typescript apparently transcribed from tapes, Lunsford Collection).

18. Lunsford taped interview with Joseph T. Wilson, 1967. The role of fiddlers' conventions in shaping Lunsford's ideas—and the larger patterns and formats for presenting traditional culture to popular audiences—is yet to be analyzed. Joseph T. Wilson's liner notes to *A Fiddlers' Convention in Mountain City, Tennessee* (County 525), and *The Hillbillies* (County 405) are suggestive in this regard.

19. For an outline, see Jones, "The Minstrel," 2-7. See also Jones, *Minstrel*.

20. From Jones, *Minstrel*, 8-25 and McLeod, "Minstrel," 27.

21. Quoted in Jones, *Minstrel*, 93.

22. Harold H. Martin, "Minstrel Man of the Appalachians," *Saturday Evening Post*, 220 (22 May 1948): 31.

23. Quoted in Jones, *Minstrel*, 93.

24. Quoted in Jones, *Minstrel*, 93.

25. Quoted in Jones, *Minstrel*, 53. Emphasis added.

26. See Jones, "The Minstrel," 89, and *Minstrel*, 29. Even the essentially admiring piece on Lunsford by Martin in the *Saturday Evening Post* came close to caricaturing Lunsford and mountain people, especially in its reliance on some suspiciously staged-looking photographs.

27. Cecil Sharp, *English Folksongs from the Southern Appalachians*, 2 vols. (London: Oxford University Press, 1932), I, xxiii.

28. Martin, "Minstrel Man," 164.

29. For portions of Randolph's collection of bawdy lore, see Vance Randolph, *Pissing in the Snow and Other Ozark Folktales* (Urbana: University of Illinois Press, 1976).

30. See David E. Whisnant, *All That Is Native and Fine: The Politics of Culture in an American Region* (Chapel Hill: The University of North Carolina Press, 1983) for a discussion of these predispositions among cultural workers in the mountains.

31. These criticisms (and others dealt with below) are raised in Bill Finger, "The Limits of a Folk Hero," *Southern Exposure* 2 (Spring 1974), 27-37.

32. Jones, *Minstrel*, 97-98. I know of no systematic analysis that has been undertaken of either Lunsford's performers during the festival's first half century or of the frequency with which any given item or form was presented.

33. From Jones, *Minstrel*, 52.

34. In each area, the impacts varied over time. Discussion here will be confined primarily to initial, short-term impact.

35. For the information that follows I am grateful to the following members of the 1928 dance teams: Charlotte Cathey, Florence Cathey, George Cathey, Lucy (Mrs. Frank) Hall, Gertie Mae (Mrs. Homer) Morgan, and Mary Luther Smathers. Interviews were conducted February 28-March 2, 1979. Crucial assistance in locating some members was graciously provided by Mrs. Mamie Medford, Mrs. Ernest Nolan, and Mr. and Mrs. Fred A. Howell. Additional information on pre-festival dance traditions was offered by Ruth Lovinggood Wilkie. Names of team members were obtained from a September 14, 1928, newspaper account of a post-festival dance exhibition held at the Asheville city auditorium. Clipping in Lunsford papers, Mars Hill College.

36. Dances held in conjunction with work gatherings were reported by only one informant, who was 86 years old when interviewed (twenty or so years older than most of the other informants).

37. I have been unable to discover any photographs of the 1928 festival, or of any of its participant groups.

38. Recent practice at the festival has, in fact, been to divide teams into "smooth" and "clog" categories for competition.

39. For examples of these opposing viewpoints, see Helen Lewis et al., "Family, Religion, and Colonialism in Central Appalachia," in *Growin' Up Country*, ed. Jim Axelrod (Clintwood, Virginia: Council of the Southern Mountains, 1973), 131-156, and Jack E. Weller, *Yesterday's People* (Louisville: University of Kentucky Press, 1965).

40. It is also important to note that sports competition was by this time very keen in the Candler community, whose basketball teams had already advanced to the state finals several times in high school tournaments. One dancer (who was also a star athlete) agreed with my suggestion that competitiveness among dance groups, once established by the Lunsford festival, quickly assimilated itself in form and scale to that already existing in the sports area.

41. Whether this pattern would be borne out among other informants, I do not know. Some interviews suggested that while smooth dancing was more common in Candler, clogging may have been more customary in other areas such as Soco Gap, further to the west.

42. Asheville *Citizen* (5 June 1928), C-1, and Asheville *Times* (5 June 1928), 1.

43. See Bill C. Malone, *Country Music, U.S.A.*, rev. ed. (Austin: University of Texas Press, 1985), 33–34, 70–72. Only one informant recalled a local "barn dance": he attended it as a CCC camp resident in the 1930s, and it was held at "Helen's Barn," which was, in fact, not a barn at all but a dance pavilion constructed to serve the Florida tourist trade in Maggie Valley, one of the prime tourist areas in western North Carolina.

44. Asheville *Citizen* (5 June 1928), 1. To explain the presence and significance of the crafts exhibits in the Rhododendron Festival—and its cultural relationship to the event produced by Lunsford—would take one far beyond the limits of this chapter and into the history of missionary, craft, and settlement schools in the mountains, and the related crafts revival movement. On the latter, see Allen H. Eaton, *Handicrafts of the Southern Highlands* (1937; rev. ed. New York: Dover Publications, Inc., 1973), and Whisnant, *All That Is Native and Fine*. Asheville was an important crafts revival center in the 1920s.

45. Knott quotations from Jones's *Minstrel*, 66–67. See also Sarah Gertrude Knott, "The National Folk Festival After Twelve Years," *Western Folklore* 5 (1946): 83–93, and Archie Green, "Commercial Music Graphics No. 32: The National Folk Festival Association," *John Edwards Memorial Foundation Quarterly* 11 (Spring 1975): 23–32. On the national festival movement, see David E. Whisnant, *Folk Festival Issues: Report From a Seminar* (Los Angeles: John Edwards Memorial Foundation, 1979). Knott's National Folk Festival Association survives as the National Council for the Traditional Arts, which produces the National Folk Festival and does consulting and contract work for federal agencies in the area of folklife policy and programs.

46. Charles Seeger to Adrian J. Dornbush, U.S. Farm Security Administration, *Miscellaneous Printed Matter*, 2 vols. (Music Division, Library of Congress, 21 August 1936), unpaged. I am grateful to Archie Green for calling this memo to my attention.

47. The Pennsylvania Folk Festival was held July 30–August 2, 1936, at Bucknell University. For account, see Angus K. Gillespie, "Pennsylvania Folk Festivals in the 1930's," *Pennsylvania Folklife* 26 (Fall 1976): 2–11. Gillespie's article reproduces the 1936 festival program, which suggests that Seeger's criticism of the festival events was, if anything, understated. Gillespie notes that folklorist George Korson got the idea for a folk festival from Sarah Gertrude Knott, who, of course, got it from Lunsford.

48. A fuller analysis of the White Top Festival is available in Whisnant, *All That is Native and Fine*, 181–252.

49. Finger, "The Limits of a Folk Hero." Finger notes especially that Lunsford made no alliance with unionized workers in western North Carolina, which, he argues, is "the most heavily unionized area" in the largely unorganized state. Although Lunsford's early festivals were, in fact, cosponsored by Asheville's Central Labor Union, I have discovered no evidence that even tentatively suggests how Lunsford and the CLU related to each other's work, if indeed the relationship was more than merely formal, as it may have been. I am also aware of no tradition of labor-oriented song among western North Carolina's unionized textile, paper and rubber workers to which Lunsford might have related. Clearly, more work is needed to answer these intriguing questions about local vernacular culture.

Chapter 8

Wild and Yet Really Subdued: Cultural Change, Stylistic Diversification, and Personal Choice in Traditional Appalachian Dance

Gail Matthews-DeNatale

I remember as a child visiting my grandparents in Canton, North Carolina. In those days, I-40 was still a dream, and it took all day to drive hairpin roads that snaked their way across the Smoky Mountains. Despite the difficulties that the terrain presented, my father seemed to be magnetically attracted to the mountains. After my grandparents died in the 1960s, he proceeded to buy land in Waynesville, North Carolina, and construct a dogtrot lodge that he built out of old handhewn logs. The Swag, a local place name for the land my father purchased, was no more than fifteen miles as the crow flies from Canton, the town where he had lived during his later childhood and adolescence. We established several close friendships with our Swag neighbors, even though we were considered to be outsiders and newcomers.

One afternoon at a beef shoot in which our new-found friend Jody Wood had won first prize, musical instruments were brought out to celebrate the victory. Instinctively my father leaned forward at the waist a bit, bent his legs at the knee, hyperextended his back, and began to move his feet, just barely lifting them off the ground, shuffling in time with the music. Our mountain friends looked on in amazement. My mother, brother, sister, and I were perplexed. Then one of our mountain friends made a comment to the effect of "why didn't you tell us you were from around here?" This was the beginning of my fascination with traditional dance.

The multifaceted importance of this dance intrigued me. It was the first time I had ever seen the percussive improvised footwork that has come to be known as clogging. My father and his friends usually called it buck dance or just dance.

I was determined to learn this dance that had the power to open doors to local acceptance. Late at night in the privacy of my own room, I did my best to mimic the dance movements that I had witnessed. I also eagerly attended Saturday night dances at the Maggie Valley Playhouse dance hall. At these dances I learned how to respond appropriately to popular square dance calls such as "The Grapevine Twist," "Georgia Rang Tang," and "Walk The King's/Queen's Highway." During the dances I also picked up the essential rhythm of the accompanying dance foot-work—feeling this rhythm through the hands of my fellow dancers so often that eventually my feet knew what to do. My favorite part of these dance events were the times, in between square dances, when a small group of self-appointed dance masters, often including my friends George and Amos Wood, got up and confidently walked toward the middle of the room. I watched with total fascination as these "buck dancers," virtuoso performers of the local style, congregated in a small conversation-like circle in the middle of the room. Responding to commonly understood cues, each buck dancer would take their turn showing off for the others while the rest held back and either clapped in rhythm for them or yelled phrases of encouragement. When Amos and George Wood eventually asked me to join them in the buck dancers' circle, I glowed inside, knowing that all those years of practice and observation had finally paid off.

After enrolling in a course on dance ethnography at Indiana University with noted dance scholar, Anya Peterson Royce, I discovered that very little scholarly research examined mountain dance. It seems that early collectors were so intrigued by Appalachian ballads and coverlets that they gave scant attention to vernacular dance. My childhood experiences and the continuing vitality of dance in western North Carolina led me to believe that dance is intimately connected with mountain identity. I postulated that a detailed study of mountain dance would provide valuable information about the cultural landscape.

In 1982 and 1983, I conducted the research for my master's thesis on dance in Haywood County, interviewing dozens of dancers, collecting their oral histories, participating in social dances at the now defunct Maggie Valley Playhouse on Saturday nights, and attending private dances as well as public competitions held at local schools. I chose Haywood County not only because of its reputation as a hotbed of traditional dance, but also because my father was raised there in the paper mill town of Canton—many of my informants went to school with him. Because I learned how to dance by watching my father, I could draw on his knowledge of the area and my own dance experience to aid my research.

In this chapter I hope to convey not only the appearance but also the spirit and meaning of traditional dance in Haywood County, North Carolina. I want readers to consider the connections between the recent proliferation of Southern Appalachian dance styles and the overwhelming socioeconomic changes in the mountains since the 1940s. When we view this traditional dance within its broader cultural context, we can better understand the connection between mountain dance style choice and larger issues of individual values and community identity.

THE ORIGINS OF CLOGGING

During the past twenty years, folk dance enthusiasts across America and Europe have taken to clogging with a fervor that rivals Jane Fonda's aerobics craze. Clogging has a strong contemporary following, but part of the dance's appeal is that it is considered to be an old dance that is part of our heritage.

As a trained folklorist, I am expected by most people to know the "true" origin of this tradition. Unfortunately, the history of using footwork while square dancing is as elusive as it is fascinating. Many scholars and popular writers who deal with clogging and traditional mountain dance base their work on outdated scholarship, impressionistic travel accounts, how-to step books written by non-Appalachian dancers or physical education teachers, and observations of non-Appalachian revival dance communities. While these sources provide fascinating primary data for studies of revival dance and the adaptation of regional dance for general audiences, they do not teach us much about earlier social dance traditions in the Appalachian mountains.

After sifting through the available information and considering other problematic works with a grain of salt, I have concluded that the reliable documentation about this dance is extremely scanty. I doubt that anyone will ever know the precise family tree of mountain dance, although it almost certainly is an amalgam of traditional West African, British Isles, German, and possibly Native American traditional step dance styles.[1]

Although the question of origins will never be answered conclusively, the people of Haywood County frequently discuss the dance's genealogy. During interviews, I would often receive unsolicited etymological information. Local interest in and opinions about this dance's origin are far more important than unverifiable historical theory; what is most important is that Haywood Countians believe that this dance is representative of their Appalachian identity.

Each person's understanding of mountain dance history is tailored to their individual perception of what it means to be Southern Appalachian. Kyle Edwards, owner of The Stompin' Grounds, a Maggie Valley dance hall that was opened in the early 1980s, perceives the culture as being relatively homogeneous: "Since our community is situated in the remoteness of the Appalachians . . . the purity of the old English style remained intact here and was not influenced by western style dancing until the advent of television."[2] In contrast, Albert Burnette, retired employee of Champion Paper Mill and caller for the legendary Champion YMCA dance team, favors a more multicultural explanation of mountain dance:

They called it [traditional dance] "buck and wing" because really it started off, it's an old dance, been handed down through the generations. I guess maybe they call it the buck and wing after maybe the Indians. . . . The Indians used to dance too, you know. That's a body expression—everybody has it . . . The Irishman, he does the jig. The Scotsman, he'll do the highland fling. The English people, they taught 'em to do the old Virginia Reel. Lot of that came down through the courts of England. They took all that stuff and mixed it up together, and when they brought it to the mountains, it stayed. They called that just buck and wing dancing. The old game rooster, he puts his spur through his wing and sort of runs sideways. He struts and cackles a little bit for the hens. So they figured that when he was dancing, he had his spur through his wing.[3]

Despite the fact that Kyle Edwards, Albert Burnette, and the other dancers in Haywood County disagree as to the cultural constituents that produced mountain square dance, they are all concerned with maintaining what they perceive to be the dance's original form, intent, or essence. Advocates of the oldest dance styles, such as Albert Burnette, hold to a conservative definition for "mountain dance," one that excludes newer forms such as precision clogging. Kyle Edwards, whose own children are the brightest stars in modern precision clogging, argues that the heritage of "mountain dance" includes a tradition of freedom and innovation—dancers should therefore be free to embrace precision styles if they so choose.

This argument about what is traditional and what is not, which dance styles are legitimate representations or manifestations of mountain culture and which are not, is as complicated as it is fascinating. I will try to explain the different dance styles and attendant aesthetics in detail. The most important thing to keep in mind is that, in their discussions about dance, these dancers are using dance as a vehicle for exploring powerful questions that concern all humans, questions such as: Which aspects of my parents' lifeways do I want to emulate in my adult life, and which things do I want to change? In embracing the conveniences of modern society, will I lose the "personal touch" and informality that make life fun? Am I losing my sense of individuality in this age of technology? How much of my original culture can I change before I lose my "self," my identity?

DANCE AND TRADITION

I will preface my discussion of Appalachian dance style with the warning that dance terms, like fiddle tunes and quilt names, vary from area to area. I worked very hard to understand how dancers in Haywood County talk about dance, but it is entirely possible that dancers in other states may describe their dance differently. There were even some inconsistencies within my own research in Haywood County. For instance, every informant told me that old-style dance, as opposed to precision dance, has no basic set of definable steps. However, as I worked with the dancers, they sometimes would show me their version of the "double shuffle" or the "Georgia backstep." I came to understand that when dancers said they had no steps, they were trying to communicate that their dance learning process does not involve isolating steps in a self-conscious manner, even though some buck dancers do name their steps.

While it is true that "clogging" hails from the Southern Appalachian mountain area, the mountain dance I learned as a child from my father and his friends in Haywood County is radically different in form, intent, and essence from the clogging I have encountered outside the Southern Appalachian area. In fact many of the old-style dancers in this area claim that the term *clogging* is relatively new to the mountains. In other words, they don't even call their older percussive style of dance clogging. When older dancers in Haywood County refer to their dance, they just call it "dance" or "square dance," omitting any reference to footwork because intermittent percussive footwork is an assumed part of the dance. The only word used by the old-time dancers themselves to refer specifically to footwork was buckdancing. When they used the term *buckdancing*, they were referring to an individual dance performed in a traditional style by virtuoso dancers within the community.

The casual observer may not notice any differences among precision clogging, freestyle clogging, old-style social square dance, or buck dance and mistakenly lump all dance that involves percussive manipulation of the feet together as "clogging." Some researchers may not even get their questions understood if they use the wrong terms, for example, by assuming that clogging means the same thing as old-style social square dancing or buckdancing. One dancer, Gertie Welch, told me that when a folklorist in Washington, D.C., referred to her old-style dancing as "clogging," she was mildly upset but did not correct the man because he was giving a speech at the time, and she "didn't want to embarrass him or hurt his feelings."[4]

It is amusing to note that although most people do not distinguish between old-style dance and newer forms of clogging, those Appalachians who perform these different kinds of dances have very strong, often negative feelings about each other's dance styles. As with the distinctions between various Protestant denominations, features that may seem minor to the uninitiated are crucial to the practitioner.

This proliferation of dance styles is congruent with the many changes that Appalachian people have witnessed during the past sixty years as they have become increasingly connected with the nonmountain world. Before World War II, many people in western North Carolina never traveled outside their home county during their lifetime. Haywood County had one of the largest enlistment percentages in the nation during World War II. According to North Carolina geographer Bill Sharpe, "In World War II the county [Haywood] sent more volunteers per capita than any other county in the United States."[5] This massive enlistment during the 1940s, extensive road improvement since the 1950s, and the spread of electricity in the 1960s that made television and telephones accessible in even remote homes had a profound impact on the cultural exchange between mountain and nonmountain people. Today the choice of mountain dance style has become one way for individuals to make a statement about their preferred lifestyle, world view, and relationship to change.

One way of exploring the cultural significance of traditional dance is to look at what can and cannot be changed from the dancer's point of view or, in other words, what is and isn't essential to the spirit of a particular dance form. For instance, a dancer could wear jeans or a tuxedo, perform in the street or a ballroom, during the daytime or at night, but in order to dance a waltz, you have to have ¾ meter music (i.e., music with a basic rhythm of *1,2,3,1,2,3*). Therefore ¾ time is essential to the spirit of a waltz. Likewise, the freestyle cloggers I spoke with did not believe that frilly clogging costumes, patent leather shoes, and electrified bluegrass or country music violated the spirit of traditional mountain dance, but they did object strongly to preordained precision steps. In addition to disliking predetermined precision steps, the more conservative old-style social dancers and buck dancers also resented high kicking and loud tap shoes. Not surprisingly, precision dancers have the least restrictive range of acceptance, only omitting what they call "tap dance" movements.

Ironically, it is often a confrontation with change that helps us clarify the essence, importance, and meaning of our traditions. Folk dance, as well as folklore in general, must continually change in order to keep up with the needs of the people who engage in it. We are constantly figuring out which new cultural options we will embrace or reject.

THE HAYWOOD COUNTY TRADITION

Old-style dancing differs radically from today's nonmountain clogging. The overall look of an old-style dancer is very similar to the limberjack or dancing doll toy. Says former dance hall owner Hazel Bradshaw, "It's just a feather dance, that's just a little toe dance. You just kind of move from your knees down. The old timers said that when you were a smooth dancer . . . you could dance with a bucket of water on your head and never spill it."[6] This stillness is not only aesthetically pleasing but it also enables the square dance group figures[7] to be executed smoothly. In traditional mountain dance, the legs are usually slightly bent to act as shock absorbers for the torso.[8]

Old-style dancers rarely raise their hands above their belt lines. Their arms are still, yet relaxed, with what Chief Howell, former Soco Gap Dance Team member, calls a "common swing."[9] The footwork is very subtle and light. The feet are rarely raised more than six inches off the floor, a radical difference from the synchronized high kicking of modern precision clogging teams. It is also markedly different from the choreographed, high-kicking dance of post-1960s revival teams such as the Green Grass Cloggers, who have a home team based in Vanceboro and a branch team in Asheville, both in North Carolina.

Traditional old-style dance footwork is not defined by a set of standardized steps such as one encounters in the waltz or the box step. Although there are step names such as "Georgia Backstep" and "Double Shuffle" (the meaning of which varies depending on whom you ask for a definition), there is no basic step as there is in precision or revival clogging. Each dancer develops his or her own repertoire of percussive foot movements that matches their own interpretation of the music.

In order to learn how to dance traditionally, a person must first learn the guidelines of the aesthetic (i.e., keep the torso still, dance with your feet low to the ground), and then develop unique dance movements that do not violate the aesthetic. This method of learning takes many years; mountain dancers not only internalize the "how-to" aspects of the dance, the dance also becomes part of their identity in the same way that we recognize individuals by their distinctive voice and speech patterns. No two mountain dancers ever dance alike. According to old-style dancer Fred Moody, "Each person had his own step. Some would dance real good, and some not, but everybody did their own thing. There's no set way to do it."[10]

Regional styles did develop over time, although today the differences are becoming less pronounced. Bob Phillips, a dancer from Canton, North Carolina, explains:

Each area had a characteristic type dance. For instance, right here we dance one way, and you can go up in Maggie Valley, and they'll be a little bit different—fact is, they call it a 'Maggie dance,' 'Maggie footwork.' It's different. Now I'd say fifteen years ago, I could go hear a team, I don't care where it was, and I could turn my back to them. Really now, I'm not exaggerating. Put ten teams up there, and I could pick out the ones from Haywood county. They had a characteristic beat. You have to hear it. You feel it.[11]

To the Haywood Countian, square dancing is a beautifully balanced combination of freedom and discipline. The square dancers come together to execute geometric group figures; this is the element of community discipline in mountain dance. Yet in freedom of footwork style, mountain dancers are able to express their individuality. Each dancer has his or her own unique movements and style. For this reason Kyle Edwards calls traditional style dancing "the freedom dance."[12]

The combination of freedom and group cooperation, in which sixteen or more dancers' unique styles interact within the precisely coordinated square dance figure structure, is similar to the excitement of hearing early hot jazz ensemble performances, in which musical improvisation occurred within a chordal structure. Both types of performance, jazz and mountain dance, involve artists who are so skilled and immersed in their traditions that they can take the risk of improvisation—which results in structured spontaneous interaction. This interaction between structure and improvisation creates a tension that traditional dancers and audiences find aesthetically appealing.

CULTURAL AND STYLISTIC CHANGE

I mentioned earlier that during the past sixty years, Haywood Countians have experienced many changes: the rise of tourism, television, radio, massive enlistment in World War II. Ironically, Haywood County's long-standing reputation as a tourist's vacation haven has helped perpetuate traditional dance in addition to encouraging dance style change. According to Sam Queen, Jr., son of the late Sam Queen who organized the legendary Soco Gap Dance Team:

The tourists started coming in here just as quick as the trains got here. The train came in here in the late 1800s. Tourists came out of the hot, malaria-infested country, they'd send their families in here. . . . In about the mid-1930s, square dancing became respectable through these mountains, and parents would let their children go, and then it mushroomed into just about the total social program by '38 'til about '50. . . . It was a real good type program, the most democratic social life you've ever seen, because you could blend any kind of a crowd, and you didn't have to rely on any kind of formalities. . . . People of all ages, especially the tourists that come in here, they really just loved it. It done a lot for the tourist program in these mountains in the late '30s and early '40s before the war, then right after the war.[13]

While some other mountain communities gave up square dance in favor of more urban amusement, Haywood Countians discovered that tourists enjoyed participating in social dances while on vacation. Many social dances or barn dances during the 1940s up until the 1980s were multilayered events that included strong local followings as well as seasonal tourists.

The building of better roads has also facilitated travel into and out of the area. Contemporary freestyle and precision clogging teams travel from western North Carolina throughout the United States, and some teams even fly to Europe. This mobility has resulted in an increased awareness of nontraditional lifestyle options and an increased diversification of square dance styles; the complications and anxieties associated with large-scale cultural change are also evident in the contemporary square dance scene.

The late 1920s witnessed the emergence of square dance teams. All evidence indicates that before this time, dances were purely social in nature, and any competition was informal. At the inception of team dancing, there was very little difference between staged performances and social dancing. The dancers danced to slower old-style music and wore their Sunday best—no set costumes. Early social dances were performed in large circles of two-couple pairs, often referred to as " big circle square dance" (Figure 8-1). There was no limit to the number of people who could participate in a dance, provided that there was enough space in the room and an even number of couples. When dancing on stage, the early teams continued to dance in a big circle but limited their circles to eight couples who, when in their two-couple pairs, formed four two-couple squares that, taken together, comprise a fifth large square (Figure 8-2). On the stylistic level, no changes were evident between the early square dance teams and the social old-style square dancers—each dancer still had an individualistic footwork style.

According to the accounts of older dancers, old-style buck dancers in Haywood County danced with their weight centered on the balls of their feet. Kyle Edwards speaks of early competitions in which chalk was drawn onto the dancer's shoe heel, and any dancer who rubbed the chalk off during the dance was disqualified.[14] The traditional buck dancers that I have documented drop their heel only occasionally for emphasis. This is what Hazel Bradshaw meant earlier when she referred to old-style dance as a "toe dance." Today the only dancers who consistently dance on the balls of their feet are often called "Maggie Style" dancers, indicating that they are dancers who learned how to dance in the Maggie Valley area where this style has persisted.

Sometime between the mid-1940s and the early 1950s, team dancing began to change. These years witnessed the birth of clogging. For the first time, team costuming became de rigueur. The female clogging costume consisted of fluffy crinoline petticoats that supported dresses with closely tailored bodices and full skirts. There was nothing traditional about these outfits; they were in accordance with the fashions of the day. Yet what began as a very contemporary costume has become a clogging tradition. The basic clogging outfit has changed very little in the past forty years. The male clogging team members simply wear matching shirts and pants.

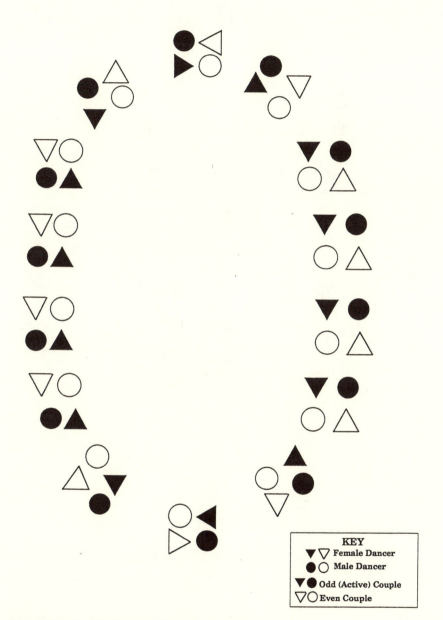

Figure 8-1. *The Big Circle social square dance layout.*

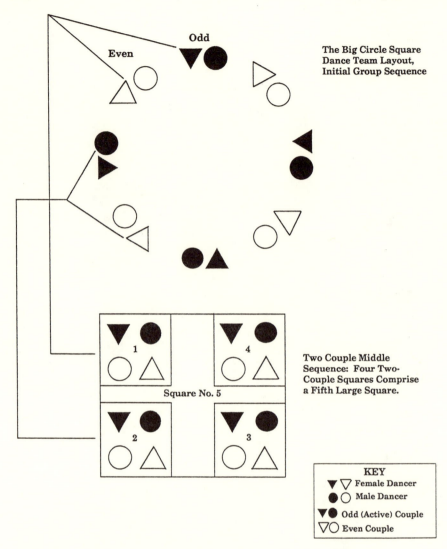

Figure 8-2. *Traditional freestyle clogging dance formations.*

With the advent of loud public address systems and bluegrass music, freestyle dancers began using taps as a practical matter so that their feet could be heard above the increased volume. Soon, however, the jingle taps became a trademark, signaling the advent of freestyle clogging as we know it today. Taps were not simply a stylistic hallmark of modern clogging. They profoundly changed the style of mountain dance in Haywood County because they only sound good when the music is fast (160 beats per minute or faster), and in order to "work" the taps, the body weight must be centered over the heel. By "work" the tap, I mean that the footwork is designed to make the taps jingle.[15] Movements that match the music without taps may not sound good with taps. This resulted in shifting the dancer's center of gravity from the toe to the heel, which contributes to the heavier looking dance style that we associate with the southern mountain area. There are still a few clogging teams that do not require taps, but most cloggers wear them.

The original clogging teams of the 1950s were all freestyle teams; thus, freestyle clogging frequently is referred to as traditional clogging. In freestyle, the freedom of individual style and footwork is maintained, even applauded. The figures commanded by the caller are executed by the group to a synchronized perfection, but the individual personality of each dancer is expressed in improvised footwork.

Precision clogging, a dance that involves two or more people executing the same step at the same time, was reportedly invented in the Piedmont during the late 1950s by James Kesterson, a dance choreographer who felt that it was time to update and modernize this traditional dance.[16] In this most recent square dance form, each dancer executes the same footwork in the same way at the same time, much like the Radio City Rockettes. Unlike all other forms of mountain dance, precision clogging footwork involves high kicks, placing an emphasis on speed and technique over individualistic expression. Likewise, precision clogging figures and music are not necessarily traditional. Many precision teams have discarded the big circle dance format for line dances. These lines do not require an even number of dancers or couples. I have even seen these modern cloggers dance to 45 rpm records of contemporary pop and rock music, such as the song "Boogie Fever" sped up to play at 78 rpm! This speeding up of the music allows precision dancers to show off an almost athletic endurance, and the dance ceases to function as a group activity in which old and young, talented and untalented dancers can recreate together.

Many mountain dancers do not accept precision clogging. They often refer to precision clogging as "flatland" clogging, not only because many of the precision teams they see hail from the Southern Piedmont but also as a way of emphasizing how removed precision clogging is from the aesthetics and ideals of traditional mountain culture. Many of the people I interviewed indicated that precision clogging is such a radical departure from other forms of traditional dance that it should not be included in the constellation.

Ironically, it is the advent of precision clogging that has stimulated a controversy among mountain square dancers about the role and purpose of traditional dance. Many community members, disturbed by the new square dance styles, consequently talk about dance with a clarity and verve that would probably not have been possible before increased style diversification. For example, buck dancer John Reeves, speaking about a precision team that he had seen performing at a festival, complains, "The thing I resented most was they were advertising them as Southern Appalachian, and it wasn't. It had nothing to do with it." Hazel Bradshaw, former owner of the Maggie Valley Playhouse, an old-style social dance hall that was built by her husband Joe Campbell in 1949, observes, "After teaching [clogging] in the schools, the teachers brought that [precision] out more. They were not from the families that did the dancing. I think they just studied it. I don't think they were from any of the original families that danced." Finally, Chief Howell, buck dancer and old-style social dance caller, isn't one to mince words. "When they first started out with that [precision]," he recalls, "I made the remark, and I won't back down a bit, that I could get out there and train some horses to do that."

Amazingly enough, all of the previously mentioned dance styles, even the old-style social dance, now coexist (albeit not so peacefully) in western North Carolina. Thus the development and history of dance style has been an additive process. Each of the people I interviewed had an ardent opinion about the "best" style of dance and described the shortcomings of other styles. Precision was the most controversial style, disliked by both freestyle cloggers and old-style dancers. Albert Burnette, freestyle caller for Canton's historic YMCA freestyle team, spoke of precision dancing as if it were a pollution of the original style. Refusing to acknowledge that precision dancing exists in his county, he said, "I think dance stayed pure here." Freestyle clogger Bob Phillips explains that his distaste for precision style clogging stems not from any lack of proficiency on the part of precision dancers, but rather from the fact that his criteria for judging dance differs from that of the precision dancers. He says, "Now they [precision dancers] are good. I'm not arguing that. It takes a lot of practice and a lot of work, and it's difficult, and I can't do it. But the point is, the best judge of what the dancers like [is] what did your daddy or great-granddaddy or mother do?"

What is the significance of this stylistic proliferation? Why are freestyle and old-style dancers so deeply offended by precision clogging? What does this dance complex as a whole mean to the inhabitants of Haywood County? And finally, what role does mountain dance play in their lives?

DANCE AND IDENTITY: LAYERS OF MEANING

There are many reasons why some people feel compelled to dance—some of these reasons are obvious, while others are more subtle. Many dancers stated that they dance because it helps to keep them physically fit. This physical exercise aspect of dance motivation is probably more important today than it was in the past when most dancers got plenty of exercise while farming. Another obvious reason for dance is social in nature: it provides nonthreatening interaction between unmarried males and females. Finally, whenever I stray too far into my own theoretical musings, the dancers whom I work with remind me that the main reason they dance is simply because the dance is fun.

A less obvious, but clearly articulated, aspect of mountain dance is its role as a source of identity for individuals within the community. Mountain dance increases self-esteem because it allows an individual to excel and master a skill that is respected by other members of the culture; it provides those who have and those who have not succeeded in other aspects of mountain culture with the opportunity to become virtuoso performers.

I mentioned earlier that traditional mountain dance entails an interaction between the opposing forces of restraint and freedom. The square dance form, in which dancers work together to respond to the commands of a caller, provides restraint within an overall geometrical structure. While adhering to the mandates of these calls, the individual dancers also have freedom to improvise their footwork within the established form. The educational value of traditional mountain dance may be found in recognizing a need for balance and the interplay between opposing forces of variation and tradition, order and freedom, and community responsibility and individualism.

This balance is one in which the dancer simultaneously engages in group cooperation to create geometric figures while maintaining a unique individual identity via dance footwork. In this stylistic fusion of freedom and group cooperation, traditional mountain dance celebrates the possibility of community members working together to achieve a goal while allowing each person to maintain and develop his or her unique identity. This ability to operate well as an independent person within a larger group effort was undoubtedly crucial to the collaborative barn raisings, farming, and harvesting of agrarian life.

When precision cloggers choreograph their footwork along with the square dance calls, they violate this traditional balanced perception of ideal order. Precision dance incurs the wrath of freestyle and old-style dancers because precision dancing's mechanical aesthetic negates the traditional dancer's personal creativity, thereby rupturing a balance and interplay between individual and community.

As it has become increasingly necessary for mountain people to know how to interact with nonmountain people, mountain dance has gradually taken on an additional educational responsibility. Freestyle clogging teams grew out of the new social educational needs characteristic of an increasingly urbane community. Says Marty Phillips of freestyle clogging:

Socially it helped me. It has helped me to develop a pretty tough skin so far as how to handle myself in a certain situation. I've been thrown in with every type of person. . . . I've also learned, too, from square dancing, that all people are alike, and there's really no difference in the person that's having a struggle to make ends meet and one that's very affluent. It has also made me able to adapt to any kind of music in any kind of dance.[17]

Not only does freestyle clogging teach the fine points of in-group interaction but also by being part of teams and touring all over the country, not to mention abroad, mountain children now learn via their dance teams how to deal with people who were not enculturated in the mountains. These touring experiences allow mountain dancers to present and share their traditional dance to outsiders within a positive and affirming context in which the outsiders want to learn more about Appalachian traditions. These tours in effect involve cross-cultural dialogue between mountain and nonmountain individuals. This is radically different from the in-group communication involved in old-style social dance. The differing stylistic formats and contexts of old-style dance and freestyle team clogging are aimed toward different educational purposes.

Compared with freestyle clogging and old-style social dance, precision clogging is a style that does not relate to the predominant values of the rural Haywood County community; rather the aesthetics, goals, and ideals of professional elite dancing and the mass media are emulated. A product of more industrial times, precision dance encourages participants to operate as functional cogs within an automated society. The tight, crisp choreography of precision dance indicates that this dance caters mostly to nontraditional audiences. Precision dancers travel around the country to competitions that name the "world champion" or "national champion" of clogging. While at home in western North Carolina, precision dancers perform more often for tourists than for fellow community members. When asked what the dance means to them, precision dancers do not usually stress the idea of heritage or tradition; they refer to the dance as a sport or an art, reflecting the increased sense of competition in precision dance.

In recent years, since the completion of my research, venues for old-style social dance have decreased and precision dance has become increasingly popular among young dancers. While I have not heard any Haywood County precision dancers describe their dance as "traditional," I do know that the national precision dance "community" sees their dance as a continuation of traditional heritage. Formal precision dance competitions have categories that include "traditional freestyle" and "buck dance" as competitive categories despite the fact that the dancers who compete in these categories regularly wear taps, perform recognized precision steps, and engage in high kicking. Perhaps my interviews were conducted at a transitional turning point that marked a stylistic shift. I know that this possibility makes some Haywood County dancers anxious about the future life of their traditional dance.

Contemporary dancers in the Southern Appalachian area have their choice among a variety of dance styles; in deciding how they will dance, they also decide where they will stand regarding issues involving a choice between innovation and tradition. Stylistic choice has become a nonverbal statement about the way an individual dancer believes things "ought" to be, about the correlation that should or should not exist among dance, lifestyle, and world view. In modern society, we are constantly making lifestyle decisions from a vast and complex system of alternatives. Our choices, and therefore our values, are evident even in something as commonplace and seemingly frivolous as dance.

NOTES

1. For more discussion and an extensive bibliography, see Gail Matthews-DeNatale, "Kinesic Conversations: Statements about Identity and Worldview in Appalachian Dance," in *Of, By, and For the People: How Dance Proclaims Political Ideals, Ethnicity, Social Class, and Regional Pride* (Riverside, California: Society of Dance History Scholars/Congress on Research in Dance, 1993).

2. Kyle Edwards, personal correspondence with the author, Maggie Valley, North Carolina, Summer 1982.

3. Albert Burnette, interview with the author, Chingquapin Ridge near Canton, North Carolina, Summer 1982. All subsequent quotes attributed to Albert Burnette are from this interview.

4. Gertrude Plott Welch, interview with the author, Hazelwood, North Carolina, Summer 1982.

5. Bill Sharpe, *A New Geography of North Carolina* (Raleigh, North Carolina: Sharpe Publishing Co., 1954), 1: 178.

6. Hazel Bradshaw, interview with the author, Maggie Valley, North Carolina, Summer 1982. All subsequent quotes attributed to Hazel Bradshaw are from this interview.

7. A "figure" is a sequence of movements that the dancers do together, such as "all join hands and circle left" or "allemande left."

8. Compare with descriptions of Newfoundland stepdancing style in Colin Quigley, *Close to the Floor: Folk Dance in Newfoundland* (St. John's: Memorial University of Newfoundland Folklore and Language Publications, 1985), 19–26.

9. Robert "Chief" Howell, interview with the author, Jonathan's Creek, North Carolina, Summer 1982. All subsequent quotes with Robert "Chief" Howell are from this interview.

10. Fred and Darlene Moody, interview with the author, Maggie Valley, North Carolina, Summer 1982.

11. Bob Phillips, interview with the author, Canton, North Carolina, Summer 1982. All subsequent quotes attributed to Bob Phillips come from this interview.

12. Kyle Edwards, field notes from an untaped interview with the author, Maggie Valley, North Carolina, Summer 1982.

13. Sam Queen, Jr., interview with the author, Hazelwood, North Carolina, Summer 1982.

14. Edwards, field notes.

15. Howell, interview.

16. Despite the fact that some contemporary dance scholars question Kesterson's role in the development of precision dance, all of my informants described Kesterson as the father of precision style clogging. Kesterson lived nearby in Hendersonville, North Carolina. One possibility is that precision dance was an idea whose time had come and was born at about the same time in several different locations—polygenesis in action. For a detailed account of the Kesterson story, see Stephen March and David Holt, "Chase That Rabbit," *Southern Exposure* 5 (Summer/Fall 1977): 44–47.

17. Marty Phillips, interview with the author, Canton, North Carolina, Summer 1982.

Chapter 9

Carrying on the Old Mountain Clog Dance: Thoughts about Freestyle Clogging

AN INTERVIEW WITH BOB PHILLIPS

Gail Matthews-DeNatale

Bob Phillips has been dancing with freestyle clogging teams since the early 1970s. He currently directs the Canton, North Carolina, team called the Rough Creek Cloggers. The team has retired from competition, but it still dances regularly as an exhibition team at the Waynesville, North Carolina, Country Club Inn and for various conventions. In addition, they have traveled to festivals, including the Mountain Dance and Folk Festival in Asheville, North Carolina. In 1980, the Rough Creek Cloggers toured in France, and together with Gail Matthews-DeNatale, Phillips has participated in the international folk dance conference, Folkmoot U.S.A. held in Haywood County, North Carolina. A firm believer in old-style mountain clog dance, he frequently serves as a judge for clogging competitions throughout the southeastern United States. He is retired from a managerial position with the Champion International Paper Mill and is the mayor of Canton. These excerpts are from an interview conducted by Gail Matthews-DeNatale in the summer of 1982.

I consider Haywood county the hotbed of the old mountain clog dance. Right here. Bascom Lunsford,[1] talking to him, he said it ran in a band from North Georgia to Virginia. It's a band right through here where you see this clog dancing. It's been performed here for a number of years.

Each area had a characteristic type dance footwork. For instance, right here we dance one way, and you can go up in Maggie Valley, and they'll be a little bit different—fact is, they call it "Maggie style," Maggie footwork. It's different. Now I'd say fifteen years ago, I could go hear a team, I don't care where it was, and I could turn my back to them. Really now, I'm not exaggerating. Put ten teams up there, and I could pick out the ones from Haywood County. They had a characteristic beat. You have to hear it. You feel it. It sounds to-ti-di, to-ti-di, to-ti-di, to-ti-di. We don't call it an extra beat. It's something that's characteristic of the footwork itself.

Now what's happened, your teams, you can't keep them together for a long time. I took a boy from over here at Candler, North Carolina. He was a smooth dancer. Brought him over here and made a beautiful clog dancer out of him. He goes back over, and they start a team over there. In the process the dance gets changed a little bit and now . . . I'm going to call it diluted. It's a lot more diluted than it used to be— on their footwork and on a lot of their calls. Course they're pretty. And usually if you go to a festival, you've done a lot of research to dig up an old figure, and those older figures are difficult to find. You do it one time, and the next time you go out, there'll be about two, three more teams will have that figure.

What we do here is all the old traditional figures. As far as the footwork goes, we instruct the individual to do his own interpretation of the music. In other words, he's interpreting the music with his feet. That's what Bascom would tell you. One way you can always kind of get this is when you hear the music going. I've got some records here that are what we dance by. Listen to the music, and close your eyes. This is the best way I've found. Close your eyes and your feet will kind of, well, want to start moving around. If you put fifty people together, I suspect you wouldn't find two that dance alike. Now my wife dances, I dance, and my son dances, and not a single one of us dance at all alike. We have our own styles. This is your true mountain dance.

This is what we teach. That's the reason I don't teach anybody to dance a certain way. I try to show them. The best way to teach them is to put them with somebody that dances good. And maybe they can just walk. They learn the figures, and first thing you know, you'll see them "te-de-dum," moving their feet around. And I prefer them not to try to imitate anybody. Let them arrive at their own style.

When I was directing a group of junior high and high school kids, I perhaps was a pretty hard taskmaster. But I demanded that they do a certain figure a certain way, and they do it right. I was an old bear, you know. But really, they were real sweet kids. They did a beautiful job. It's a matter of work. That's all in the world it is. Instead of dancing, we spent as much time walking to learn the figures: "Walk, walk. You're not doing it right. Do it again. Do it again." I had them one night do it twenty times on one figure. I said, "You're going to do it 'till you get it right."

We went to the Washington Senate Rotunda, and Senator Byrd, he plays the fiddle, you know, he was up on the balcony, and they did the "couple star." That was a beautiful thing when it's done right. I went up [on the balcony] and that thing was as pretty . . . It couldn't have been done any better. They didn't take a back seat to anybody. And they cut it just perfect. See, we have a certain way how we pivot. Everything was worked out. In other words, I say "No loosey goosey. Make it crisp, make it sharp, make it good." I said, "Just like you've got a two-by-four nailed to your back." I said, "Make it come around." And we hammered, and we hammered, and we hammered, and we hammered. But it paid off.

Over here, they have another dance they call precision clog. You've probably heard of that. I feel like where it came from was from James Kesterson[2] in Hendersonville, North Carolina. I saw him years and years ago do this. He took the mountain clog dance, and he jazzed it up to bring it up more like a modern dance. They used quite a bit of clog steps, you know, as far as their footwork. But each dancer is dancing exactly like the next one. The Rockettes would be a good example. They might not be the same kind of footwork, but they kick the left leg together, the right leg together. Kesterson said anybody can do the old mountain style. What he wanted to do was liven it up. Well I don't go that way. I try to stick to what is the old way, near as we can.

The people are so confused today. It's utter chaos really. I judge, and it's gotten so bad that now in some areas I refuse to judge. I mean when it comes down to that, I'm blunt. I'm blunt because it's been a battle for a number of years. So many of the directors honest-to-goodness don't know the difference. They really don't know the difference of what they're teaching. All they're doing is they're teaching the footwork. I went over where they brought out a duo, where they're going to play a record. That's my first exposure to this type of thing, and they played "Boogie Woogie." I 'bout died! I honest-to-goodness about croaked!

After it was over, we the judges called the man over that was running the thing and said to him, "By no stretch of the imagination can that be old mountain clog dancing." And we're just not going to judge them. We got kind of frank. He went over and talked and came back and said, "I'll tell you what. If you'll judge it on through this," see, he was kind of in a bind, "then I'll promise you, next year we won't have any such thing." I said, "Fine." So we went ahead.

But during the dance contest, I'm sure it was very obvious on my face how I felt. I was sitting there with a kind of disgusted look on my face. He came over and said that one of the directors over there was kind of afraid that their duo was not getting a fair judging. "Oh," I says, "they're getting a fair judging, but I don't have to like it." And I don't.

If I catch one doing a step that is not traditional, where it's obviously a modern figure or footwork, I'll stop them. Let me give you a couple of illustrations. Every once and a while, you'll see a dancer [gets up and clicks heels together]. You know what that is: that's a Charleston step. Then there's this one [swings one leg in a circle behind him]. I'll knock off points on that quicker—that's Wringing the Cow's Tail. One of the judges of a dance team said there wasn't any cows that had any tails in Georgia because every one of them had been wrung off that day. What you've got to watch for are Virginia Reel figures, formations. You've got to watch for Charleston steps. These are basically what you've got to watch for.

Usually precision dancers will use traditional figures, but they're inclined to throw in figures that are not as traditional. They have on their judging sheets sometimes "variety" or "originality," something similar to that. Now on the old freestyle, they nailed one old team director and knocked off a couple of points 'cause they went into four circles and used some Western club square dance figures. Some of the teams that have won in the past have added a lot on them, and they couldn't even cut it anymore in competition because they've added so many goofy figures in there. Oh, some of them are real elaborate.

It's getting far afield. You see it spreading, and the people take it, and they'll make up a figure, and they'll do this and they'll do that. It's just so mixed up. We had a group that come in here from East Tennessee. Good dancers, good precision team, did real good. And they went through the whole dance and did not do one corner figure. I murdered them on the score. Because this is what it is—it's a square dance with clog footwork. Well, so much for that.

What makes a good dancer? There's several things. I think you have to have a desire to want to dance. I don't care how potentially good a dancer is, if he doesn't have a desire to dance, he's not going to be good. I mean, he might be pretty good, but he's not going to be just really top flight. Number one: the ability to really relax and enjoy himself. That's the key right there. The freestyle dancer, if he's *really* relaxed—and this is the key to the whole thing—if he's really relaxed, he's not going to be very tired. He'll be hot, maybe, but he's not going to be very tired. You don't fight it. You relax and just "wheererrreer," let it go, you know. I've seen people come off the floor, young people, just keel over. They're fighting it instead of relaxing and enjoying it.

You can spot a precision dancer [snaps his fingers] usually that quick. They've got a characteristic about them. They're not free-flowing. I sit here and watch harness racing on TV Saturday nights, with little sulkies behind them. They have two types: trotters and pacers. Your trotter is more of a natural gait. A pacer is more of what I call artificial. It's more of what the old timers call racking. But on a pacer, you know, both legs on this side go together like this, and a trotter's picking one up at a time. This is what I compare the precision dance versus your freestyle. One's an artificial type dance, and one's a free-flowing individual type dance.

When I get out and try to kick up in the air and do this high stuff, that's not dancing to me. When you dance, you have a good time. Also, you'll find what creeps in is a lot of skipping. The caller will run the tune too fast. If you're really and truly dancing, you're not going to move too awful fast. If the team gets to whistling along, the girls will kind of skip to get through the figures in time. A lot of times on these evaluations, I'll put down "*Dance*, don't skip."

You don't have to be so spectacular. If you'll listen at them [freestyle cloggers], it's just beautiful to listen at them: "bep-ti-de-bep-ti-de-bep," you know, right down the line.

What makes a bad dancer? Attitude. Really, that's more than anything else, I think. Attitude—which wraps up a whole lot of things. I can tell if a dancer's mad or something's wrong. I had a team I judged awhile back. I noticed one girl. Something was wrong with that girl. She was sour looking. She wasn't enjoying herself. It hurt the whole team's effort.

The main thing in mountain clogging is pure enjoyment. This is my relaxation. It's not for the glory. I just thoroughly enjoy it, and I also would like to think maybe that we're carrying on something that has meant so much over the years to so many people in the original form, without diluting it and polluting it.

NOTES

1. Mars Hill, North Carolina, native Bascom Lamar Lunsford was a promoter of mountain music and mountain dance, and organized the first Asheville Mountain Dance and Folk Festival in 1928.

2. For a detailed account of the Kesterson story, see Stephen March and David Holt, "Chase That Rabbit," *Southern Exposure* 5 (Summer/Fall 1977): 44–47.

Chapter 10

"Clogging Is Country": A Precision Clogger's Perspective

AN INTERVIEW WITH BARBARA BOGART

Jane Harris Woodside

Barbara Bogart admired Ralph Sloan and his team of exhibition precision clog-gers, the Tennessee Travelers, whenever she caught their brief appearances on television. In the middle 1970s, she began dancing, starting out with Western club square dance. In 1978, she discovered precision clogging classes in Knoxville, Tennessee, and today she is the director of the Kingsport Country Cloggers, a precision clogging team based in Kingsport, Tennessee. The Coun-try Cloggers perform for many private shows, conventions, and other area func-tions, participate in local festivals, and occasionally travel as far as Opryland in Nashville or to South Carolina to do special shows. Bogart also holds down a full-time job at a large printing company during the day.

Clogging is a very popular and dynamic dance form in the Appalachian region, with clear links to the older traditional solo flatfooting or buckdancing, the old-time social square dance that Mrs. Veronia Miller calls,[1] and the freestyle team clogging style described by Bob Phillips[2] and discussed by Gail Matthews-DeNatale.[3] Many precision cloggers use a basic step consisting of a double toe (also known as a "shuffle") with the left foot, a step on the left, a rock on the right, then a step back onto the left foot. As Bogart learned from another clog-ging instructor, the leg in precision clogging is generally raised more than six inches off the ground. (In many—though not all—communities, raising your foot less than six inches is, by definition, flatfooting. To Bogart, flatfooting means more of a smooth scooting or shuffling of the feet instead of a strictly up-and-down motion.) Bogart points out that the basic step is very similar to tradi-tional solo flatfooting and buckdancing forms in the region. Her group simply adds what she calls "a modern flair."

Though utilizing them far less exclusively than freestyle clogging teams, precision cloggers do sometimes borrow old-time square dance figures for their routines. Unlike freestyle teams, of course, individual precision team members synchronize their steps. Also the precision team's repertoire includes a much larger stock of figures and formations than those found in old-time or freestyle team dance. In a typical hour-long performance, Bogart places a circle dance performed by the entire team at the beginning, middle, and end of the show. In between, she has couple dances, all-female production numbers, and line dances.

Other clogging groups have departed further from traditional social dance, leaving behind all vestiges of old-time square dance figures and often blurring what had been well-defined gender roles. At its most extreme, these new-style cloggers dance to disco and other pop music, add karate moves to their routines, execute various acrobatic moves, or imitate robots.

Like Western club square dance, precision is a national phenomenon, but there seems to be more regional variation in precision than exists in Western club square. "You go to a different area, and they have a totally different style. The steps are basically the same deep down, but everybody's got their own different style," says Bogart. There are national precision clogging conventions, workshops, and competitions. Based in Durham, North Carolina, the National Clogging and Hoedown Council legislates competition rules.

The following is an excerpt from a 1990 interview with Jane Harris Woodside.

We do the old clogging style (Figure 10-1). Clogging normally has a main beat, a steady beat, and you emphasize that beat either with a heel or a flatfoot step. The count we call a downbeat, then in between is an upbeat, and you have your double-toes, toes, or rock steps between the downbeats. So actually, you've got a step on the upbeat and a step on the downbeat, which is generally about all the amount of steps or sounds that you have within a beat. The younger people do what they used to call modern buckdancing. It's more just a hopping motion, just an up-and-down hopping motion, and you've got a lot of extra sounds or movements in the same amount of beats. The new modern buck dancers count the basic step, "A, E, and uh one; A, E, and uh two." The old basic is counted "And one and two." In the new style, you've got a lot of heel-toe, and you're jumping on the ball of your other foot. You are hopping up and down on one foot, while you're doing different things with the heel and the toe of the other foot. In my opinion, the young kids are the only ones who've got the stamina that can handle the new style of clogging today.

I prefer the traditional type clogging steps because I think they are prettier and have more form to them. To me, in the modern clogging, they have changed the whole style. They say it's progress, but to me, it is not traditional. I think what we do is more in keeping with what was traditional, even though we may have a little bit of a modern flair to the steps and make them look different. Even though you may be doing different steps in the more modern style clogging, the steps generally all look alike.

A true traditional clogging team dances the old-time square dance figures while doing freestyle footwork. The couples team of the Kingsport Country Cloggers do

Figure 10-1. *The Kingsport Country Cloggers, Kingsport, Tennessee, 1990. Photograph by Barbara Bogart.*

the old-time or Appalachian square dance figures; however, we hopefully do the same steps in precision. Once you do precision dancing, it is harder to do just freestyle clogging where no two cloggers are in step with each other.

I dance with the couples team and call the dance. However, my calling of the dance is at a minimum because of how I write our routines. Listening to the music will tell the dancers when to change from one figure to the other on most figures. There are a few figures that, depending on how many couples we have—sometimes we may have four, six, or eight, or even an odd number of couples—it will change the timing. So I usually have to cue them a little bit. When I do yell a cue, it is not to tell them *what* to do but *when* to start the movement. Those are the only times that I really need to cue a particular dance.

To put a little variety in our shows, the team does dances other than the Appalachian square dancing. We do line dances with the whole team. The girls' team does production or team numbers. They intertwine with each other and do different formations, circles, and/or lines during a particular routine. They do not do any of the Appalachian square dance figures but other types of figures. Most of the teams of today do only line dances because that is about the only thing they teach at workshops. But when you are doing a thirty-minute to an hour show, doing the same type of dance over and over gets old or boring to a lot of people, no matter how good you are at your craft. I always try to put a variety in our shows to keep a little more interest.

The other dances we do, with the exception of the couples' and girls' team numbers, are choreographed to the music we select. The music is usually one of the current Country and Western songs. We have it on tape, and the dance has been choreographed specifically for that particular arrangement. I hear a tape I like, and I just kind of feel the music, try to match steps with the feel of the music. The clogging steps have a definite sound to them, and I try to match the sound closely to the rhythm or melody of the songs. You have to dissect the music, break it up into the intro, verse, chorus, ending, and any breaks in between that it might have. Music usually runs in eight-beat phrases, except for the transitional breaks. It is kind of easy and fun if you hear a song that you just have a feel for, and steps just pop into your mind that seem like they fit perfect, as if a certain part of that song was just made for a particular step. I start choreographing from that point and then jump around to different parts of the song until I get it written. I don't usually just take any song step by step from beginning to end. There has to be something with a song that I particularly like and feel. I can just see that step go with it and sort of go around about that with variations. You also want to put a little movement with the dance rather than standing in one spot during the whole dance. Most of your audience can't really associate with the steps unless those steps are done in connection with some sort of teamwork, which adds some kind of design or flair to the dance.

We do not go to competitions. I don't think much of competitions, personally. It is not much fun. There is so much jealousy, and to me, it just isn't worth the time and trouble. I got into clogging for the fun and enjoyment of the dance, and I particularly get a charge in teaching beginners and experiencing the thrill with them of learning and sharing their joy.

I also get other rewards from teaching. People who have taken my classes come to me and tell me how much it has helped them. It will take their minds off their personal problems and give them strength. Or they come just for the exercise. It is a good aerobic exercise, but it does not feel like you are exercising, and therefore it makes it easier to stick with it and help control your weight if you do it often. I had one man who said to me that he had high blood pressure. He came to my classes and enjoyed them so much. He became real good at it, too. He said he lost twenty-five pounds, and he does not have to take any blood pressure pills any more. He said his doctor told him it was the best thing he could have done.

But then, most people take the lessons just for their own enjoyment. There are many places in the community where they have live bluegrass bands, and people can go out for a night and just enjoy dancing.

When we do shows, I want to let people feel the excitement, the enjoyment we feel. We try to convey to our audience what we feel. Most of these people who go to the bluegrass festivals and enjoy that type of music enjoy the clogging, too. I like bluegrass music for dancing because that is where clogging comes from—from the old Appalachian, the old bluegrass music. Clogging is country.

NOTES

1. See Miller, "You Have to Watch Your People," in this volume.
2. See Phillips, "Carrying on the Old Mountain Clog Dance," in this volume.
3. See Matthews-DeNatale, "Wild and Yet Really Subdued," in this volume.

Chapter 11

"I Want To Show These Young People What We Used To Do": A Cherokee Revivalist Remembers

AN INTERVIEW WITH WALKER CALHOUN

Jane Harris Woodside

Walker Calhoun is one of the leaders of the current attempts on the part of the Eastern Band of the Cherokee to revive traditional dance on the Qualla Boundary Reservation in North Carolina. Born in 1918 in the small, isolated mountain community of Big Cove, he has experienced the shift from a culture supported by subsistence agriculture to one based on tourism and light industry. In this edited excerpt from a 1989 interview conducted by Jane Harris Woodside, Calhoun remembers his youth in Big Cove and the attempts of his half-uncle, Will West Long, to keep the vestiges of traditional Cherokee culture alive. He describes the Booger dance, a fascinating form that straddles dance and drama. And he speaks about the Raven Rock Dancers, his own troupe of traditional dancers consisting of one of his nine children, Bernice Bottchenbaugh, her husband Rick, and many of Calhoun's grandchildren.

All this hillside was in corn when I was a child. I mean *all* over this hillside. We did a corn dance and a green corn dance. The corn dance—they do that, celebrate the corn harvest. Green corn—they done that dance in August. Down here, close to the river, we had a ball field. It growed up now. That's where they done that green corn dance. Womenfolks cooked the corn, beans, 'taters—whatever they had, they cooked it, took it down to the ball field, and they called it dinner-on-the-grounds. And while we was waiting to eat, that's when the men done this green corn dance around the food.

We didn't have stores around here. Every time we want something, we have to go to Cherokee to get it and carry it home. One man had a yoke of steers, white-faced, and a wagon. And he used to go out once in a while, all the way to Whittier, which must have been about thirty-five miles from here. A train stopped there. There was a little depot; it's still there. He took the wagon to haul in sugar, coffee, salt, whiskey. A lot of people sent for those things by this man with a wagon. Took him about—I don't know—took him about a day-and-a-half to get there. You know, the steers are slow, and it was a rough road.

All the young people—there was nothing much to do. We didn't have many sports back then. We just had Indian stickball and bow-and-arrow shoot. We didn't know anything about basketball or baseball and all that. The young people would help raise food, and sometimes they'd build a house, a log house. Keep busy. They hewed the logs, made one side flat, notched them. They done a good job. That was a way of life. That's the way they kept busy.

We had a free labor group, a *gadugi*. Some person sick, couldn't work—these people get together. We had a group organized. We had the boss, the headman. Will West Long was the headman for the free labor group. He'd go around and visit the homes and find out, see if anybody needs help. If he find out somebody needs help, Will West set a time and let the rest of the community people know where we going to meet, where we're going to do the work. And when the day was over, we quit work, and he used to talk with us. To love one another, keep this, keep that going. He was a good man, all the way around. People come to him for medicine, to be doctored. Herbs, a lot of herb medicine. I know some of them.

And we'd dance at least two times a month, or three, just at somebody's home. Right over here at my aunt's, we used to do our dances. That was something. It's something like social dance. Just everybody, just anybody come to the dance. It was all night long. This dance we did at home, I call it Six Nations dance because that's what they call it: they got a record or tape where Will West sings from that Museum, the Cherokee Museum. There's a lot of them that could lead the dance. Every man used to lead the dance.

I was a teenager, the last time I did the Booger dance. Used to be a bunch of them sitting in the house on the bench. And they start the singing, the Booger dance songs. I know about six of them. While the boogers are getting ready, putting their things on, Will West Long and older folks just sit inside and sing, beating on the drums, rattler, tin can, or just whatever they get a hold of. Boogers come to the door, and they quit singing, let them come in and set on a bench. There's a bench for them to sit on while they's waiting to dance. They always have a leader. He come in first, sit down.

There used to be another man questioned these boogers. They couldn't speak out 'cause if they did, they get recognized. You're not supposed to know who they are. Some of them have a blanket over them, a mask. So they had to have a man to ask questions, ask them their name, and then he'd announce it to the audience. Question all of us. Ask them their name, ask them what they was, what they was doing here. They would give a funny name.

After that, they start singing again. The leader danced first. The leader put on the action, you know, any funny act people can think of. So when the leader's through, then another one would get up. They call another one to dance, and they do the same thing. Sometimes there'd be about a dozen of them. And they wore homemade masks. Will West Long—he used to make his own masks out of buckeye, soft wood. When they were dressed up, you couldn't tell who they were. You know, it was just supposed to be a fun dance. People used to believe in witches. They just sort of made fun of the witches, I believe, in this dance. Drive them away or something like that. That was the purpose of that dance: to drive away evil spirits.

All of them dances have meaning. Beaver dance—it's not a beaver dance. Beaver can't dance. It's a beaver hunter's dance. They done it before going to hunt the beaver so the dance would give them luck. That's the way I understand it.

When Will West Long died, that's when it started going down. They kept the simple dances, like the Friendship dance, the Beaver, the Quail. That's about the only thing they was doing. They didn't know the Eagle dance, the Peace Pipe, the Green Corn Dance, the Bear Dance. That's the ones I brought back. Some of them anyway. There's a few of them that's just gone: like the Ground Hog, Snake, Buffalo dance, Horse dance. Will West Long wasn't doing those dances when I was a kid. All the dances, I call them sacred because they honor the animals. Sacred dances.

I just want to show these young people what we used to do. In my own family, my oldest child remembers a little bit about Will West Long. The rest of them didn't know what I was talking about. And then I got them started. They get the most applause for the Beaver dance. They carry a stick to kill the Beaver with. They dance with them sticks. First they go around and join them sticks together while they dance. Then when I tell them to go beaver hunting, a pair goes from the main dance, they go the opposite way, they go hunt beaver. Two men pull the Beaver on a cord, and the hunters try to hit it with a stick.

The Peace Pipe's supposed to be seven men and seven women. And every dance is sevens. All the dances are supposed to be representing the seven clans. Even them feathers [indicating the rods of feathers used in certain dances] seven, seven feathers on them. The women hold their feathers under the men's.

This singing, it's a spiritual thing. We can't, we don't understand it. Most of this I say when I'm singing, it don't mean nothing to me. God knows what you sing, but we don't know. Was a gift to them many years ago, nobody knows when. There's a legend about these songs Indians sing. A boy and girl were killed by evil people, and as they were being burned to death, they sang, and their song drifted up in the smoke. And whoever hears that song, it sticks to his memory.

Some people's interested in this tradition. When we practice, people get interested. Join in. If I had a room, if I had a place, I'd invite different communities from all over the reservation. Most of the young people, it's something new. There is a few of us left that knows all about this, the old dances—just half a dozen left.

My dancers are named the Raven Rock Dancers. The reason I named it this: they call this Big Cove Community; the Indians, they call it the Raven's Place. The reason the Indians named it that is 'cause there's a big rock right up there, not too far. You can see it when you come around below here, up on the mountain, a big rock.

That's where ravens used to raise little ones. So they named this Raven's Place. In English, they call it Big Cove. I don't know how they named it Big Cove. But to the Indian-speaking people, it's Raven's Place. Still got that Indian name. That's why I named the dancers Raven Rock, Raven Rock Dancers.

Chapter 12

"Everybody Needs Identity": Reviving Cherokee Dance

Jane Harris Woodside

The culture, history, and language of the Eastern Band of Cherokees are dying out. Traditions once passed on orally from generation to generation now reside largely with the elderly members of the band and are in danger of being lost forever. There is a need of preserving the culture while it is still available and of engaging the youth with the notion of what it means to be Cherokee.

> Alvin Smith, "Cherokee Culture," *Cherokee One Feather*, August 13, 1975

It is impossible, at this late day, to distinguish accurately between ancient traditions of the Cherokees and modern fictions, or between those which are purely original, and those which have been derived, wholly or in part, from intercourse with the whites. Their traditions are fading from memory, and only a few aged men can give much information respecting them.

> "Cherokee Traditions," *Cherokee Phoenix*, April 1, 1829

The first weekend of March 1991 was meant to be a Desert Storm rally, but after the United States and its allies made quick work of Iraq, the North Carolina Cherokee quickly recast the event into a victory celebration. On Saturday morning, a parade made its way down U.S. 441, one of the main highways through the off-season tourist town of Cherokee on the Qualla Boundary Reservation. A special honor guard of Oklahoma Cherokee veterans came for the occasion. In the Boundary's multipurpose building, red, white, and blue bunting, children's patriotic drawings, and a plentiful supply of yellow bows decorated the walls. The patriotic speeches began mid-morning, followed by country and western bands and amplified gospel groups that played while community members gathered just outside the building for dinner-on-the-grounds.

And they danced. On a rainy Friday evening, the community organized a modern version of a traditional Cherokee 49er, a dance originally held to honor warriors as they returned home. For hours, twenty or thirty Cherokee—men and women, mostly young, some older—wore elaborate regalia and performed the rapid, intricate footwork of pan-Indian Pow Wow dance.[1] Even more people participated in the Pow Wow during the dance held Saturday afternoon to honor the soldiers who would soon be returning.

Between the lunchtime gospel music and Saturday afternoon's Pow Wow dance, Walker Calhoun led out his troupe of Raven Rock Dancers. For the next ten minutes, Calhoun's daughter Bernice Bottchenbaugh, along with several of his grandchildren, did the centuries-old Cherokee tribal dances: the bear, quail, and beaver hunt dances. Cherokee traditional dance is quite simple, especially in contrast to Pow Wow dance; this tribal dance form is principally intended for group participation rather than for the display of individual expertise.

An elderly, dignified man, Calhoun is one of the leaders of the Cherokees' latest attempt to resuscitate the old dances. The crowd, consisting almost exclusively of Cherokee, watched respectfully during this brief and symbolic reminder of their tribal identity and applauded. Then the pan-Indian Pow Wow dancing resumed.

Dance to the modern-day Cherokee is no mere entertainment. It remains, as it was for their ancestors, a fundamental cultural idiom, one that they reach for time and time again when they need to express their deepest feelings about war and peace, about human experience, gratitude, God, or friendship. Both the traditionally derived and the thoroughly modern elements of the Desert Storm rally hint at how complex a task it is for the modern-day Cherokee to formulate his or her identity—as an Eastern Band Cherokee, as a Native American, and as an American citizen.

With its central place in their culture, dance has played an important role in the Cherokees' efforts to work out a viable identity for hundreds of years. But those attempts to formulate an identity take place in an increasingly complex environment, where not all the members of the community have arrived at the same solutions to the dilemmas posed by change, further complicated by increased contact with cultures other than their own. At least some Cherokee see traditional dance as one way to survive spiritually, psychologically, and, to some degree, economically.

CHEROKEE TRADITIONAL DANCE

The majority of the sedate Cherokee dances that Calhoun and his family dance in public are dances in which the performers mimic the animals after which the particular dance is named. For example, the dancers perform the bear dance to Calhoun's brisk, rhythmic chant punctuated by a gourd rattle. It opens with the dancers trotting around in the counterclockwise circle characteristic of Cherokee dance. At intervals, every other person in the circle turns and faces the dancer behind him or her; they both claw the air and growl. In the middle section, the pace slows, and the dancers all face forward, hunch over and imitate a bear's lumbering walk as he gathers acorns. They then repeat the first movement of the dance until its conclusion. The ideal is to become so involved with accurately portraying the animal that the dancers forget the presence of any onlookers.

In addition to animal dances such as the bear, the quail, the beaver, and the eagle, the Raven Rock Dancers also publicly perform nonmimetic, more abstract dances such as the Friendship and the Peace Pipe. In the Friendship dance, for example, the group—using slow shuffling steps—begins by circling single file and counterclockwise. As the tempo picks up, the dancers move at a trot. Next, they join hands. A dancer breaks the circle and leads the group, first back and forth, serpentine-fashion, then winding the ensemble into tight, concentric circles, much like the "wind the clock" figure found in old-time Appalachian square dancing. Finally the leader forms the circle again, the group resumes its quick-paced, single-file trot, and shortly afterward, the dance ends.

In the place of the skins and wooden masks worn by their ancestors, today's Cherokee traditional dancers wear dress that reveals recent and sometimes disparate influences. At the Desert Storm rally, most of the dancers wore Pow Wow regalia since many traditional dancers are also avid and skilled competition dancers. Some, however, wore the outfits that I have seen them wear when performing before predominantly non-Native American audiences. These particular outfits resemble the colorful variations on European-American dress that the nineteenth century North Carolina Cherokee adopted.[2] The women are attired in calico dresses in colors such as bright blue, dusty pink, or orange, with long full skirts decorated at the hem with bands of ribbon. The men wear equally bright "ribbon shirts," tunics decorated with ribbons at the collar, cuffs, and yoke. From the front and back yoke, two pairs of ribbons flutter with the dancer's movements. These ribbon shirts trace their origins to recent history. They were worn during various Native American protests beginning in the 1970s (Figure 12-1).

During the past forty years, Cherokee traditional dances have come close to disappearing entirely. Today, among the Eastern Band of Cherokee, various people, with equally varied motivations, are trying to give these old dances new life.

The leader of the Raven Rock Dancers, Walker Calhoun, is a World War II veteran who saw service in Europe, a retired factory worker in his seventies, and a highly respected spiritual leader and elder. He is from Big Cove, a once-isolated mountain community located fourteen miles from the town of Cherokee on the Qualla Boundary. The Qualla Boundary consists of 56,621 acres located west and slightly south of Asheville, North Carolina, principally in Jackson and Swain counties, the home of almost 9,600 Cherokee tribal members as of January 1990.[3] Big Cove, always one of the most traditional of the nine communities that comprise the Boundary, had long been a stronghold of the old dance. But even there, traditional dances were rapidly dying out.

Revival efforts have met with limited success. On the one hand, Calhoun has won considerable respect and recognition both on and off the reservation for his

Figure 12–1. *Cherokee children performing the Beaver Dance, mid-1980s. Photograph by Kenneth Murray.*

efforts to keep traditional dance alive. In 1988, his cultural preservation work earned him the first Sequoyah Award ever awarded, a prize established by North Carolina's Eastern Band and Oklahoma's Cherokee Nation. The following year, he was one of seven recipients of the North Carolina Heritage Award, and in 1992, the National Endowment for the Arts awarded him a National Heritage Fellowship. Traditional dances are frequently part of Cherokee cultural and educational programs, often aimed at children. But despite all this recognition, performances of the ancient traditional Cherokee dance form are infrequent; it does not enjoy nearly the grass-roots popularity that the pan-Indian Pow Wow dancing does.

Still, this modest, limited dance revival is significant for the part it plays in helping the Cherokee regain a sense of what it means to be Cherokee, in reclaiming pride in their ethnicity, a pride that has been under attack from many quarters over the years, and in reforging bonds with the much larger Western band of Cherokee in Oklahoma.

EARLY CHEROKEE DANCE AND RELIGION

When the Raven Rock Dancers performed at the 1991 Desert Storm Rally, they simply danced without offering any explication. When they appear before non-Native American audiences, an individual sometimes explains the meaning of the dance. For example, Gilliam Jackson has on occasion served as a facilitator for the Raven Rock Dancers' performances. Jackson is from Snowbird, another highly traditional Cherokee enclave located about fifty miles from the Qualla Boundary in Graham county. He has been a traditional dancer and is currently director of Cherokee Tribal Child Care Services.

When Jackson interprets Cherokee traditional dance for outside audiences, he speaks of his ancestors' world view and belief systems. The animal dances, he explains, were originally part of rituals intended to honor and give thanks to animals such as the bear, the horse, the turkey, the eagle, and the quail as a way of guaranteeing a successful hunt. "Our belief system held that all the animals were in the spirit world, just as we are, and that we needed to give thanks in order to continue receiving the things they give to us: the skins, the tools that we could make from their bones," Jackson says.[4] Dance, he continues, affected the natural and human worlds in very concrete and immediate ways. The Cherokee divided their year into two seasons: winter and summer. They danced certain dances—such as the green corn dance—only in summer since they associated such dances with crops and vegetation. A dance common to many tribes, the green corn dance was a ritual performed as part of an annual ceremony to celebrate the harvest. The Cherokee believed that winter dances, such as the eagle and the bear, attracted cold and death. To perform a dance in other than its appropriate season was to upset the balance and invite catastrophe.

Today's presentations of Cherokee traditional dance are attempts to reconstruct the way the Cherokee saw the world and how it felt to be Cherokee before the Europeans came. Although DeSoto ventured into Cherokee territory in 1540,

European contact did not begin in earnest until the late seventeenth and eighteenth centuries when Europeans set up trading outposts. However, written descriptions of Cherokee life do not appear until the early to mid-eighteenth century.[5]

At the time of those first written accounts, European contact had already had some influence on the Cherokee. Nonetheless, between sixteen thousand and twenty thousand Cherokee still lived much as they had for centuries. They lived in a loose confederation of approximately sixty autonomous villages spread over forty thousand square miles in parts of North and South Carolina, Georgia, Alabama, Tennessee, Kentucky, Virginia, and West Virginia. Each village consisted of a cluster of log-and-clay homes, surrounded by fields, gardens, and pastures. The economic base was cooperative agriculture, mainly the women's province, supplemented by the men's hunting and fishing. The matriarchal and matrilocal clan system held the highly decentralized system together by means of customary laws. Each of the seven clans was usually represented in any given village.[6] Local chiefs led by trying to achieve consensus.

Dance was an important part of Cherokee religion and ritual. As anthropologist Charles Hudson writes in *The Southeastern Indians*, "Indeed, no clear line can be drawn between dancing and ritual because both were believed to contribute to the health and happiness of man."[7] Descriptions of the religion are sketchy, but historian William McLoughlin gives at least a glimpse of pre-Christian Cherokee beliefs in his books, *Cherokee Renascence in the New Republic* and *Cherokees and Missionaries*. As with several other Native peoples, the Cherokee believed that they were "the principal people" and that their home in the Southern Appalachians was the center of the earth. Theirs was an animistic system full of rituals and myths. The ideal was harmony and balance.

To achieve and sustain that harmony, the Cherokee not only offered individual prayers to their Mother, the Earth, and their Father, the Great Spirit and giver of breath, they also observed six seasonal festivals tied to the growing season. At these festivals, "all-night dances accompanied these ceremonies, in which both women and men participated, to the music of drums, flutes, and gourd or tortoise-shell rattles."[8] These all-night ceremonials, or Stomp dances, took place at special ceremonial grounds around a mound on which a sacred fire was lit.

The Cherokee today often ascribe all or most of the erosion of their traditional culture, including their religion, to their forced removal to the newly established Indian Territory in Oklahoma in the early nineteenth century. In reality, the Cherokees' traditional way of life began to disintegrate approximately forty years prior to the Removal, shortly before the first Protestant missionaries managed to establish a firm foothold in Cherokee territory early in the nineteenth century.[9] In 1794, the Cherokee concluded their unsuccessful war against the American colonists, siding first with the British during the Revolution and then fighting on alone for more than a decade, attempting to hold onto what little territory they still possessed. By the end of the eighteenth century, many of the fewer than ten thousand surviving Cherokee lived on only a quarter of their original land holdings,[10] located principally in northern Georgia with additional territory in southeastern Tennessee, southwestern North Carolina, and eastern Alabama.

Suffering from defeat and twenty years of devastation, with their old social order in shambles, many Cherokee abandoned at least portions of their traditional religious practices. According to McLoughlin, they concluded that those traditions had not helped them prevent or control the recent disasters.[11] In addition, some Cherokee ventured into the world of European-style subsistence farming with its individualistic ethos, as opposed to their earlier communal style of agriculture. As McLoughlin observes, "Much of their ceremonial life was related to hunting and war or concerned with sustaining communal harmony. If they dispersed to become farmers, they would have to give these up. Of what use now were the Scalp Dance, the War Dance, the Buffalo Dance, the Eagle Dance?"[12]

Leaving their traditional religious beliefs behind also meant, of course, leaving behind the religious festivals of which dance was so important an element. By the turn of the nineteenth century, they were observing only two of their seasonal festivals: the green corn dance and the purification ceremony. At least one early nineteenth century traveler, John Norton, concluded that while the Principal People had preserved their dance forms in great purity, the underlying religious system had not been so fortunate. He relayed the comments of a Cherokee acquaintance about the green corn ceremony: " 'It now appears only a matter of mutual congratulation and rejoicing, that the crops have so far ripened, as to become fit for food.' "[13]

NINETEENTH-CENTURY REVIVALS

The current revival of traditional dance is certainly not the first of its kind. By the early 1800s, for example, the Cherokee faced the task of coming up with a new blueprint for reassembling the pieces of their culture to fit their radically altered circumstances. In anthropologist Anthony Wallace's terms, they needed to "revitalize" their culture. This could be most effectively done not by simply returning to their old ways, but by creatively blending elements such as old traditions, modified customs, and selected European cultural traits into a new workable whole.[14] But as the new century wore on, the Cherokee increasingly had to try to reformulate their culture under the threat of forced removal from their ancient homeland.

There were two competing revitalistic movements: the acculturationists and the traditionalists. A powerful minority of Cherokee—the educated, English-speaking, mixed blood, and wealthier individuals—favored acculturation. They believed that the United States was serious when it formulated a policy that encouraged the assimilation of Native Americans into the newly independent country. They set about reconstituting the shattered Cherokee society into a far more centralized, formal governmental system, using the young United States as a model. The acculturationists adopted Christianity slowly and, at first, superficially. At least some of them lived on plantations in large, well-appointed houses, owned slaves, and sent their children to mission schools. They took up reels and country dancing (termed "English dancing"), and the violin.[15] Still, they did not want to assimilate completely, to disappear into the larger European-derived culture. Their hope was that if the Cherokee could prove they were capable of "civilization," the United States would allow them to coexist in their homeland with their former enemies.

Traditionalists, in contrast, believed that they could best deal with the emerging (and encroaching) culture of the United States by holding fast to the old Cherokee traditions and culture, or at least what remained of that culture after several hundred years of contact with Europeans. In contrast to the acculturationists, the traditionalists tended to be older, less affluent full-bloods who lived in the North Carolina mountains and on the southern and western borders of the Cherokee Nation. These Cherokee participated in only sketchily documented revivals including the Religious Revivals of 1811 to 1813, White Path's Rebellion in 1827, and a diffuse but persistent series of revival attempts in the 1830s. Not surprisingly, a resurgence of the all-night dances that were the main form of worship in traditional Cherokee religion accompanied each of these revivals. While the acculturationists were intent on spurning and denigrating traditional culture, the traditionalists "revived their religious dances of ancient origin with as much solemnity as ever was seen in worship in our churches," as Colonel Return J. Meigs, a Federal agent stationed among the Cherokee at the time, characterized it.[16] In addition during this period, visions warned of the consequences of not respecting the ceremonies and spirit of traditional Cherokee religion.[17] Although a single charismatic leader never emerged in any of these traditional movements, shamans played an important role. During this series of revivals, the Cherokee were not intent on bringing back the dance itself, but rather on bringing back as much of the old Cherokee religion and the traditional life as possible—a religion and a way of life that only recently had begun to disintegrate.

In 1838, the struggle between the acculturationists and traditionalists became a moot point. Both sides lost as Federal soldiers escorted seventeen thousand Cherokee on a forced march to Oklahoma. On this infamous "Trail of Tears," approximately four thousand men, women, and children died.

EARLY TWENTIETH-CENTURY REVIVAL

Will West Long was Walker Calhoun's half-uncle and an important early influence. Sometimes called the Father of Cherokee Indian dance, Long is credited with having kept the traditional dances alive during the early part of the twentieth century. He lived from 1870 until 1947, a period during which his small mountain community's contact with the outside world increased dramatically. Like his early nineteenth century ancestors, Long found himself at a crossroads, faced with new options. Dance played a prominent role as he struggled with questions of identity, first for himself and then for his community.

Long was an Eastern Band Cherokee. Today's Eastern Band members are the descendants of the eleven hundred Cherokee who managed to avoid the Removal and stayed behind in the North Carolina mountains. Most of these Cherokee were such committed traditionalists that they had seceded from the Cherokee Nation proper by 1819. With the help of William Holland Thomas, a white trader with close personal ties to the Cherokee, these Indians argued long, hard, and ultimately successfully that they were North Carolina citizens who had a right to stay where they were.

After the Removal, the North Carolina Cherokee lived in relative isolation for decades. Around the turn of the century, mainstream twentieth-century culture began to make its presence felt, first with the arrival of the lumber industry and the railroads and later with the Depression's federally sponsored programs. External forces began to influence the culture, even in isolated communities such as Big Cove. By at least the 1930s, the material culture of these rural Cherokee living on small subsistence farms was not very different from that of the mountain whites living nearby.

What remained uniquely Cherokee were the nonmaterial aspects of culture.[18] Among the nonmaterial aspects that persisted were vestiges of Cherokee religious beliefs. By the end of the nineteenth century, although the Cherokee were mostly Christian, they practiced their own highly syncretic versions of the Baptist or Methodist faiths.[19] Traditional healing practices and private rites lived on in the North Carolina mountains.

Will West Long's father was John Long, a Cherokee Baptist preacher. Long grew up, however, in the household of his mother, Sally Terrapin, who belonged to a well-known traditional family. During his youth, his maternal relatives instructed him in a wide range of Cherokee traditions. But he was exposed to non-Cherokee culture as well when, as a sixteen year old, he attended Trinity College near High Point, North Carolina.

Even after he returned to Big Cove in the late 1800s, Long continued to live in both the Cherokee and white worlds. He had already begun collecting and studying conjurers' books when he met James Mooney on Mooney's first field trip to the Qualla Boundary in 1887. Mooney, a journalist turned ethnologist, did some of the first important studies of Native Americans during his career with the U.S. Bureau of American Ethnology. Long became Mooney's interpreter and friend, and Mooney, in turn, encouraged Long to further his education. Anthropologist John Witthoft, who worked with Long toward the end of the Cherokee's life, reports that during this period of Long's life, "the white man's world had begun to seem quite attractive to Will."[20]

In 1895 at the age of twenty-five, Long studied at the Hampton Institute in Virginia where he received a combination of academic and vocational instruction designed to prepare young Cherokee for employment outside the reservation. After leaving Hampton, he continued his schooling in New England and then worked in Boston and in various other New England towns. During this sojourn, he seems to have experienced an identity crisis. Witthoft writes, "He worked hard at his studies, and felt that he was making progress away from his Indian background, but he was frequently troubled by doubts and homesickness."[21] His health suffered. He returned to Big Cove in the fall of 1904, shortly before his mother's death. From that time on, he made Big Cove his home. There his health improved, his fascination with the white man's world waned, and his faith in the Cherokee way of life revived.

Walker Calhoun describes his uncle's traditional lifestyle with approval. "He farmed. Sometimes he got a job, little jobs. He was just like us, the rest of us. He raised food. He could have had a good job, I guess. He went to college, but he chose to live just like the rest of us."[22] Long urged his fellow Cherokee not to trade their own unique culture for white ways and became a community, political, and spiritual leader, often championing traditionalist positions and causes.

Additionally, he kept traditional dance alive. While Long was alive, Big Cove was the major center of traditional dance on the Boundary. He taught the eagle, the peace pipe, the beaver, the bear, the quail, and the green corn dances. With his encouragement, dancers gathered two or three times a month for all-night social dances held in a nearby home. There were still occasionally green corn dances on a ball field by the Raven's Fork River in August. "Women folks cooked the corn, beans, taters, whatever they had. They cooked it, took it down to the ball field, and they called it dinner-on-the-grounds," Calhoun recalls. "And while we was waiting to eat, that's when they done this corn dance around the food."

Long had become, in effect, a participant-observer in his own culture. He frequently served as liaison between the Cherokee and a long line of anthropologists who made their way to Big Cove, attracted by its conservative bent. During the 1930s, he collaborated with anthropologists Frank G. Speck and Leonard Broom on the research that resulted in *Cherokee Dance and Drama* (1951), the only book-length study of Cherokee dance to date. Long shared his expertise and offered his services at a fair market price, becoming, to borrow Finger's phrase, a "small-scale capitalist."[23]

He was instrumental in Cherokee traditional dance's evolution from a purely social, participatory event to serving, at least on occasion, as an exhibition, performed for both tourists and anthropologists. For example, Witthoft reports that at some point when Speck was conducting his fieldwork in the 1930s and 1940s, Long led the Big Cove community in a re-enactment of the entire Cherokee ceremonial cycle so that the anthropologist could document it. "Most of these rituals had been last performed in the 1880s," Witthoft reports, "and the combined tradition and memory of the whole community were called upon for guidance in this resurrection."[24]

Traditional dance had been under attack from several quarters for some time. First missionaries and then teachers in the federally run boarding schools punished children for speaking Cherokee. Speck found that the most vigorous assaults came from fundamentalist Cherokee preachers.[25] Furthermore, he observes in *Cherokee Dance and Drama* that the spiritual content of dance had nearly vanished. "Cherokee animal dances are now mainly social forms," he concludes.[26]

However, at the same time, there were forces that worked to preserve at least some semblance of Cherokee traditional culture, including the dance. As the lumber industry collapsed in the 1920s, there was "a prescient awareness that tourism might someday offer the Eastern Cherokees the best chance of earning a living in their own homeland," writes Finger.[27] They were correct, although it took sixty years before tourism began to realize its potential as an economic base. Tourism in the area began with railroad excursions into the western Carolina mountains. It was further fostered by the construction of paved roads, the establishment of the Great Smoky Mountains National Park adjacent to the Qualla Boundary, and the selection of Cherokee, North Carolina, as the southern terminus for the Blue Ridge Parkway in the 1930s.

Furthermore, during the 1930s, John Collier became the first commissioner of Indian Affairs to work on the assumption that it was possible for Native Americans to retain their cultural identities and still function within the larger national context. This philosophy was embodied in the Indian Reorganization Act of 1934. It became both practically and ideologically acceptable, at least in some quarters, to encourage Native American crafts, arts, and customs.

Long assisted at the birth of the Cherokee tourist industry. In 1914, he was on the committee that organized the first Cherokee Fair, a forerunner of today's annual Fall Festival. The Cherokee began the Fair in part to promote interaction between the Cherokee and their white neighbors and to bring visitors to the reservation who would appreciate and buy Cherokee crafts. Long often directed traditional dance performances at the fair and at other tourist events. A 1937 photograph shows Long with male and female dancers, most attired in long fringed shirts worn over pants or long skirts (Figure 12-2).

Calhoun, born in 1918, remembers how beginning in August, Long used to hold practices in his yard. "People who lived way down this side of Cherokee used to come. They'd have to walk to come dance and walk back home. That's how interested they were."[28] Calhoun's mother, Sally Ann, was one of Long's dancers, and it was at these practices that Calhoun first learned how to do the traditional Cherokee dances.

Sometimes I'd dance with them at the tail end [of the line] 'cause I was a little boy. He [Long] let the kids dance at the tail end so they could learn. Will West Long never did get us kids to do the dances till we were grown. He used to start about a month and a half before fair time practicing the dances. Every Saturday, Sunday evening, he'd build a big fire and dance around the fire. It was nice like that. Some nights it lasted [until] about almost midnight.[29]

During the early part of his life, then, Long had to work out for himself just how much he wished to adapt to the white man's outlook, beliefs, and assumptions. The white world was a world in which Long was well equipped to function, both by virtue of his abilities and his education. Ultimately he decided to adhere to and actively promote what remained of the customs and culture of his ancestors. Once he had solved this problem for himself, he encouraged others in his community to share his belief in the Cherokee culture. Long's dilemma was essentially the same dilemma the Eastern Band faced as a whole as their mountain communities became less and less isolated: to what extent did they wish to participate in the non-Cherokee culture that came in with the lumber industry and the railroads and the tourists; to what extent did they want to hold onto what was left of the old ways? This was

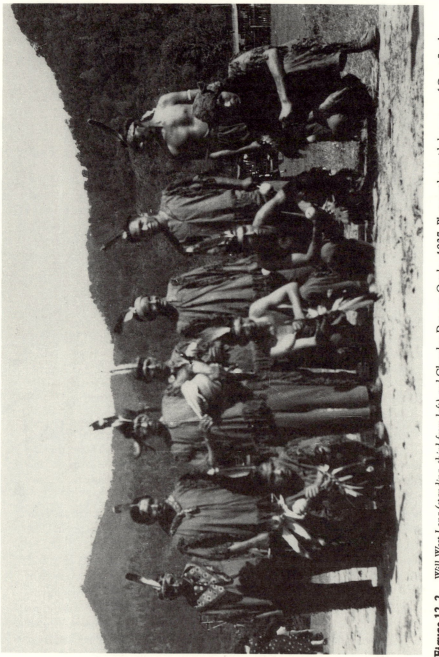

Figure 12–2. Will West Long (standing, third from left) and Cherokee Dancers, October 1937. Photograph provided courtesy of Great Smoky Mountains National Park.

essentially the same dilemma that the Cherokee faced in the period immediately preceding the Removal, and it was a dilemma they were to face yet again.

There are, however, important differences between revival movements of the early nineteenth and early twentieth centuries. Unlike the nineteenth-century revitalization movement, Long's crusade was not, as far as we know, accompanied by visions. Instead, his main sources of inspiration seem to have been the scholarly, methodical study of Cherokee culture that he probably learned, at least in part, from observing ethnologist Mooney at work.

The destabilizing forces in Long's time were evolutionary rather than catastrophic, as they had been a century before. During this time of social change, Long did his best to preserve the surviving intangible underpinnings of Cherokee culture—the values, beliefs, and assumptions, and surviving practices such as dance and the *gadugi*. These underpinnings gave the Cherokee a sense of being Cherokee, of being different, no matter how much their lives might outwardly resemble those of their white neighbors.

Long was a realist, however. Witthoft sums up Long's attitude toward his culture by noting "he wanted to see it preserved and interpreted, and he needed the wages he received for his work . . . "[30] By participating in events such as the Cherokee Fair, Long demonstrated that he knew that simply preserving old beliefs was not enough. He also attempted to use Cherokee culture itself to attract much-needed tourist dollars to the reservation. These sometimes conflicting needs—to preserve a sense of Cherokee identity and the equally insistent need to make a living—continued to characterize subsequent revivals as the century progressed.

Will West Long died in the late 1940s when Walker Calhoun was twenty-eight. When Long died, people such as Walker's older brother, Lawrence, and Lloyd Sequoyah tried to carry on. And Calhoun and his family still often danced informally at home after supper. But as Calhoun observes of the community's enthusiasm for dance, "When Will West died, that's when it all started going down."

MAINTAINING AN IDENTITY IN CHANGING TIMES

Working out an identity has become a complicated matter for the late twentieth century Cherokee as their position within society has become more complex. After years of wrangling, the Cherokee are finally acknowledged to be both North Carolina and American citizens with voting rights. A locally elected tribal council governs some aspects of their life, but the federal government holds their land in trust. The federal government also supports and administers their schools and health services. Although they are subject to some state laws, they are exempt from others. Enrolled members of the tribe, who are entitled to access to reservation land and federal benefits and to privileges such as eligibility for tribal office, must currently prove that they have at least one-sixteenth Cherokee ancestry. These "objective" criteria for tribal membership create considerable friction and division within the community and generate endless discussions about who should and should not be entitled to membership benefits.

There are also issues of identity within the context of the larger Native American community. They are Cherokee, but they are Eastern Band Cherokee. They share a common heritage with approximately 100,000 of their kin in the Cherokee Nation of Oklahoma, but years of separation have shaped their cultures in different ways. They are Native Americans, but among Native American groups they are conservative. For example, although the Eastern Band Cherokee followed with interest the activities of the American Indian Movement and other militants during the sixties and early seventies, they eschewed its radical tactics, preferring instead to work within moderate pan-Indian organizations. As Finger notes, the Eastern Band Cherokee "generally viewed the growing 'Red Power' movement as a threat to their satisfactory working relationship with the BIA [Bureau of Indian Affairs]."[31] Still, the heightened ethnic consciousness of the 1960s has not left them untouched and undoubtedly played a role in subsequent traditional dance revivals.

Finally, decades of intermarriage and varying choices about whether to assimilate have produced a community on the Qualla Boundary that generally falls into three groups: the affluent, assimilated "white" Cherokee who are, according to French and Hornbuckle, "not easily distinguishable from other middle class Americans;"[32] the traditionalists such as Walker Calhoun who do their best to preserve what remains of the old ways; and the many individuals and families caught between the Cherokee and white worlds.[33] Social worker Gilliam Jackson characterizes the members of this last group as "the in-betweens who are in a state of confusion, who are basically lost. They don't have a strong philosophical base, they don't have a clear cultural identity, they don't have a strong spiritual connection, and they don't have a strong value base. When the storms hit, they get knocked off their feet quite easily."[34]

Rapid change has come to the reservation over the last forty years. Until the 1940s, the economic base was still largely subsistence agriculture. But during the 1940s, just as the population began to increase due to improved medical care, the land base began to disappear as decades of soil erosion, resource destruction, plant disease, speculation, and national economic changes took their toll.[35] During the 1940s and 1950s, housing, health care, and schools were all uniformly poor. During the 1950s, Collier's policy encouraging diversity was replaced by yet another federal policy, rather ominously labeled "termination," a policy predicated once again on the belief that assimilation was in the Indians' best interests. Under termination, as tribes demonstrated their ability to function independently, they would lose all federal services. At least some Native Americans saw this policy as a way for the government to renege on their treaty obligations by prematurely withdrawing badly needed support and protection.[36]

Some light industry arrived on the reservation in the 1950s. But it was the tourist boom and the infusion of War on Poverty funds during the 1960s that radically changed Cherokee life. By the early 1980s, only one percent of the reservation's land was used for agricultural purposes, while ninety percent of the Band's income came from its six-month tourist season.[37]

With its seasonal employment, the tourist industry is a mixed blessing. The unemployment rate in the 1980s ranged from around three percent in the summer to as high as sixty percent during the winter months.[38] In 1990, the per capita income was just over $6,600 compared with a national per capita income of $18,685.[39]

DANCE REVIVES ONCE AGAIN

The tourism boom of the late 1950s and 1960s began to create a demand for something resembling Native American dance as a way of entertaining the tourist. However, as Speck notes, the new industry resulted only in "the preservation of superficial aspects of the dances adapted for the entertainment, if not the edification, of tourists."[40] For example, choreographers incorporated a version of the Eagle dance into the Cherokee outdoor historical drama, *Unto These Hills*. That version had much deeper roots in Broadway than in Big Cove.[41]

A newspaper photograph from the 1950s illustrates another effect that tourism had on dance. It shows a group of male Cherokee dancers performing what is called a "native dance," but they are wearing Sioux Indian headdresses "in deference to tourists who demand that the Cherokee look like the Indians of their imaginations."[42] Once the Boundary became the premier tourist Indian reservation of the East, many Cherokee began to feel pressure to become Plains-like Indians.

By at least 1970, however, the Cherokee reintegrated traditional dance into reservation life. Accounts from 1969 to the present in *Cherokee One Feather*, the weekly Qualla Boundary newspaper, refer to traditional dance in a variety of settings. Most of the dance groups consisted of school-age children. Pre-schoolers in the Big Cove Day Care danced. Elementary school children danced. The very first elementary school dance troupe grew out of the Follow Through program, a Head Start-type program for children in the early grades. In 1976, another elementary school dance program, the Cherokee Children's Dance team, resulted from the efforts of music teacher Leo James, along with Mike Crowe and Myrtle Driver; together they worked to incorporate Cherokee dance and song that was as authentic as possible into the grade school curriculum. They went back to Speck's books and his 1934 disc recordings of song, some of which featured Will West Long. In addition, they tapped the memory of Big Cove resident Lloyd Sequoyah.[43]

High school students danced as well. In 1978, students in the Cherokee High School Bilingual program presented a performance that included four traditional dances in addition to an Indian fashion show. Children and teenagers performed in a variety of contexts. One high school student performed the eagle dance in a senior talent show, which also included students' impressions of pop culture figures ranging from Gomer Pyle to Gypsy Rose Lee. Young dancers appeared at festivals, were invited to American Legion birthday celebrations, performed at numerous building dedications, and danced at reading incentive award programs.

Most of the reasons given for such cultural programs had to do with recovering a way of life believed to be lost, or nearly lost, to Cherokee children. The denigration of Cherokee culture over a long period resulted in widespread demoralization among both children and adults. As Bernice Bottchenbaugh says, "At one time, a lot of Indians walked with their heads down because they didn't want to be seen as an Indian. They were picked on, they were put down, they were called names. It made them feel almost ashamed to be an Indian."[44] By using their dance traditions to help the young rediscover their heritage, the elders hoped to give the children's self-esteem a badly needed boost. "If we continue to teach our Indian children the true history and culture, they will learn that we were not the dirty, animal-like, less than human beings as some textbooks, television and movies portray us," asserts an article on the elementary school program.[45]

There were adult groups as well—groups with agendas that were a complicated mix of cultural preservation and public relations. In the spring of 1974, for example, a group of Indian dancers, craftsmen, stickball teams, and others incorporated as "The First Americans." The First Americans realized that the upcoming Bicentennial would create a demand for Indians at various patriotic observances, and they positioned themselves to meet that demand. Asking for industrial backing and promising to distribute brochures for local Cherokee businesses and tourist attractions, the First Americans felt that "the opportunities for such a group to advertise Cherokee and the Qualla Boundary to the rest of the U.S.A. is limitless and will surely increase our tourist trade and add to our many thousands of friends."[46] Two years later, however, the group recast its goal as it applied for a National Endowment for the Arts grant to develop curriculum materials: in 1978, it was "to maintain and retain Cherokee history and culture."[47]

Even before the First Americans came into being, there was Richard Crowe. Crowe, born in 1927, was for years one of the most prominent figures on the traditional scene in Cherokee. A native of the Boundary, he got his first taste of acting when he earned a speaking role in *Unto These Hills.* After trying to establish an acting career in New York, he returned to the Boundary in the 1960s. He needed to earn a living and hit on the idea of demonstrating Cherokee crafts, foodways, and dance at the shopping centers that were beginning to open throughout the region. He and his wife Berdina made appearances up and down the eastern seaboard as well as on the Qualla Boundary.

He also organized several dance troupes, each of which disbanded after a time. In 1974, for example, Crowe and his Qualla Boundary Dancers performed at a press conference designed to boost tourism,[48] appeared at a U.S.S.R.-U.S. track meet in Durham, North Carolina,[49] and entertained seventy-five Amway sales representatives at a sales meeting at the Cherokee Holiday Inn.[50] At the same time, he often served as a resource for the children's dance programs. Crowe's involvement in traditional Cherokee dance, then, reflected his lifelong love of performing, his need to make ends meet, his desire to market Cherokee as a tourist attraction, and his genuine pride in his ethnicity. "I'm always saying I'm proud," he explains. "I'm proud to be who I am, and I say, you should be proud of who you are. Knowing who you are: that's identity. Everybody needs identity."[51]

A young Cherokee, Jean Mansfield, enlisted Richard Crowe's assistance as she helped to reorganize the Qualla Boundary Dancers once again in 1984. They performed that April when the Eastern Band and the Cherokee Nation held a historic joint Tribal Council meeting in Red Clay, near Cleveland, Tennessee. It was the first such meeting between the two branches of the Cherokee people since shortly before the Removal. The Qualla Boundary Dancers asked Walker Calhoun to act as the driver, an individual who generally served as the master of ceremonies. Calhoun agreed and offered to sing for them. "They was pleased with my singing, and they kept me a long time," he remembers. It marked the first time that Walker sang for someone other than his family in nearly thirty years.

As a result of their experience in Red Clay a number of Qualla Boundary Dancers, including Gilliam Jackson, formed their own troupe, the Seven Clans Indian Dancers. Calhoun served as their primary teacher. "We really didn't understand what we were doing at first. It was all for show," explained dancer Vangie Wolfe Stevens in a 1985 *Cherokee One Feather* article. "We are getting away from that now and getting into the culture."[52]

"Then this dance troupe scattered, and I started with my grandchildren," Calhoun recollects. When asked why he continues to be involved in traditional dance, he says, "I just want to show these young people what we used to do. It's something new to them. There's a lot of them just hungry for the dance." Adds his daughter, "It's just now, these past few years, that my Dad realized that most of our own people didn't know what the dances were. He said it scared him."

Calhoun measured the Raven Rock Dancers' performance against his memories of his mother's dancing. Bottchenbaugh remembers her father's teaching methodology during the early days of the troupe. "My Dad would watch our dancing, and if somebody didn't have the step that he remembered or just the right movements, he would tell us about it. He'd even show us sometimes. He'd show us how grandmother'd [Sally Ann Calhoun] done it. We tried to imitate her."

Calhoun's participation in Red Clay had another long-lasting effect. In time, with the strengthening of ties, a religious and cultural exchange project between the two branches of the Cherokee people was born. While the Eastern Band had preserved more fragments of the Cherokee dance tradition, the Oklahoma Cherokee had retained more of the old religious ceremonies and beliefs. Members of both tribes began putting the pieces of their once common culture together, with Calhoun playing an important role in the process.

In *Cherokee One Feather*,[53] Robert Thomas, an Oklahoma Cherokee by birth and an anthropologist by training, wrote that in 1988 Gokski Smith and two young Oklahoma Cherokee traveled to North Carolina to learn the eagle dance. Gokski Smith was the head medicine man of the Redbird Fire in Oklahoma, a Fire laid down in 1902 by Redbird Smith to serve as the ceremonial site for the Stomp dances that took place around the sacred mound.[54] Redbird Smith was the religious leader responsible for the re-establishment of the old Cherokee Keetowah religion among members of the Cherokee Nation, partly in reaction to the cultural and social threat posed by the federal policy of allotment.[55]

Thomas reports that the absence of the old Cherokee ceremonies in North Carolina appalled Gokski Smith. After meetings between Calhoun and Western Cherokee spiritual leaders, held both in North Carolina and Oklahoma, they made arrangements to conduct the ceremonial lighting of the Big Cove Fire on September 29, 1989. "After 150 years they had brought the Fire back to the 'old country,' to the Cherokee Holy Land," writes Thomas.[56]

The Fire still burns in Big Cove. During the spring of 1991, Stomp dances generally took place once a month. Walker Calhoun served as the chief ceremonialist, and his daughter attended regularly. Bottchenbaugh cannot estimate how many people were coming to what she often referred to as the Stomp Dance church in the spring of 1991, but she was pleased at the number of teenagers and young adults who were rediscovering this revived version of the old religion. "I think we have more of those than we do adults," she notes. "They're just so hungry to learn about themselves that they're coming out."

"Not anybody can go," explains Bottchenbaugh. Performing the animal dances in public, even for Amway sales representatives, is an acceptable way to share their culture with others. "But the religion we want to keep sacred, more private because that was something that was taken from us that should never have been taken. Well, I really don't think it was taken from us," she corrects herself. "I think we were influenced by the new religion. It sounded so great and grand."

To protect this traditional Keetowah religion, she was guarded about giving an outsider too much detail.[57] She would say that the Stomp dance was a simple dance done in characteristic counterclockwise motion around the sacred mound. They dance counterclockwise, she said, to undo the damage that has been done. The group has also reconstituted the green corn dance; the last one had taken place in Big Cove in 1937. "Then we include all the dances. We just have a good time. You know, it's a celebration. We include all the dances because those dances are honoring dances too."

According to Bottchenbaugh, the Keetowah religion is a simple affair. "The Cherokees' religion wasn't hard. Don't abuse each other, take care of each other, and take care of the earth, appreciate what God gave us. And that's really all there is to it. All these dances and everything, that's just like saying thank you. Anybody can say that. But this is showing that we really mean it."

In her childhood, Bottchenbaugh attended both the Baptist and Holiness churches in Big Cove. In a 1957 masters thesis, John L. Grant described the religious life in Big Cove during the period when Bottchenbaugh was growing up.[58] On the one hand, Grant observed that Big Cove was "thoroughly churched and missionized."[59] However, although most Big Cove Cherokee claimed to be Baptists, there was very little denominational loyalty. People would attend the Straight Fork Baptist Church some Sundays, Holiness services on others, and drop in on the Mormons from time to time. The Cherokee congregation sat through these services with "remarkable reserve," in distinct contrast to the arm-waving, shouting white preachers who promised prompt punishment for any and all sins: "If you don't do right, you'll pay, you'll pay."[60] While both Baptist and Holiness white preachers tended to treat the Cherokee as if they were children, the Mormons straightforwardly informed their Indian congregation that they were a race cursed by God because of the sins of their ancestors.

Bernice Bottchenbaugh still occasionally attends Holiness services and reads her Bible. But she says, "I never felt like I belong there. And with the Stomp Dance church, I do. It's like there was something missing all my life." At the Stomp dance grounds, Bottchenbaugh says she finds a fellowship and an acceptance that was missing in her experiences in Christian churches. "It's like one great big family. You make friends for life. That's how I can say it. You know, you can't hardly wait to see each other again, and that draws you back together to the next Stomp dance." Even those who are reluctant at first usually join in the dance eventually. "They know nobody's going to make fun of them 'cause there's nothing to make fun of. Everybody's doing the same thing. It's just like a confident kind of feeling. You can dance for hours, and when you leave and go home, it's like a peaceful kind of rest when it's over."

CONCLUSION

In the 1829 *Cherokee Phoenix* excerpt[61] that serves as one of the epigraphs for this chapter, an anonymous writer predicted the imminent demise of the "ancient traditions of the Cherokees." Almost 150 years later, Alvin Smith is still worried about the imminent demise of Cherokee traditions and the culture those traditions embody.[62] Meanwhile, distinctively Cherokee traditions have ignored such predictions and continued.

In many respects, of course, the traditions of the 1970s, which Smith and other segments of the Cherokee community are so intent on preserving, look, sound, and undoubtedly function differently from those that the 1829 writer had in mind. The Cherokee have performed traditional dance over time in a number of varied contexts; it has often served quite diverse functions. Those changing contexts and functions invariably leave their mark. Traditions of any sort must adapt to the present as well as preserve what has come before if they are going to survive.

Contemporary interpretations of Cherokee traditional dance are in part the "modern fictions" of which the 1829 *Cherokee Phoenix* author speaks. The eagle dance provides a good example. Eighteenth- and nineteenth-century accounts of the eagle dance describe an all-male group, naked except for a loin cloth and covered in paint and feathers, alternating the dance steps with spirited narratives of their war and hunting exploits.[63] The sacred eagle they celebrated most often seems to have been the fierce bird of prey. In contrast, in the mid-1980s, college-educated Vangie Wolfe Stevens of the Seven Clans Indian Dancers called the eagle the most powerful of birds, representing "wisdom, strength, and courage. It flies the highest and represents someone who wants to attain the highest goals."[64] Today's eagle dance is dignified, performed in ribbon shirts, with no narratives interspersed among the movements.

Even if the traditional forms themselves have evolved and their functions have changed, one purpose has remained constant. Over the years, Cherokee traditionalists have called on dance and other traditions to help articulate and maintain a sense of identity that sets the Cherokee apart from their neighbors. Tribal identity is one important piece of an increasingly complex sense of identity. For example, even though the pan-Indian Pow Wow dancing predominated at the Desert Storm Rally during which the Cherokee frequently asserted their allegiance to the United States, it was still symbolically important to have the presence of a respected elder such as Walker Calhoun and an interlude of tribal traditional dance to remind the community of, in Alvin Smith's words, "what it means to be Cherokee."

The Cherokee, we have seen, have been reviving their tribal traditional dance off and on for almost 200 years. Not surprisingly, it is especially during periods when they are faced with new choices generated by substantially changed circumstances, when their sense of identity has to absorb and accommodate those changes, that traditionalists reconstitute their traditions in order to shore up a sense of Cherokee identity. During the early nineteenth century, traditionalists countered the acculturationists' attempts to cope with the encroaching white settlements and with the cultural wreckage left by the Revolutionary War with the revival of a culture that had begun to disappear only recently. Railroads and the lumber industry brought Will West Long and his community face to face with an outside, newly industrialized culture that offered new rewards, exacted new costs, and posed new risks. Late twentieth century Cherokee found themselves marketing their culture to visitors from all over the country as their economic base shifted to tourism and to a cash economy. At the same time, they were affected by the rise of ethnic consciousness and pride that was taking place throughout the nation.

During these periods of increased contact with a culture other than their own, Cherokee individuals have had to decide how much of the new to incorporate, how much to reject. To some degree, all Cherokee during these times of rapid change had to ask themselves if they could change without breaking too abruptly with the past, if they could better their chances of survival by borrowing some features of the dominant culture without being engulfed by that culture.

As with all identities, Cherokee identity is rooted in a sense of difference. They distinguish their own culture from that of the largely European-American culture that surrounds them, and it is that sense of difference—more than any particular discrete, inviolate traditional forms—that Cherokee traditions help to celebrate and sustain. The Cherokee are Americans whose cultural differences have long been seen as debilitating liabilities by the federal government and by many members of mainstream culture. Today, the Cherokee are attempting to rediscover and reassert those differences with pride, even while acknowledging their common bonds with other Americans and Native people.

When asked why it was so important to keep specifically Cherokee traditions alive, Gilliam Jackson replied, "I think that God made us different, and He must have had a good reason. Not that He made us better or not that He made us inferior, He just made us different. I think we have a lot to be proud of; our traditions add to our identity, add to our self-esteem, add to the whole person. When these things are gone, I think we're going to be in a state of confusion: we're not going to know who we are."[65]

Whether the Cherokee will be able to use their traditions to maintain this sense of difference is difficult to say. Jackson has his doubts. After all, there are still powerful forces promoting assimilation, and just because the prophecies of the death of Cherokee traditions have not come to pass over the past century or two does not guarantee those traditions' survival in the future. Certainly Cherokee traditions are not as plentiful as they once were, and, as Calhoun notes, it is ironically the *novelty* of Cherokee traditional dance that is the source of its attraction to many youngsters. But distinctively Cherokee traditions have survived in large measure because of their ability to persist without becoming anachronistic, to change without changing beyond recognition.

The current revival both resembles and does not resemble its predecessors. It is especially intriguing to note that while the nineteenth-century dance revival was a by-product of largely religious traditional movements, today the process is happening in reverse. This latest in a series of revival attempts began with a revival of a traditional art form sparked in large measure by the need simply to make a living, to survive economically by marketing their culture through tourism. After Red Clay, however, this revival deepened into something more, into a revitalization movement that attempts to recreate and reaffirm the values, beliefs, and perspectives grounded in a Cherokee past and contained in traditional Cherokee religion, an alternative world view that will answer present needs. The Cherokee are trying to heal themselves, to fill in the vacuum left by years of having their traditions suppressed and devalued. As they move counterclockwise through their dances, they are trying to undo the damage.

NOTES

1. Pow Wow dance draws on the traditions of many North American tribes; it is competitive, with dancers vying for substantial prize money at intertribal gatherings held throughout the United States and Canada from the early spring until late fall.

2. See for example John R. Finger, *The Eastern Band of Cherokees 1819–1900* (Knoxville: The University of Tennessee Press, 1984), 62, and John Witthoft, "Will West Long, Cherokee Informant," *American Anthropologist* 50 n.s. (1948): 357. Finger describes mid-nineteenth century dress in the North Carolina mountains. ". . . Cherokee eclecticism and fondness for color appeared in startling array on dress up occasions with calico dresses, turbans, shawls, bright handkerchiefs, feathers, 'scarlet belts, and gaudy hunting shirts' "(p. 62). The shift from the more traditional Cherokee dress of buckskin seems to have occurred later in the isolated community of Big Cove. Anthropologist John Witthoft notes that when Long returned to Big Cove in the late 1880s, he discovered that ". . . factory-made shoes had only recently appeared at the first store at Smokemount, and calico and Kentucky blue jeans cloth had replaced buckskin and homespun woolens" (p. 357).

3. John R. Finger, *Cherokee Americans: The Eastern Band of Cherokees in the Twentieth Century* (Lincoln: University of Nebraska Press, 1991), 159.

4. Walker Calhoun and Gilliam Jackson, interview with the author, Big Cove, North Carolina, 12 August 1989.

5. See James Adair, *Adair's History of the American Indians*, ed. Samuel Cole Williams (Johnson City, Tennessee: The Watauga Press, 1930), and Henry Timberlake, *Lieut. Henry*

Timberlake's Memoirs, 1756-1765, annotated, indexed and with an introduction by Samuel Cole Williams (Johnson City, Tennessee: The Watauga Press, 1927).

6. See Laurence French and Jim Hornbuckle, "The Cherokees — Then and Now: An Historical Glance," in *The Cherokee Perspective*. eds. Laurence French and Jim Hornbuckle, pp. 3-14. (Boone, North Carolina: The Appalachian Consortium Press, 1981), 5-8.

7. Charles Hudson, *The Southeastern Indians* (Knoxville: The University of Tennessee Press, 1976), 400.

8. William G. McLoughlin, *Cherokee Renascence in the New Republic* (Princeton: Princeton University Press, 1986), 15.

9. For an account of the early Protestant missionaries, see William G. McLoughlin, *Cherokees and Missionaries, 1789-1839* (New Haven: Yale University Press, 1984), 35-81 and 102-123. The Moravians established the first permanent mission on Cherokee territory around 1800. In 1804, these Moravians, a "small, pietistic and pacifistic, German-speaking sect," (p. 36) opened a mission boarding school in northern Georgia, fifty miles southeast of Chattanooga. The next major wave of Protestant missionaries did not appear on the scene until 1817 when the American Board of Commissioners for Foreign Missions, a Boston-based organization consisting of Presbyterians and Congregationalists, arrived in northern Georgia, followed closely by Baptists and Methodists.

10. McLoughlin, *Cherokee Renascence*, 25.

11. McLoughlin, *Cherokees and Missionaries*, 24.

12. McLoughlin, *Cherokee Renascence*, 30.

13. John Norton, *The Journal of Major John Norton, 1816*, ed. with introductions and notes by Carl F. Klinck and James J. Talman (Toronto: The Champlain Society, 1970), 79.

14. See Anthony Wallace, "Cultural Composition of the Handsome Lake Religion," *Symposium on Cherokee and Iroquois Culture*, eds. William N. Fenton and John Gulick, Smithsonian Institution Bureau of American Ethnology, Bulletin 180 (Washington, D. C.: U. S. Government Printing Office, 1961), 143-151.

15. See John Ehle, *Trail of Tears: The Rise and Fall of the Cherokee Nation* (New York: Anchor Books/Doubleday, 1988), 95; McLoughlin, *Cherokees and Missionaries*, 92-93, 332, and Norton, *Journal*, 50.

16. Quoted in McLoughlin, *Cherokees and Missionaries*, 92.

17. For a description of the visions, see McLoughlin, *Cherokees and Missionaries*, 84-86.

18. See Finger, *Cherokee Americans*, 20-21, 67, and Witthoft, "Will West Long, Cherokee Informant," 357.

19. See Finger, *The Eastern Band of Cherokees*, 151.

20. Witthoft, "Will West Long," 357.

21. Witthoft, "Will West Long," 357.

22. Walker Calhoun and Gilliam Jackson, interview with the author, Big Cove, North Carolina, 12 August 1989. Unless otherwise noted, all subsequent quotations from Walker Calhoun are from this interview.

23. Finger, *Cherokee Americans*, 71.

24. Witthoft, "Will West Long," 358.

25. Frank G. Speck, and Leonard Broom in collaboration with Will West Long, *Cherokee Dance and Drama* (Berkeley: University of California Press, 1951), 6-7.

26. Speck, Broom and Long, *Cherokee Dance*, 7.

27. Finger, *Cherokee Americans*, 54.

28. Calhoun and Jackson, interview.

29. Michael Kline, "Where the Ravens Roost," *Old-Time Herald* 2, no. 5 (August–October, 1990): 27.

30. Witthoft, "Will West Long," 359.

31. Finger, *Cherokee Americans*, 154.

32. French and Hornbuckle, "The Contemporary Scene," *The Cherokee Perspective*, ed. Laurence French and Jim Hornbuckle (Boone, North Carolina: The Appalachian Consortium Press, 1981), 26–43. This quote is from p. 27.

33. See French and Hornbuckle, "The Contemporary Scene," 27–28; Finger, *Cherokee Americans*, 67; John Witthoft, "Observations on Social Change," in *The Cherokee Indian Nation: A Troubled History*, ed. Duane H. King (Knoxville: The University of Tennessee Press, 1979), 205–207, and John Gulick, *Cherokees at the Crossroads* (Chapel Hill, North Carolina: Institute for Research in Social Science, 1960), 124–131.

34. Gilliam Jackson, interview with the author and Susan Spalding, Cherokee, North Carolina, 10 July 1991.

35. Witthoft, "Observations on Social Change," 207.

36. The policy was ultimately rescinded by Congress in 1988.

37. French and Hornbuckle, "The Contemporary Scene," 39.

38. Jonathan L. Taylor, "Principal Chief's Report to the People," *Cherokee One Feather* (8 March 1989): 1–3. This quote is from p. 1.

39. U. S. Census, 1990 Census of Population and Housing, Government and Business Services Branch, North Carolina State Library, Raleigh, North Carolina, for the state per capita figure; Survey of Current Business, U. S. Department of Commerce, Bureau of Economic Analysis for the national per capita figure.

40. Speck, Broom, and Long, *Cherokee Dance*, 6.

41. Document Associates, "Cherokee," 26-min. VHS 1/2 inch videotape (New York: Document Associates, 1976).

42. "Cherokee Dance," *The Spartanburg Herald Journal Mountain Vacation*, (Johnson City, Tennessee: Archives of Appalachia, East Tennessee State University, n.d.): Joe Jennings Collection, Old Finding Series 6, Box 3, Folder 14.

43. "Traditional Dances Taught in School," *Cherokee One Feather* (11 February 1976): 1 and 3, and "Cherokee Children's Dance Team in School Dedication," *Cherokee One Feather* (14 April 1976): 2.

44. Mary Bernice Calhoun Bottchenbaugh, taped phone interview with the author, 7 March 1991. All subsequent quotes from Bernice Bottchenbaugh are from this interview.

45. "Traditional Dances Taught in School," 3.

46. "New Group Formed on Qualla Boundary," *Cherokee One Feather* (30 April 1975): 1.

47. "Cherokee Group Receives Grant for Cultural Work," *Cherokee One Feather* (18 August 1976): 7.

48. "Media People, Other Visitors Impressed by What Cherokee Has to Offer," *Cherokee One Feather* (22 May 1974): 1.

49. "Cherokee Dance at USSR–U.S. Track Meet," *Cherokee One Feather* (10 July 1974): 1.

50. "Qualla Dancers Reorganize Club," *Cherokee One Feather* (4 December 1974): 1.

51. Richard Crowe, interview with the author, Cherokee, North Carolina, 1 March 1991.

52. "Seven Clans Indian Dancers to Perform at Dillsboro Heritage Festival," *Cherokee One Feather* (19 June 1985): 7.

53. Robert K. Thomas, "Cherokee Religious and Cultural Exchange Project," *Cherokee One Feather* (8 November 1989): 11.

54. For more on the Redbird Fire in Oklahoma, see Robert K. Thomas, "Cherokee Religious and Cultural Exchange Project," *Cherokee One Feather* (8 November 1989): 11 and 13, and Robert K. Thomas, "The Redbird Smith Movement," in *Symposium on Cherokee and Iroquois Culture*, eds. William N. Fenton and John Gulick (Washington, D. C.: U. S. Government Printing Office, Smithsonian Institution Bureau of American Ethnology, Bulletin 180, 1961), 161–166.

55. Embodied in the General Allotment Act of 1887, allotment was a tactic of the Federal government designed to promote assimilation. The underlying assumption was that replacing the Native Americans' pattern of tribal land ownership with individual ownership would automatically result in acculturation to mainstream values.

56. Thomas, "Cherokee Religious and Cultural Exchange Project," 13.

57. For a description of a modern Stomp Dance among the Oklahoma Cherokee, see Hudson, *The Southeastern Indians*, 473–475.

58. John L. Grant, "Behavioral Premises in the Culture of Conservative Eastern Cherokee Indians" (Masters thesis, University of North Carolina-Chapel Hill, 1957), 108–123.

59. Grant, 109.

60. Grant, 112–113.

61. "Cherokee Traditions," *Cherokee Phoenix* (1 April 1829): 1–2.

62. Alvin Smith, "Cherokee Culture," *Cherokee One Feather* (13 August 1975): 2.

63. See for example J. P. Evans, "Sketches of Cherokee Characteristics," *Journal of Cherokee Studies* 4, no. 1 (Winter 1979): 19–20, and Norton, *Journal*, 114–115.

64. "Seven Clans Indian Dancers to Perform at Dillsboro Heritage Festival," *Cherokee One Feather* (19 June 1985): 7.

65. Gilliam Jackson, interview.

Part 3

Inventing Traditions

Like the indigenous preservationists of "Conserving Tradition," the dancers included in Part 3 often have a sense of mission. The historical reconstructionists and the so-called revivalists of "Inventing Tradition" share the belief that they are trying to give new life to a form of dance that has vanished, or very nearly vanished, from view. However, unlike the indigenous preservationists, the leaders of these movements have not been born into the tradition that they are attempting to keep alive. They come from places, communities, and times other than those that produced the vernacular dance that the "revivalists" so wholeheartedly espouse. As Dudley Culp, a founder of the Green Grass Cloggers, puts it, "We're revivalists because the dance is not native to us."[1]

Folklorists, and to some extent the dancers themselves, often distinguish between "revivalists," individuals participating in groups such as the Green Grass Cloggers or the Princeton Contra Dancers, and "genuine" participants in the traditional process. Yet on closer scrutiny, we realize that few of these revivalists are engaged in the straightforward task of restoring a vernacular dance to life. For example, what folklorist Douglas Day charts in "Folk Dance in the Early Years of the John C. Campbell Folk School" is the importation during the 1920s and 1930s of a version of Scandinavian folk dance into the western North Carolina mountains by the Folk School's founders, Olive Dame Campbell, Marguerite Butler Bidstrup, and her Danish-born husband, Georg. Culp in the interview excerpt, "We Tended to Project a Lot of Energy," and Phil Jamison in "The Green Grass Cloggers" describe the birth during the early 1970s of this dance troupe in eastern North Carolina. The

Green Grass Cloggers, consisting of college students and recent graduates imbued with back-to-the-land ideals, toured internationally, performing an energetic style often misrepresented as Appalachian "clogging." As Culp and Jamison demonstrate, what the Green Grass Cloggers actually did was invent an entirely new dance form based on a synthesis of elements drawn from old-time Appalachian solo and square dance, freestyle, and precision clogging as well as Western club square dance. They then elaborated on these borrowed elements with innovations of their own.

Contra dance provides yet another example of a "revival" dance form that is not really a simple revival. Contemporary contra or country dance is a vernacular dance form that first emerged during the early twentieth century in the northeastern United States; it was based on the collecting work of early folklorists such as Cecil Sharp and on printed sources, some dating back to the seventeenth century. Eventually, contra has become a national phenomenon, with groups in Appalachian towns and cities such as Johnson City and Knoxville, Tennessee, and Boone, North Carolina. Musician, contra dancer, and dance publisher Richard Carlin contributes his study of contra dance entitled "Yuppies Invaded My Tradition at Midnight," an essay which is a rare combination of solid demographic analysis and humor. Carlin describes how a group of students and young professionals, a group that seems to have much in common with the Green Grass Cloggers, began with "traditional" contras, which featured simple figures. In time, however, these dancers began to invent their own "modern," "progressive," or "zesty" contra dances, dances with a faster-paced, high energy style featuring far more complicated figures.

Folklorist Richard Blaustein presents a historical overview that points out the mutual influence between "elite" and "folk" and between "traditional" and "revivalist" dance in his essay, "Old-Time Fiddling and Country Dancing in North America." He sets the stage for Merry Feyock's article, "Dance, Our Dearest Diversion," which approaches dance history from another, more practical angle. Feyock has been involved in the dance program as a teacher, researcher, and dancer since 1979 for Colonial Williamsburg, the restored colonial capital city in Tidewater Virginia. She walks the reader though the complicated, often difficult, and surprisingly creative process involved as a group of twentieth-century Virginians attempt to recreate a reasonable facsimile of eighteenth-century dance.

DISCUSSION

These vernacular dancers frequently speak of how their activities either benefit "the tradition" or have potential educational value. Many revivalists believe they are performing a valuable service to the tradition and to society at large by preserving these dance forms. For example, speaking of Appalachian dance and music, former Green Grass Clogger Dudley Culp asserts, "I see the revivalists as the ones who are keeping those traditions alive."[2] Richard Carlin notes that such dancers "like the notion that they are upholding some 'ancient art' and are carrying it forward in the face of terrible odds."[3]

Many of the proponents seem to be well-educated, middle class individuals—often professionals—who see these forms of dance as a way of turning back the clock to a simpler time, one with more humane values that contrast sharply with the contemporary industrial, or "plastic," culture. Although by and large they are people who are succeeding in mainstream society, at least some of their values are at odds with that society.

Advocates of these dance forms often see them as performing a valuable educational function. As Feyock shows, Colonial Williamsburg saw research into eighteenth-century vernacular dance as part of a larger educational effort designed to give visitors a glimpse into the past. Day illustrates how the Bidstrups and Mrs. Campbell, following the lead of art critic John Ruskin, believed that "folk" dance could and should be edifying as well as entertaining.

There is no question that vernacular dance serves the dancers' needs as well. On a superficial level, participation in such traditional dance groups gives their members a chance to meet new people and socialize with old acquaintances. For example, Feyock observes that the Colonial Williamsburg dance troupe attracted a large number of young, unmarried museum professionals, helping to create a greater sense of cohesion among staff members.

However, these revival and historical reconstruction dance groups serve a deeper function than mere socializing. What becomes clear is that for the dancers, gathering together in these dance groups often helps supply a sense of community and continuity missing from their lives. Culp notes that his family did not belong to any particular ethnic group. He goes on to speculate that his involvement in the Green Grass Cloggers—in dancing that was closely identified with what the Cloggers viewed as a stable, conservative mountain culture—may have compensated for that lack of ethnic affiliation. And Carlin states that for the Princeton, New Jersey, contra dance group, it was the dance that literally created the community. (This was true, remember, for some old-time square dance groups and for the African American steppers as well.) One of the respondents to his survey commented, somewhat wistfully, "It's the closest thing I have found to a neighborhood or community."[4] In each case, the dancers have established a community, one based on values rather than on geographic proximity or a shared history.

In this section, the various authors and dancers often have differing opinions as to what tradition is and where it resides. Day sees the indigenous community as the agent that perpetuated true Appalachian dance, traditions that the John C. Campbell Folk School staff increasingly ignored during its early days. The Bidstrups, on the other hand, seemed to take a view commonly found among revivalist dancers that tradition was somehow contained within the dance form itself. If tradition is an inherent property of the dance, then the revivalists are able to dismiss the arguments of people who claim that their participation in contra dance or clogging is inauthentic because the revivalists have appropriated someone else's tradition. For Feyock and the Colonial Williamsburg dancers, of course, the important standard is not authentic tradition but historical authenticity.

Finally, the Bidstrups and Carlin clearly hold quite different views as to what dancers should do with tradition once they have received it. While teaching Scandinavian dance at John C. Campbell, the Bidstrups insisted that their students perform the dances according to the instructors' exact notions of correctness. Neither innovation nor input from the group was encouraged. Much like the original eighteenth-century minuets described by Feyock, the Bidstrups used their folk dances to exclude certain people who did not measure up to their standards. Carlin, on the other hand, subscribes to the view that tradition is a process. The Princeton contra dancers, in fact contra dancers everywhere, serve tradition not by preserving these country dances intact but by creating new dances and a new dance style based on what came before them.

Although Feyock and Carlin both contribute insights into the nature of vernacular dance and its relationship to community and the traditional process, the main point of both their papers is a description of a particular technique of studying historical and vernacular dance. Feyock delineates in a straightforward way the method involved in historical reconstructions. Of particular importance is the use of primary sources to construct an image of the dance and its sociocultural context. Reliance on descriptions or notated scores is not enough. She also recognizes the importance and validity of the creativity of both the reconstructionist and the dancers themselves as they develop these performances.

Feyock is aware that to some extent these historical recreations are modern creations. Since the information about eighteenth-century American vernacular dance that has survived to the present day is so sketchy, a point also made by folklorist Richard Blaustein, guesswork on the part of the reconstructionist is unavoidable. Furthermore, she makes the point that even in their own time, the manuals used by dancing masters provided only the barest of details. The dancing masters, therefore, had to interpret the vernacular dances according to their own understanding of the contemporary aesthetic. Feyock describes a process of piecing together clues that resembles, in part, the method by which the Cherokee reconstructed their own tribal dance by going back to written sources and anthropologists' field recordings.

Carlin contributes a direct and simple questionnaire designed to discern the composition of a dance group. Rarely has anyone undertaken such a demographic survey of a dance community. The result is that we as researchers often have only general impressions and educated guesses, rather than hard data, about who exactly is doing any given type of vernacular dance. In Carlin's case, some information surprised him, even after his many years with the group. Carlin's form is short enough to be completed during a break in the dance and can be modified to produce a profile of any dance community. In addition, it allows participant-observers to test their subjective impressions against more objective information.

Ultimately, these essays point out the many intriguing parallels to be found among traditional, revivalist, and reconstructed dance forms.

NOTES

1. Culp, "We Tended to Project a Lot of Energy," in this volume.
2. Culp, "We Tended to Project a Lot of Energy."
3. See Carlin, "Yuppies Invaded My Tradition at Midnight," in this volume.
4. See Carlin, "Yuppies Invaded My Tradition."

Chapter 13

The Green Grass Cloggers: The Appalachian Spirit Goes International

Phil Jamison

With flying feet, swirling calico skirts, and high-kicking legs, clogging burst on the national folk festival scene in the early 1970s, personified by a group of long-haired young people from North Carolina known as the Green Grass Cloggers. Since then, countless groups modeled after them have sprung up across the United States and as far away as England and Japan. With respect for the styles and attitudes of older traditional dancers, the Green Grass Cloggers combined the traditions of North Carolina clogging with their own innovations to develop a distinctive style and approach. Since their inception in 1971, they have traveled, performed, and taught their style of clogging throughout the Southeast and far beyond to thousands of people across the United States and around the world.

THE BIRTH OF THE GREEN GRASS CLOGGERS

In the spring of 1971, Dudley Culp, then a student at East Carolina University, went to the Fiddlers' Convention at Union Grove, North Carolina. In addition to hearing old-time music, he saw precision and freestyle cloggers as well as traditional buck dancers, and he became infatuated with the dancing in general, but especially with buck dance. That fall, he and Toni Jordan Williams, went to Harper Van Hoy's Autumn Square-up at Fiddler's Grove. At this festival, which featured a competition for traditional clogging teams, they learned a few steps from some of the dancers. They also met Willard Watson, a traditional flatfoot dancer from Deep Gap, North Carolina, who was to have a major influence on the Green Grass Cloggers' style.

Inspired by what they had seen and learned, and encouraged by Willard Watson, Dudley and Toni started a clogging class at East Carolina University in Greenville, North Carolina, where they had previously been part of a Western club square dance class. Out of this group, the original Green Grass Cloggers formed. A few of them had recollections of grandparents or other family members flatfooting or buck dancing, but most of them were starting from scratch, knowing very little.

For the most part they were learning on their own, living as they were in the eastern part of the state where they were isolated from the traditional cloggers of the mountains. When they had the opportunity, they watched other clogging teams and learned a few basic steps, but the biggest influence on their style came from the older generation of buck dancers whom they met at festivals and fiddlers' conventions. These older traditional dancers did not have a uniform style, and they did not approve of the increasing conformity of newer clogging styles. They stressed the importance of each dancer's individuality.

This attitude was embraced by the Green Grass Cloggers, who were eager to find alternatives to the styles of the 1950s and early 1960s. This was in the early 1970s, and many young people rebelled against the establishment by pursuing "back-to-the-land" ideals. They became interested in the old-time ways that had been rejected by their parents' generation. Dancers like Willard Watson epitomized these ideals. Two other old-time dancers who were particularly influential in teaching the Green Grass Cloggers were Hansel Aldridge of Mecklinburg County and Robert Dotson of Sugar Grove, North Carolina.

Besides their steps, these old-time dancers taught appreciation for the old-time music they favored over postwar bluegrass. These dancers of the older generation became mentors in much the same way and for the same reasons that musicians such as Tommy Jarrell, the noted old-time fiddler from Mount Airy, North Carolina, became models for the young old-time music scene. Rejecting postwar styles of music and dance, these older dancers maintained that the best music for dancing was the old-time traditional Appalachian music that had evolved alongside the dance over many generations.

These attitudes corresponded to the back-to-the-land ideals espoused by many of the Green Grass Cloggers, who were mostly students enrolled at East Carolina University. The back-to-the-land crowd felt ready to turn the "establishment" upside down and shake it up, but at the same time, they respected that establishment's roots. In addition to clogging and Western square dance, the students' dance background included the popular music and dance of the time. This combination of experiences and beliefs may be the source of the high energy, high spirits, and "wildness" that characterized their performances.

Another aspect of traditional clogging preached by the old-timers was that dancing is meant to be fun rather than competitive. They had seen competitive dancing come to dominate the clogging world, and the growing competitive attitude and standardization had created a new generation of cloggers who could only perform memorized sequences of steps and did not know how to listen to and dance to the music. What was being lost was the individuality and spirit of old-time buckdancing and freestyle clogging that comes from the heart. The Green Grass Cloggers adopted the idea that clogging could be just for fun. As it had been for previous generations, old-time music and dance became incorporated into their social scene and their lives so that no party or get-together was complete without live old-time music and clogging.

To a lesser extent, the style of the Green Grass Cloggers was influenced by the traditional freestyle clogging teams that they saw performing or competing at festivals. They learned some steps from these teams, and they adopted a few of the large group figures such as "the King's Highway," "Tunnels," and "the Clover Leaf" into their dance routines. However, aside from this, their choreography borrowed little from the North Carolina tradition of team clogging. Instead of forming a traditional big circle set, they arranged their dancers in Western club-style square sets. With four couples in each, the two square sets would dance independently most of the time, only occasionally joining together as one big set. Rather than using the two-couple or "circle-up-four" mountain dance figures common to traditional freestyle clogging teams, they fit their steps to four-couple Western club square dance figures. Some of these had been learned at their square dance class, and others were taught to them by a caller named Betty Casey.[1] In their eagerness to learn, the Green Grass Cloggers traveled not only to music festivals but also to the homes of the older dancers, thus becoming perhaps the first dance group actively collecting dance steps from various regions. Out of this, an eclectic dance style developed rather than a strictly regional one, as found in more traditional groups.

THE STYLE

Traditionally, there were no standardized names for clogging steps. Names for a particular step would vary from region to region. As the Green Grass Cloggers learned new steps, they named them. Old-timers encouraged the younger dancers not only to collect steps from traditional sources but to invent their own steps as well. The results included steps involving head-high kicks and other nontraditional and unconventional movements. Sometimes the Green Grass Cloggers named a step either after the person who invented it or the individual who taught it to the group. Steps used in their first routines included the "Basic," the "Earl," the "Eddie," the "Indian," the "Grand Square Kick," and "Karen's Kick."

These steps, together with the dance figures, created a new style of team dancing. The Green Grass Cloggers used taps on their shoes in order to make the steps more audible, despite the fact that the older dancers had not used them. Making use of fast-paced figures in short energetic routines, the younger dancers consciously designed much of their choreography to interest the audience. However, they synchronized their footwork much as modern precision clogging does. Precision clogging, a style that developed in the 1950s in which all the dancers execute the same step at the same time, is usually done in lines rather than in the square dance figures—either big circle or four-couple—used by traditional teams and the Green Grass Cloggers.

Organized group clogging was born at Bascom Lamar Lunsford's first Mountain Dance and Folk Festival at Asheville in 1928. When first seen by the clogging world at festivals such as the Asheville Mountain Dance and Folk Festival or the Union Grove Festival, the Green Grass Cloggers' lively, free-spirited dancing must have seemed as radical as their scruffy, long-haired appearance. While traditional cloggers keep their feet close to the floor, the Green Grass Cloggers with their head-high kicks and other unconventional steps had an unmistakably original and uninhibited look. In their first few years as a group, they performed solely in North Carolina, and while they were entertaining to watch and popular with audiences, some of the cloggers on other teams did not approve of these wild "hippie stompers." Willard Watson and other mentors approved, though, and continued their encouragement. Their attitude was that clogging steps and style need not, in fact should not, be standardized.

THE STYLE TAKES OFF

Due to their eagerness to travel and to a growing reputation, the Green Grass Cloggers were the first cloggers seen by many folk festival audiences outside the Appalachian region. By 1974, they had an established reputation for audience appeal, and they received many offers to perform all over the United States and Canada. For example, during the mid- to late-1970s, they appeared at the Philadelphia Folk Festival, at the National Folk Festival, and the Great Hudson River Revival, as well as the Chicago, Winnipeg, and Vancouver folk festivals. In addition to performing at these large Northern festivals, the Cloggers eagerly shared their passion for their dance form by teaching workshops where as many as three thousand people at a time learned the basics, Green Grass Clogger-style. Most of these people had never seen Appalachian clogging, and many may have erroneously assumed that the Green Grass Cloggers represented a traditional North Carolina style.

Before long, dozens of new clogging groups formed all around the country in the many places where the Cloggers had given performances and conducted workshops. Far from the Appalachians, and with only the Green Grass Cloggers as models, these new dancers in turn taught others. By the end of the 1970s, there were cloggers all across the United States who had learned second-, third-, or fourth-hand. Some had never heard of the Green Grass Cloggers but knew their steps—the "Earl," the "Indian," and others—believing these to be traditional Appalachian clogging steps. As they have continued to be disseminated through workshops, dances, and other means—both formal and informal—the steps and style have now become widespread. In fact, by the mid-eighties, the style spread far from its source in North Carolina not only to groups all across the country but also overseas. In Japan, for example, the Corn Creek Cloggers danced "Indians" and "Earls" and wore imitation Green Grass Clogger costumes.

In 1977, half of the Green Grass Cloggers decided to form a full-time, professional touring group. They hit the road in an old converted bus, presenting old-time music and clogging at festivals, concerts, and schools in many parts of the country where people had never heard of clogging before. The "road team" relocated to Asheville in 1980. They have continued to travel, perform, and teach their style of clogging all across the United States and, in recent years, in eleven foreign countries located in South America, Europe, and Asia. After a decade of year-round touring, they are no longer out on the road full-time. The Asheville group, as well as a "home team" still based in Greenville, continue to dance and perform on a part-time basis.

Stylistically, there are many clues to identify the influence that the Green Grass Cloggers have had on other clogging groups, groups modeled after themselves and after modern precision teams. Most obvious are the use of high kicks and the other Green Grass Clogger-devised steps and the use of four-couple square dance formations. In general, their steps all start with the right foot stepping on the beat of the music rather than starting with the left, as most modern precision groups do.

The costuming of dancers generally reflects the styles of the day, so it is not surprising that the Green Grass Cloggers rejected the clean-cut, uniformed look of the 1940s and 1950s in favor of the look of the 1960s and early 1970s. Their first outfits featured long "granny dresses," later replaced by calico square dance dresses minus the bulging crinolines that are associated with precision and freestyle cloggers today. The men wore blue jeans and work shirts with calico yokes, thus stating a connection between traditional clogging and a down-home country lifestyle. Depending on one's viewpoint, it was either a very relaxed or a very scruffy appearance. In their search for affordable leather-soled shoes, the women in the group went to second-hand stores where they found stocky-heeled, orthopedic shoes, or "granny shoes," as they called them. Unlike the red, white, or lime-green tap shoes of other contemporary cloggers, these shoes appealed to the group because they added to the old-time look of the costume. Today, dancers across the country can be seen wearing this type of shoe for dancing—a custom started by dancers unable to afford good new shoes and by the desire for a traditional look. These shoes, the lack of crinolines, and the characteristic style of dance are all signs of the influence of the Green Grass Cloggers.

CONCLUSION

Just as Bill Monroe and his Bluegrass Boys spawned a new style of music that combined traditional Appalachian music with new innovations, the Green Grass Cloggers have done so with clogging. What was once viewed as radical has now joined and blended with and, in some cases, changed the older traditional forms. Other dancers and audiences have accepted this new clogging style as a legitimate one.

It is important to note that the Green Grass style is not the only form of clogging that has become widespread in the 1970s and 1980s. Modern precision clogging is now also found throughout the United States. National precision clogging organizations promote this form in part by sponsoring and sanctioning competitions. Since contests require consistent judging criteria, these competitions have, in turn, resulted in a standardization of steps and routines. Modern precision clogging is more often performed to pop country and rock and roll than to traditional Appalachian music.

Some proponents of this branch of clogging have moved far afield from its Appalachian roots in other ways as well. Although some precision teams perform only for fun, there are many young cloggers today who look at the dance strictly in terms of competition; to these thousands of dancers, clogging has become a competitive sport rather than something done just for fun and in order to enjoy the music. Many do not even realize that it is possible or desirable to dance to live traditional music. Instead, they dance only to recorded pop songs such as "That Old Time Rock and Roll," "Nine-to-Five," or "Elvira." Many do not know that it is possible to dance without wearing loud tap shoes.

While traditional mountain-style clogging is still popular in Asheville and other areas in the Appalachian mountains, modern precision clogging and the Green Grass Clogger style are the two predominant forms that are currently being taught outside the local region. If the modern precision and Green Grass Clogging styles are compared today, what was viewed twenty years ago as the radical Green Grass style now, in fact, appears closer to the Southern Appalachian tradition than its modern precision counterpart. Although the Green Grass steps and style are a departure from the traditions of North Carolina team clogging, it is a style that is now accepted by traditional mountain-style cloggers, and it is a style that is rooted in traditional Appalachian music and dance. But more than their steps and style, the most important contribution that the Green Grass Cloggers have made to the traditions of Appalachian clogging is keeping the spirit of traditional clogging alive. This spirit, as exhibited in their attitude toward dancing, embraces the importance of individual expression, the appreciation of live traditional music, and the enjoyment of noncompetitive clogging, all important aspects of traditional Appalachian dance.

NOTE

1. Betty Casey has written several square dance books, including *The Complete Book of Square Dancing* (Garden City, New York: Doubleday & Co., Inc., 1976).

Chapter 14

"We Tended To Project a Lot of Energy": Reminiscences about the Early Days of the Green Grass Cloggers

AN INTERVIEW WITH DUDLEY CULP

Susan Eike Spalding
and Jane Harris Woodside

Dudley Culp was a founder of the Green Grass Cloggers. Although he is now a jewelry maker and goldsmith living in the western North Carolina community of Burnsville, he still calls contra and square dances in the region from time to time. In this excerpt from a 1991 telephone interview with Susan Spalding and Jane Woodside, he gives details of how he and the early Green Grass Cloggers invented this new, traditionally inspired dance style. Specifically, he shows how they blended together the footwork of mountain dance and the figures of western club square dance, then added innovations all their own.

I was born in Greenville, South Carolina, in 1948. I lived there a short time and then moved to Greensboro, North Carolina. That's where I grew up. My father was in textile manufacturing, a salesman, and my mother was a homemaker. My family didn't have any particular ethnic identification, and I think that was something that was missing, something that all the folk stuff replaced.

I went to East Carolina University and studied art. That's in Greenville, North Carolina. I used to go to the Union Grove Festival in western North Carolina—the one that got to be so big—while I was in college. Towards the end of college, I saw the first clogging team.

At first when I went to the Fiddlers' Convention, either there wasn't any clogging, or I just didn't tune into it. Immediately after I graduated, I went to the spring one. There were two very good clogging teams there, and they were just really dynamic. One of the two was the Smoky Mountain Cloggers. I think they were from Avery county in North Carolina, but I'm not sure. Their dancing was more the precision type of dance. There were eight couples, and they did lots of rhythm changes, lots of the Southern Appalachian big circle type figures.

They were just very much together. It was like one person dancing. Those sixteen individuals were dancing as one person. They were with the music. A lot of clogging teams don't pay attention to the music, but this team did. And the way they pulled off the rhythm changes was just phenomenal. It blew my mind. I'd never seen anything like it before. You know, it takes a lot of practice to pull that off.

I'd always done rock and roll dancing, all through grade school, high school, and college. But when I saw that clogging, that's when I really got the bug. I drove my roommate crazy with it because I did it so much. I was so enthralled with these two clogging teams I'd seen in the spring—I guess it was 1970—that I wanted an exhibition group to perform at Union Grove. That was always in the back of my mind.

I got more serious about organizing the group in the fall of 1971 after I'd been to the Annual Autumn Square-up, sponsored by Harper Van Hoy in Fiddler's Grove, North Carolina. When Toni Jordan Williams and I were there, we learned more steps, and we got lots of inspiration from seeing so many excellent groups compete in both the precision and traditional categories. We left there really determined to get things going.

In eastern North Carolina, we were geographically protected, and we were made to rely on our own devices and creativity—and there was a lot of that. Toni Jordan Williams helped me start the group. We had gone together to a square dance class offered by the university; it was just college students doing Western club square dance figures. She had also gone to the Fiddlers' Convention, and I had taught her a couple of steps, so we just thought about putting the steps with Western club square dance figures. The only reason I did it was because I didn't know the Southern Appalachian figures at that point. And so I just did what I knew.

That Western club square dance class only lasted three months. And then I connected with another woman who was a square dance teacher, Betty Casey.[1] So we hired her for a short time. She had all of these square dance records and books, and she helped me with some organizational skills. I just got into calling out of necessity because there was no other caller.

Our first real performance was at Cherry Hospital in New Bern in February of 1972. We also performed at the large Union Grove Festival in April of '72, the one sponsored by Pierce Van Hoy. And then exactly one year after going to the Annual Autumn Square-up, the Green Grass Cloggers returned to Fiddler's Grove. Toni's the one who came up with the name. In any case, we came back to Fiddler's Grove and participated in the traditional clog team category. At that point we only had four couples. We won first prize that year. Shortly after we won that competition, our team size doubled, and we performed with eight couples for many, many years.

And we kept going back each year to the festivals in western North Carolina. At the festivals, there were people at camp sites doing their own thing, their own little buck dances. Dancing around, just little bands playing around the whole festival, you know. And people would just start dancing. And I would corner people there and make them teach me a step that I didn't know. I was pretty obnoxious about it.

Remember when I mentioned that Smoky Mountain Clogging team? They performed the year after we formed the Green Grass Cloggers. There was one very difficult step that I really wanted to learn. It had been raining a lot of the festival, and I hiked across this horrible field in a foot of mud to learn that step. I just went up on their school bus and said, "You can't go until you teach me this." [*Laughs*] I wouldn't let them leave until they taught me that step. And they did. We called that step the Smoky Mountain step.

We met the dancers Willard Watson and Hansel Aldridge at Union Grove. And then there was another woman, Evelyn Farmer. She helped me in the very, very beginning with the basic step of clogging. Willard and Hansel helped us with styling, you know, because that style of dance was not indigenous to any of us. It just helped seeing people who had done it all their lives: the way they held their body and some of the rhythms. Willard and Hansel were always extremely supportive because they loved the dance, and they loved the music.

Now, getting paid for it or going anywhere else, that wasn't important. When we did perform, we got asked by other people to perform at their festivals. That part just sort of grew haphazardly. We never made any money. We just got gas money. And we would perform at local bars. Rock and roll places. They would periodically have a bluegrass night. There was a band in Greenville, North Carolina, called the Flatland Family Band who played old-time, as opposed to bluegrass. We connected with them. And we would always make a little bit of money, but we always had a very good time, and we would involve all the people at the bar. And they had their strobe lights and black lights. We'd be wearing our costume: the boys in cotton blue jeans, and the girls wore black tights and the same style of old-fashioned calico or gingham dresses but in different colors. We would always get dressed up, and we would wear taps. We just fit right in. [*Laughter*]. Of course there was lots of alcohol, and that seemed to loosen people up. It was rather loose.

We were lucky. In those early years, there were so many creative people. We would try one thing. If it didn't work, we'd try something else. We would just have a bunch of people brainstorming and trying to fit whatever they came up with into a certain square dance figure. I know that one theme that evolved over the years was a certain economy. You trimmed the excess and pared it down to show the most variety in the fewest steps. We would edit a lot of things as time went on. It was really unique there in those formative years because everybody was always so willing to try this or that variation or come up with something else. It was fun.

From those very beginnings, we tended to project a lot of energy. Our figures are done with a lot of energy. We tried to smile, you know, and always pull something out of the hat. We had a lot of variety and a lot of change, we put in a lot of high kicks, and we were able to project a burst of energy, and I think that had a broad appeal.

I remember when I was first starting the group, it was very difficult to have to ask somebody to leave, but I did have to do it. The reason was that they couldn't dance.

They didn't have a sense of rhythm, they weren't in the right place during a figure, and they got confused. They didn't have any presence, any dance presence. They couldn't keep the right posture. Even though you're presenting all this energy, you have to keep your upper body still, and you have to have a certain poise. Some people just don't have the knack for it. When I had to ask somebody to leave, it was always a very difficult thing to do, especially when they were enthusiastic. But it wasn't fair to all these other people who are putting in all this time and effort to have a whole team compromised by one or two people.

You know, I'm not a native of the mountains, and I'll never be a native of the mountains. It's just a fact of life. None of the early Green Grass Cloggers were natives of the mountains. In the beginning, I remember, there used to be two blacks. The rest were all white. There was one fellow who was Indian. There were a number of professionals. I remember Doug Baker was an alcoholism rehabilitation administrator. There were a couple of clinical psychologists, and there was one fellow who could not read. He was from Canada. It was a broad range. It was just a whole hodge podge, melting pot. On the whole, though, we were the college kids, the radicals.

We're revivalists because the dance is not native to us. And I don't see anything wrong with being a revivalist because after having lived in Yancey County, a mountain county, for eleven years, I know that many of the natives here couldn't care less about traditional dance or music, playing banjo, fiddle in their homes. You know, they're plugged into their TVs and satellite dishes and modern culture.

I see the revivalists as the ones who are keeping those traditions alive. Maybe it'll change, you know. Maybe it does run through cycles. Just go to a fiddlers' convention, like Mt. Airy in North Carolina, and you'll see that. All the people playing old-time music are the college kids, or well, they've long since graduated, and it's the people from larger urban areas. Most of them have more of the longish-hair type lifestyle, and they're the ones who are interested in keeping the traditional old-timey music alive, and dance, too. They're putting their own slant on it. You know, using the basic formats and traditions and going off from there as an offshoot. There's lots of room for creativity.

NOTE

1. Betty Casey is author of several square dance books, including *The Complete Book of Square Dancing* (Garden City, New York: Doubleday & Co., Inc., 1976).

Chapter 15

Folk Dance in the Early Years of the John C. Campbell Folk School

Douglas Day

An article in a 1970 issue of the *Greensboro Daily News*, entitled "Culture Goes Folksy to Music Cum Good Old Song,"[1] describes the first annual Brown-Hudson Folklore Award presented by the North Carolina Folklore Society. Among the recipients that year were Bascom Lamar Lunsford[2] and Georg and Marguerite Bidstrup. The Bidstrups were honored for their contribution to folk dancing in North Carolina. The couple made that contribution during their more than forty years on the staff of the John C. Campbell Folk School in Brasstown, a small rural community in the southwestern corner of the state. The irony of the award was that the Bidstrups had never promoted indigenous forms of mountain dance in their long careers but instead had been agents of cultural change in their fervent advocacy of English and Danish folk dance. How did the Campbell Folk School, despite its avowed mission of preserving "all that is native and fine" in mountain life, and despite its jealously guarded reputation for Appalachian authenticity, come to shun local dance forms in favor of "superior" dances from abroad?[3]

On Friday evenings back in the late 1920s and early 1930s, Brasstown, North Carolina dancer John "Budgie" Brendle took John C. Campbell Folk School up on its somewhat qualified invitation to attend its Community Night Dances. Brendle and his neighbors were welcome to come to the dance as long as they refrained from the traditional Appalachian dances they'd been doing all their lives. It was not the local dancers but the so-called "star team" that dominated those evenings, a group of students who had mastered the imported European "folk" dances taught in Folk School recreation short courses and favored by the Schools' founders, Olive Dame Campbell and Marguerite Butler Bidstrup. Marguerite Butler Bidstrup's code name for this star team was "those who know."

"Unless you were in the short course, you just didn't dare go into the dance," Brendle recalled in a 1989 interview. Brendle parked himself in the School's library, took down one of the dance manuals used as a text in the course, and committed an English folk dance to memory. One night Marguerite announced that the next number "for those who knew" would be the very dance that Brendle had memorized. Brendle not only came forward ready to dance, but he asked Marguerite to be his partner.

"But Budgie," she responded to his overture in astonishment, "you don't know this one."

"But Marguerite," he assured her, "I do."

When Brendle made it through the dance without missing a step, his partner asked him how he'd learned to dance like that. "Watching people," he said, stretching the truth a bit.

"She never questioned me after that," Brendle remembers.[4]

Appalachians in this area of southwestern North Carolina had danced for as long as anyone could remember, and most had, in fact, learned by "watching people," namely their family and neighbors at numerous social gatherings. They did not learn by taking courses or referring to manuals, and these descendants of predominantly British and German settlers certainly did not draw from a largely Scandinavian repertoire. But this was precisely what Marguerite Butler Bidstrup and Olive Dame Campbell would have had them do. Bidstrup and Campbell were cultural politicians: they formulated a cultural agenda they then employed to establish and maintain a power relationship between the school staff and the people they set out to serve, all in the name of improving their students' lives. It was this relationship Brendle subverted—but only for an evening.

"The politics of culture," as applied to the cultural history of Appalachia by scholar David Whisnant in *All That is Native and Fine*, has been one of the most influential analytical tools for studying culture to emerge in the recent past. It works particularly well in the case of the Campbell Folk School. The interaction that especially interests Whisnant is that which occurs between two relatively distinct social groups, with one group holding more power than the other. Taking advantage of that power differential, the dominant group engages in systematic cultural intervention. Whisnant explains: "By that I mean simply that someone (or some institution) consciously and programmatically takes action within a culture with the intent of affecting it in some specific way that the intervenor thinks desirable."[5] Such interventions can be passive or active; they can either encourage or suppress certain cultural traits, depending on the interventionists' estimation of their desirability.

In *All That is Native and Fine*, Whisnant focused on the "politics of culture" as practiced at the Pine Mountain and Hindman Settlement Schools in Kentucky, at the White Top Folk Festival in Virginia, and at the John C. Campbell Folk School. This chapter focuses more narrowly on the folk dance movement as it was promoted at the Campbell School. I recently had the opportunity for a different vantage point on the Folk School's activities, having worked "on the inside" from June of 1988 until April of 1991 as a National Endowment for the Arts-funded public sector folklorist. While at the Folk School, I had the chance to talk with some of the school's alumni and to go through Folk School papers that Whisnant and others had not.

Whisnant was, in the main, kind to Mrs. Olive Campbell, the school's founder, describing her as one of the more sympathetic and culturally sensitive of the region's "culture workers." In contrast, I have found that the school's co-founder, Marguerite Bidstrup, was a far more heavy-handed interventionist, at least when it came to dance. To me, the Folk School's dance programs seem emblematic of the kind of distortions that have characterized "the invention of Appalachia" in the American mind.

Although I am narrowing the field of inquiry, I am addressing basically the same questions Whisnant asked in *All That is Native and Fine*: How did the Folk School's dance programs come to center so strongly on imported rather than local forms? Why did they emphasize Danish and English folk revivals rather than local play-party games, buck dances, big circle dances or, later, developments such as freestyle clogging and Western Square? What were the beliefs, ideologies, and theories of folk culture held by Olive Dame Campbell, Marguerite Butler Bidstrup, and Marguerite's husband, Georg Bidstrup? Or, absent explicitly articulated philosophies, what were their assumptions about what it was they were about?

THE EARLY DAYS OF THE JOHN C. CAMPBELL FOLK SCHOOL

Olive Dame Campbell, born in 1882 and raised in New England, accompanied her husband, John C. Campbell, during his arduous field research for a social survey of the mountains. This research was funded by the Russell Sage Foundation in 1908 (fieldwork actually began in the winter of 1907) and was designed to identify the Southern Highlands' most pressing needs and the best methods to meet those needs. While John Campbell was chiefly concerned with social conditions, his wife became fascinated by mountain culture. During her travels, Olive Campbell collected over 250 ballads and folk songs. Her collaboration with the British folk song and dance scholar Cecil Sharp produced the definitive *English Folk Songs of the Southern Appalachians* in 1917.[6] When John Campbell died in 1919, Olive finished his work, writing most of the enduring classic, *The Southern Highlander and his Homeland*, although it was published under her late husband's name.[7]

Olive and her friend, Marguerite Butler (later Bidstrup), a social worker and teacher from Ohio then at the Pine Mountain Settlement School in Kentucky, traveled to Scandinavia in 1922 and 1923 to study the teachings of nineteenth-century poet, theologian, and Danish nationalist, Bishop Nicolai Grundvig, and to observe the various folk academies that had grown from the Grundvigian philosophy. The Campbells found in the Scandinavian folk school a viable model for adult education in the states. Here was a model of liberal, democratic, nonauthoritarian pedagogy that could be adapted for use in America's "benighted South," particularly among the "poor whites" of the Southern Appalachians.[8]

Campbell and Bidstrup intended that the Folk School be grounded in local conditions and culture, that it " 'enrich the whole content of rural life,' to build up 'an enlightened and enlivened citizenship, which will . . . realize of its own initiative, a full and satisfactory rural life.' "[9] With land and labor donated by local people and with funds secured from northern churches and the Carnegie Foundation, the school was built in Brasstown in the southwestern corner of North Carolina, very near the Georgia and Tennessee state lines. Following the Danish custom, the Folk School was divided into two seasons: winter and summer. The School's curriculum was noncompetitive: there were no grades or accreditation. Working off their tuition, usually by laboring on the model farm, all students boarded at the school and during the winter months studied academic subjects such as arithmetic, geography, and history. In addition, there were practical courses. Boys took agriculture, blacksmithing, and woodworking courses, while the girls supplemented their basic studies with classes in weaving and home economics.

During the first years of the school, Danish-born Georg Bidstrup taught physical education, which included not only gymnastics but also the highly aerobic Danish and English singing games. Marguerite Butler and Olive Campbell had met Bidstrup in Denmark; he had been teaching gymnastics and Danish dances at one of the Danish folk schools. The two women actually hired Bidstrup to manage the farm at John C. Campbell, but Georg Bidstrup's first love and real forte was folk dance. Over the years, he taught the summer "short courses" in folk dance and singing, which were attended by both locals and recreational groups, home extension agents, and teachers from much farther afield. The short courses were among the most successful programs the school sponsored and gained a nationwide reputation for providing an authentic "Appalachian experience" for those from outside the region. For example, Arthur Morgan sent his daughter to the short courses to provide her with an exposure to "mountain life and work."[10] Morgan was the president of Antioch College who chaired the Tennessee Valley Authority's first board of directors from 1933 to 1938. During his tenure, he argued that cultural and social considerations should play an important role in development policy.[11] Whisnant reports that in the very early days of the Folk School, local traditions were at least sometimes featured alongside of Danish dances and songs, with an occasional popular tune sung in "good old Danish folk school fashion."[12] But as time went on, Scandinavian songs, dances, and games dominated the curriculum despite the knowledge of Appalachian traditional music that Campbell had acquired while assisting Sharp. Ironically, then, as Whisnant points out, "The school's own residential students, as well as the hundreds who came to 'recreation' short courses, thus learned Danish songs and danced Danish dances in the name of preserving 'all that is native and fine' in Cherokee County, North Carolina."[13]

The irony of the situation escaped Georg Bidstrup. He believed that while Danish and English dances had originally been introduced into the Folk School's program to serve as a bridge to local traditions, they had become "traditions of the people" by the time he had become the school's director in the 1950s. These imports were in fact "on their way to being incorporated into the Southern mountain dance form."[14] As Whisnant notes, Bidstrup overestimated the European imports' acceptance. In fact, traditional Appalachian dance forms can still be found throughout the region, while the Folk School-introduced dances have by and large vanished. But while the Folk School had little impact on the local culture of the Appalachian region, it has created an image of mountain culture that has been widely accepted by some segments of society. Whisnant observes: "The folk school has been able to establish its version of mountain culture as the legitimate one. Indeed, among the culture-conscious middle and upper classes both within and beyond the region, it is more often than not the settlement school/Berea College/folk school/Southern Highland Handicraft Guild version of 'authentic' mountain culture that predominates."[15]

FORMATIVE INFLUENCES ON THE FOLK SCHOOL'S DANCE PROGRAM

At the John C. Campbell Folk School, the relationship of music and dance—particularly dance—to authentic mountain culture was tenuous at best. Because of the profusion of promotional literature written by and about the Folk School's recreation short courses, dance instruction, and Community Night Dances, it has proven difficult to sort out fact from fiction about the Folk School's dance programs over the years. Some of the available evidence on the earliest years of the Folk School comes from the school's own archives: hundreds of books and articles on folk dance, many with notes and comments written in the margins by the Bidstrups, along with hundreds of dance records, old 78s and 45s dating mostly from the 1920s through the 1950s. In 1989 and early 1991, I conducted interviews with Folk School alumni from the 1930s, arguably the school's heyday. By piecing together a plausible historical narrative from these sources, we can begin unraveling "the tangled skeins of culture" (a metaphor referring to the revival of weaving at the folk and settlement schools) that critics have described.

The oldest books on dance in the school's library include works such as Elizabeth Burchenal's *Folk-Dances and Singing Games* (1909), *Dances of the People* (1913), *Folk Dances of Denmark* (1915), and *Folk Dances of Finland* (1915),[16] as well as Viggo Bovbjerg's *Swedish Schottische* (probably dating from the 1930s).[17] Bovbjerg's books were published by the Recreation Training School of Chicago at Jane Addams' Hull House settlement school. Burchenal was the organizer and first chairman of the Folk Dance committee of the Playground and Recreation Association of America, and her books were also used at Hull House. These were apparently brought to the Folk School by Marguerite Butler Bidstrup, who may have used them at the Pine Mountain Settlement School before helping to found the Campbell School.

Other early books belonging to Marguerite Bidstrup further illustrate the roots of the Folk School's dance program in the work of government agencies, play institutes, and in the urban settlement house movement. These included Raymond

Hoyer's *Games for Play Institutes* (1921);[18] Dagny Pedersen and Neva Boyd's *Folk Games of Denmark and Sweden for School, Playground and Social Center* (1915);[19] Anna Spacek and Neva Boyd's *Folk Dances of Bohemia and Moravia for School, Playground, and Social Center* published by the Recreation Department of the Chicago School of Civics and Philanthropy in 1917;[20] *Social Plays, Games, Marches, Old Folk Dances and Rhythmic Movements for Use in Indian Schools*, published by the Office of Indian Affairs in 1911;[21] and Charles Williams' "*Cotton Needs Pickin'* ": *Characteristic Negro Folk Dances*, collected when he taught at the Hampton Institute in the 1920s.[22] The international folk dance movement began at the institutions mentioned above; the rationale for folk dancing was that it was wholesome exercise, that it helped in the process of assimilating recent immigrants, Native Americans, and southern African Americans. (There is a wonderful photograph in the Hampton Institute collection of African American children, all dressed in white, performing a Maypole dance.)

In addition to the influence of the urban settlement houses, government agencies, and play institutes, Folk School dancer John Brendle recalls that Marguerite Butler Bidstrup's approach to dance was shaped by Cecil Sharp's revival of English folk dance while she was still at the Pine Mountain Settlement School in eastern Kentucky. Whether Bidstrup actually met Sharp is uncertain, though she was likely still at the school when Sharp and Maud Karpeles, his collaborator, "discovered" what they dubbed the "Kentucky Running Set" being danced by the students. The influence of Sharp on the Campbell Folk School was ensured by Mrs. Campbell's collaboration with him on the definitive ballad collection, *English Folk Songs from the Southern Appalachians*, published in 1917. Found among the Folk School's papers are copies of the 1920 edition of Sharp's *Folk Dancing in Schools and Folk Singing in Schools*, published by the English Folk Dance Society. Both have Mrs. Campbell's signature on the covers, and her pencil marks underline passages she found of interest. One passage Mrs. Campbell apparently felt resonant with her own philosophy of art and education reads:

Now the end of Art is not merely to amuse; indeed, as Ruskin has well said, 'Art which proposes amusement as its end, or which is sought for that end, must be of an inferior, and is probably of a harmful class.' We must be careful, then, not to estimate the educational value of dancing solely by its capacity to amuse. If, for instance, dancing in the school is to be permitted to degenerate into a disorderly romp, to become a mere outlet for high spirits, it may, and very likely will, amuse the children; but this is, surely, a form of amusement that is calculated to do them quite as much harm as good. It will not stimulate the imagination, discipline the emotions, nor have any of those effects which is the especial function of art, educationally considered, to produce. If, therefore, dancing is to be justified as a school subject, and to be accepted as an aid to education, it must be treated seriously like all other arts that are taught in school and adequate attention paid to its technical side. The steps and figures must be taught carefully and accurately and the children trained to dance in the proper way, just as in music class they are taught to sing in the proper way. Restraint, so far from suppressing self-expression or diminishing enjoyment, will have precisely the contrary effect. To confine the mill-stream is to increase its power and usefulness.[23]

FOLK SCHOOL DANCE VERSUS LOCAL DANCE

It is clear by all accounts that the Folk School's founders not only went to some lengths *not* to appropriate and build on local dance traditions (as called for in Danish folk school theory), but they also sought to avoid any appearance of complicity in the sins of local dance traditions. The reels and big set dances as well as the flat foot and buck dance solo dance forms were supposedly associated with drinking and wickedness. Campbell and Marguerite Bidstrup told the students again and again that their own mountain culture considered the fiddle "the devil's instrument."[24] Fred Smith, a Folk School student in the early 1930s, and Caroline Scroggs Anderson both recall that square dancing in particular and local styles in general were "absolutely forbidden" at the Folk School. Smith's cousin, J. G. "Slim" Martin, an excellent old-time fiddler who eventually went on to play with bluegrass musician Charlie Monroe, was not allowed to play his fiddle while he was a student at the school. Fred Smith recalls:

Back then, when I came, they didn't use any local people [as dance musicians] because all the kind of dancing they were doing . . . see, [the Folk School wasn't] doing the regular old hoedowns and square dances or nothing like that, the traditional mountain stuff that'd been going on here for years. See, they did the 'traditional folk,' that is, English and Danish, and sometimes German and Slovak . . . but more of the English and Danish than anything else.

The extent to which this prohibition was actually the case in the community at large is open to question, however. While many Brasstown families did not dance or drink, many did. Several of the more prominent families held dances in their homes; the Brendles, the Claytons, the Caldwells, the Greens, even the Scroggses—who donated most of the land that became the Folk School's large campus—were all known as "dancing families." They would take turns hosting "get-togethers," and local fiddlers, banjo players, and guitarists would play and call the figures.

The earliest dancing permitted at the Folk School were the English and Danish "singing games." Mrs. Campbell helped to form the Brasstown Women's Club, which met at the School's Farm House and then at the homes of local women; the meetings would often begin with the singing of a ballad and close with an English singing game from one of Sharp's books. These were not considered "dancing" because there was no instrumental accompaniment. The singing games, though their sources were literary, were also quite similar to the indigenous "play-party" songs, which were also not considered dancing, though they involved physical movements in time to the music. Georg Bidstrup began teaching Folk School students Danish folk dances as part of his gymnastics and exercise classes. It is unclear when the school first acquired a piano and record player, but that was when "dancing" began in earnest. It is known, however, that the completion of the Community Room in 1926 provided the school with an excellent dance floor made of oak strips an inch-and-a-half wide.

Marguerite Butler Bidstrup was once quoted as saying that because all the dances were memorized in advance, European traditions were superior—faster, more polished, more graceful.[25] In contrast, Marguerite pointed out that Americans needed to have their dances called for them. The star dancers who dominated the Friday evening Community Nights specialized, of course, in the European imports. They were members of "Marguerite's select group," the sons and daughters of local dancing families such as the Hollands, the Smiths, the Brendles, the Days, and the Andersons who met on Tuesday nights to practice the more complex, polished Danish and English dances. This group traveled throughout the region to demonstrate "folk dancing;" Fred Smith, Wayne Holland, Bert Smith, Frank Hogan, and Ralph Day constituted the Folk School's Morris team in the 1930s.

The use of recorded music was one of the strongest agents for change among Brasstown's dancers. It was far easier to dance "with precision" to the records of English and Scandinavian dance music, for example, those manufactured in London by RCA for the English Folk Dance and Song Society. The local string bands could only play Southern-style, and their tempos were "uneven." Fred Smith, like most of the Folk School dancers, preferred the records to local musicians. "They had awfully good records, see? And when they got to getting people in to play the music for 'em, if it's off . . . When they'd been trained just to perfection, you know, if the music was off the least bit, it'd just . . . bother. It's hard. If the timing's off a little or something. Later on [i.e., the 1970s], the live music got much better."

Folk School dance alumni say that one reason the Folk School dance program eventually lost its local base of support was that the Bidstrups failed to "raise up" any local dance instructors. On Community Nights, local callers John Brendle or Wayne Holland might be permitted to call the final big circle, but local people were not trained as recreation leaders. Brendle, who married Folk School student Opal Green and was one of the Bidstrup's star dancers, eventually went on to get a degree in recreation. He was the recreation director at the Fontana Dam, a Tennessee Valley Authority recreation facility located in western North Carolina, and later introduced Western club square dance in the Raleigh, North Carolina, area. But, says Brendle, what training he got as a recreation leader, he got on his own.[26]

Instead, the Folk School relied almost exclusively on imported experts. In addition to Marguerite and Georg Bidstrup, instructors for the summer short courses included popularizers of folk materials Richard Chase, Frank Smith, and John Jacob Niles, folk singer Jeanne Ritchie, and the Country Dance and Song Society's May Gadd and Phillip Merrill. Gadd and Merrill were particularly active in the introduction of English country dances, Morris dancing, and New England style contra dancing. Lynn and Katherine Rohrbough of the Cooperative Recreation Service in Ohio—publishers of the "handy kits," influential pocket-sized collections of "folksongs," singing games, and play parties distributed throughout the country, including songs compiled and plays written at the Campbell School— taught international folk dance in Brasstown.

Despite its cultivated reputation for the preservation of "all that is native and fine" in mountain culture, the Campbell Folk School never actively researched or documented local dance traditions, never encouraged the use of authentic local forms. What they did offer was an amalgamation of dance forms from foreign and indigenous sources, with the foreign element far outweighing the native. There were implicit as well as explicit messages in the rejection of the local in favor of the imported. Rejected was all that was "vulgar": vulgar dance at the folk cultural level—the mountain big circle, buck dance or flat foot—rejected because of associations with uncouth behavior, and vulgar dance at the level of popular culture—jitterbugging, clogging, or Western club square—rejected because they smacked of cheap commercialization. Folk dancing, as taught at the folk and settlement schools, was derived from loftier sources: from the gentility of upper-middle class New England and England. It was, in fact, a strong streak of Anglophilia that was the source of the English dance revival in the States, and that was behind most of the early folk song collecting in the mountains as well. This Anglophilia was simultaneously and inevitably a rejection of the native—both traditional and modern—and an assertion of the old WASP elite values. (The apotheosis of this impulse was the establishment of composer John Powell's Anglo-Saxon Club in Virginia, also described in Whisnant's *All That is Native and Fine*.)[27] The cultural workers of the folk and settlement schools saw themselves as a bulwark against the tide, upholding the old rural, agrarian values (the Folk School's motto is still "I Sing Behind the Plough") against a swell of urban, industrial coarseness—gin and jazz. It was the classic struggle of Romanticism and Modernism.

This polarity is found time and again in the promotional literature of the related folk and settlement school movements, the arts and crafts revival, the play, dance and recreation movements, and the early folk song revival. The "wholesomeness" of "true folk art" is juxtaposed against the pollution of the modern world. What the romantic impulse led to, more often than not, was cultural isolationism. For example, beginning in the 1930s, the image of the Campbell Folk School as portrayed in its own promotional literature evolved from a place devoted to the betterment of the rural community to a place where weary modern urbanites could retreat to sing, play, and make crafts.

CONCLUSION

It has been the analysts employing the "politics of culture" approach that have described in detail the agendas and power relationships between cultural workers such as the Bidstrups and the people they were purportedly trying to assist. While much of that work has been very illuminating, a criticism that has been leveled against the "politics of culture" approach is that too often the indigenous "native" people are portrayed as passive victims of cultural imperialism perpetrated by more powerful outsiders. The critics have a point. In reality, the case is not so simple as the imperialist model would suggest.

First, by no stretch of the imagination were the visionaries who ran the Folk School part of a monolithic cultural majority in American society-at-large. The ballad hunters, craft revivers, and dance instructors were marginalized within their own society. They rejected the lifestyles of their upper- and upper-middle class, northern, educated families to work in the mountains—though most maintained their ties with "civilization." Mrs. Campbell, for example, vacationed at her home in Cape Cod. As mildly bohemian, nonconformist, "artistic types," the Southern mountain workers were the direct ancestors of the 1960s and 1970s "back-to-the-land" counter-culture, what some in Cherokee County call "trust fund hippies." It is thus an oversimplification to see the mountain workers as agents of the hegemonic order, when they saw themselves as counterhegemonic (or whatever the equivalent term was in the first half of the century).[28] Secondly, the students of the folk and settlement schools hardly saw themselves as imposed upon. The cultural agenda of the Folk School, as "conflicted and bizarre" (to quote Whisnant)[29] as it may in retrospect seem, was only one of a number of options available to the young people of Cherokee, Clay, Polk, Townes, and Union Counties. All the time the Folk School was trying to protect its students from the corrupting influence of the modern world, the world continued to change around it. While the Folk School offered up old English ballads and carols, Morris dances, and the Anders Hop, the students could and often did also travel five miles away to hear the Monroe Brothers and the Stanley Brothers play the new-fangled music called bluegrass.

While many Brasstown families were certainly known as mountain-style square dancers and buck dancers, those were not the only dance forms in which they excelled. Well-to-do residents of Murphy, the county seat eight miles down river, could send their children for tap dancing lessons in the early 1920s. John Brendle notes that he learned to do "social dancing," such as waltzes and fox-trots, from friends and relations who had "been away" long before the Folk School was ever started. Many local families had sons working in textile mills in Charlotte, North Carolina, at the Alcoa plant in Maryville, Tennessee, or at rubber plants in Akron, Ohio; innovations in social dancing probably came from all these sources. For example, at first I thought that the transition in old-time square dance from the older practice of "swinging your partner" while holding hands to the newer fashion where the man places his hand around the woman's waist was due to the Folk School's influence. But John Brendle is probably correct when he asserts that the change was due more to a change in fads that took place much farther away.

The school's brand of "folk dancing" was eagerly adopted by a small group of local young people precisely because it was new and different. The Brendles say that the young people were "eager to know the new dances."[30] Caroline Scroggs Anderson says that the folk dancing they did at the Folk School was "an art form," whereas the local traditions were artless or, in her words, "just someone telling you what to do." Marguerite's star dancers, and by extension most of the Folk School students, were, in fact, cultural innovators, not unlike the first string band musicians to take up the guitar or the first dancers to put taps on their shoes in festival competition. While this new and different dance was "better," more refined and sophisticated than the local traditions, it was not as "uncouth" as jitterbugging or as "hoity-toity" as some ballroom dancing. Perhaps they saw Danish folk dancing as a less threatening innovation. But mostly, Folk School dancers saw themselves as special; they had mastered difficult dance forms that were unusual, graceful, and spectacular. When they gave demonstrations and workshops at schools and festivals around the region (including the Mountain Dance and Folk Festival in Asheville, the National Folk Festival in Chattanooga, the Southern Highland Handicraft Guild Fair in Gatlinburg), the dancer's sense of pride in their accomplishments was reinforced.

Most of the folk school alumni, while admitting that Marguerite sometimes came off as snobbish, say they loved both the Bidstrups. Many met their future spouses at Folk School dances and now talk wistfully about the warm summer night dances when, as Ruby Day recalls, "that was the only time you could get a boy to put his arm . . . around you . . . we had curfew at 9 o'clock, and the sun still up!"[31] Many of the old Folk School students don't take well to the arguments of cultural imperialism in Appalachia, at least in *their* Appalachia. They simply don't see themselves as victims of interventionism.

Still, despite the relatively benign effects of the Folk School experience on the local students, the question that a "politics of culture" approach raises is the extent to which the Folk School set itself up as an arbiter of "mountain life" to the outside world. What damage did it do—either to the native mountain folk culture or to the national mass culture—for the outside world to imagine that the Folk School version of mountain culture was authentic; that by coming to the Folk School and dancing English and Danish folk dances, one was experiencing Southern Appalachia? Seen as a single instance of a larger pattern of cultural distortion, of the hegemonic "invention" of Appalachia by privileged outsiders with little or no input from the "indigenous populace," the Community Room of the Campbell Folk School becomes a contested arena. When it came to deciding whose culture would hold sway in that arena, as John Brendle observed, "Marguerite ruled that dance floor."

NOTES

1. Burton, "Culture Goes Folksy to Music Cum Good Old Songs," *Greensboro Daily News* (5 December 1970).

2. See Whisnant, "Finding the Way Between the Old and the New," in this volume.

3. My thanks to Tom McGowan at Appalachian State University for looking up the award citation in the papers of the North Carolina Folklore Society.

4. John and Opal Green Brendle, interview with the author, Brasstown, North Carolina, 26 October 1989.

5. David E. Whisnant, *All That is Native and Fine* (Chapel Hill: University of North Carolina Press, 1983), 13.

6. Olive Dame Campbell, and Cecil J. Sharp, *English Folk Songs from the Southern Appalachians* (New York: Putnam, 1917).

7. John C. Campbell, *The Southern Highlander and His Homeland* (New York: Russell Sage Foundation, 1921).

8. Others drawn to the Danish folk school were John Glenn of the Sage Foundation; Warren Wilson, founder of Warren Wilson College; Arthur Morgan of Antioch College and later the Tennessee Valley Authority (TVA); and Myles Horton of the Highlander Folk School in Tennessee.

9. Quoted in Whisnant, *All That is Native and Fine*, 139.

10. "Mountain Life and Work" became the title of the publication of the Council of Southern Mountain Workers. The Council of Southern Mountain Workers was begun in 1913 with the goal of facilitating the exchange of ideas and techniques practiced by a variety of social, educational, and religious workers as they labored in the Southern Highlands. The Folk School was a primary training ground for the Council's recreation leaders.

11. See David E. Whisnant, *Modernizing the Mountaineer: People, Power, and Planning in Appalachia* (New York: Burt Franklin & Co., 1980), 58–61 and 276–277.

12. Whisnant, *All That is Native and Fine,* pp. 155–156.

13. Whisnant, *All That is Native,* 156.

14. As quoted in Whisnant, All That is Native and Fine, pp. 168–169.

15. Whisnant, *All That is Native,* 169.

16. Elizabeth Burchenal, ed. and trans., *Folk-dances of Denmark* (New York: G. Schirmer, 1915); *Folk-dances of Finland* (New York: G. Schirmer, 1915); *Dances of the People* (New York: Schirmer Music, 1913); and *Folk-Dances and Singing Games* (n.p., 1909).

17. Viggo Bovbjerg, *Swedish Schottische* (Chicago: Recreation Training School of Chicago, n.d.).

18. Raymond A. Hoyer, comp., *Games for Play Institutes* (Louisville, Kentucky: The Community Council Recreation Committee, 1921).

19. Dagny Pedersen and Neva Boyd, *Folk Games of Denmark and Sweden for School, Playground and Social Center* (Chicago: H. T. FitzSimons Co., 1915).

20. Anna Spacek and Neva Boyd, comp., *Folk Dances of Bohemia and Moravia for School, Playground and Social Center* (Chicago: Saul Bros., 1917).

21. *Social Plays, Games, Marches, Old Folk Dances and Rhythmic Movements: for Use in Indian Schools* (Washington: Office of Indian Affairs, 1911).

22. Charles Williams, *"Cotton Needs Pickin' "*: *Characteristic Negro Folk Dances* (Norfolk: The Guide Publishing Co., 1928).

23. Cecil J. Sharp, *Folk Dancing in Schools* (London: English Folk Dance Society, 1920), 13–14.

24. Fred Smith, interview with the author, Brasstown, North Carolina, 21 April 1989, and Caroline Scroggs Anderson and Tommy Anderson, personal communication, Brasstown, North Carolina, 2 January 1991. All subsequent quotes from these individuals are from these interviews.

25. John C. Campbell Folk School Archives, Box No. XII, Brasstown, North Carolina.

26. John Brendle, interview with the author, 31 January 1989.

27. Whisnant, *All That is Native and Fine,* 240–242.

28. *Counterhegemony* refers to the efforts of a cultural minority to resist the imposition of the values, perspectives, and customs by those in power.

29. Whisnant, *All That is Native,* 155.

30. John and Opal Green Brendle, interview.

31. Ruby Lee Corn Day, Gladys Holland, Muriel Martin, Sue Roper, and Alice Tuckwiller, interview with the author, Brasstown, North Carolina, 29 March 1989.

Chapter 16

Old-Time Fiddling and Country Dancing in North America: Some Reconsiderations

Richard Blaustein

The connections between old-time fiddling and country dancing in North America seem self-evident. On closer inspection, complex questions arise to which there are no simple or definitive answers.

An authoritative history of old-time fiddling and country dancing on either side of the Atlantic has yet to be written. Primary historical resources dealing with old-time fiddling and country dancing are fragmented, scattered, and largely ephemeral. While information concerning the music and dances of the literate elite can be readily gleaned from printed and written sources such as diaries, travelers' journals, etiquette manuals, ball programs, advertisements, and instructional books, primary data concerning the music and dance of the unlettered classes is mainly to be found in regional fiction, journalism, and oral history. Oral history, while highly valuable, can only reach as far as the memories of the oldest informants. Memory is always selective and can be deceptive.

The vagaries of folk memory are not nearly as troublesome to the contemporary student of North American music and dance as the selectivity of earlier scholars, particularly folklorists, who tended to concentrate exclusively upon the traditions of poor, isolated, and unschooled people. Until relatively recently, many folklorists believed in survivalism, a theory that postulated that the supposed insulation of such rustic folk from urban popular and elite influences resulted in the survival of cultural patterns that had disappeared in a more highly evolved, mainstream society. Since colonists such as the early settlers of North America were presumed to be removed from the main currents of fashion, it would seem to follow that their descendants would be living repositories of traditions long since extinct on their ancestral soil.

When Cecil Sharp, the noted English collector and promoter of British folk music and dance, came to the Southern Appalachians, he was hoping to discover such cultural survivals, and consequently he was uninterested in the full range of music and dance styles coexisting in the region. Sharp dismissed from serious consideration any Appalachian song or tune that was not of ancient, anonymous, and British origins. His investigation of southern mountain dancing was similarly framed by his criteria of folkloristic authenticity. While Sharp's collecting work encouraged American folklorists to study the living folk music and dance traditions of Appalachia and other parts of the United States, the inherent biases of his approach encouraged the perpetuation of a number of questionable notions, among them the belief that the cultural traditions of colonies are necessarily purer and more archaic than those of their homelands. More recent works suggest that the cosmopolitan cultures of Britain and North America had more in common with one another than with their rustic peripheries and that the American back country was not necessarily more conservative than the British hinterlands, as Sharp contended. Consequently, there is a need for a panoramic view of the development of old-time fiddling and country dancing.

Cultural fashion cycles on the peripheries have never been totally out of touch with their metropolitan centers. Approaching old-time fiddling and country dancing in terms of "folk," "popular," or even "vernacular" culture does not really do them justice. An overview must take account of the interplay between urban, elite, literate subcultures, on one hand, and rural, nonelite, nonliterate subcultures, on the other; professional and amateur performing traditions; public, formal, and competitive contexts as well as private, informal, and noncompetitive performance situations. While we see concrete evidence of the perpetuation by nonelites of cultural forms once fashionable among cosmopolitan elites, we can also observe the continuous adoption and reinterpretation of rural cultural styles by cosmopolitan romantics who have come to identify with "the folk." None of these factors can be excluded if we are seeking an understanding of the evolution and the current state of old-time fiddling and country dancing in North America.

EARLY FIDDLE MUSIC AND PERFORMANCE STYLES

There is reason to believe that the fiddle music and performance styles that French and British settlers brought to North America in the seventeenth century were considered old-fashioned by elite cosmopolitan standards of that era. According to David Boyden, a leading authority on the history of the violin, the French and English resisted adopting major innovations that were transforming musical life in Italy and Germany during the late sixteenth century, innovations such as the long bow and the modern violin itself, which first emerged in Italy around 1550.[1]

The violin music of the British Isles, heavily influenced by that of France, was primarily dance music, which employed a short arched bow and associated performance techniques predating the appearance of the first early violins. Sixteenth-century performance techniques included the use of *bourdons* (or drones), little or no use of vibrato, elaborate cross-bowing with short strokes produced with the upper end of the bow, variant tunings, and holding the bow several inches above the frog with the thumb and fingers on the bow hair to produce a shorter arc of stroke than would be possible using a modern violinist's bow grip.[2] In addition, sixteenth-century fiddlers held the neck of the instrument with a flat rather than an arched palm and cradled it in the arm against the player's collarbone or chest instead of under the chin.

COUNTRY DANCE COMES TO AMERICA

Despite their relatively conservative performance techniques, the fiddling and dancing of the British Isles and France that the settlers brought with them to the New World were nonetheless closely connected with broader western European traditions of group and solo dances of their time. The most prevalent and enduring dance tune types in the early American colonies were the reel, hornpipe, and jig, which comprise a major part of the repertories of North American fiddlers to this day. A particularly fashionable type of social dance of this period was the country dance, which was danced in square, round, and longways formations. Displacing older courtly dances, the country dance became popular in England during Cromwell's Commonwealth[3] and had become the fashionable social dance in Western Europe by the end of the seventeenth century. According to English folk dance collector Cecil Sharp, it was known as the *contretanz* in Germany, the *contradanza* in Spain, and in France as the *contredanse*, which by a curious twist of linguistics was reintroduced into England as contra dance. The country dance was also popular in Austria, Italy, and the Netherlands.[4] In any event, the country dance, though English in origin, had become part of international cosmopolitan social and cultural life by the turn of the eighteenth century. John Playford's country dance manual, *The English Dancing Master*, first appeared in 1651 and reached seventeen editions by 1728.

Dancing masters, who were commonly fiddlers as well, appeared early in the North American colonies. According to square dance historian S. Foster Damon, dancing masters were teaching country dances and step dances, and ministers were celebrating their appointment to new pulpits with "Ordination Balls" in Puritan New England before the turn of the eighteenth century. The Reverend Timothy Edwards gave such a ball in Boston in 1694.[5] An entry in the diary of Bostonian Samuel Sewell in 1685 makes mention of a "Dancing Master who seeks to set up here and hath mixt dances." In 1716, an advertisement in the *Boston Newsletter* informs the public that instruments, instrumental instruction books, and music paper were to be had at the "Dancing School of Mr. Ensloe."[6] By the eighteenth century, itinerant dancing masters moved from town to town in the north and from plantation to plantation in the south, teaching dancing and violin playing to their well-born patrons. The most popular dance instruments of the day were the fiddle, the flute, various types of viols, and early keyboard instruments. Elite compilations such as Playford's tune books and *The Fitzwilliam Virginal Book* do not begin to suggest the actual range of dance music performed by all classes of Americans; it is impossible to say with any degree of certainty how much aurally transmitted country dance music of the prerevolutionary era has actually survived into modern times.

Even so, it is clear that we are dealing with something far more complex than a purely aural folk tradition. Indeed, it is impossible to understand North America's instrumental music and dance traditions unless we take account of this formal, literate dimension of country dance music, particularly in the North. Along with this genteel tradition, which is amply documented, we can safely assume that settlers of lower social status were carrying on and developing their own traditions of instrumental music and dancing without formal tutelage, especially in the colonial back country.

EARLY AFRICAN AMERICAN CREOLIZATION

While the instrumental music and dance styles of educated classes of the North during the colonial period had not significantly diverged from their British and French sources, creolization between European and West African music and dance traditions took place almost immediately in the Southern and Caribbean colonies. Dena J. Epstein in *Sinful Tunes and Spirituals* and Lynne Fauley Emery in *Black Dance from 1619 to Today* have added greatly to our detailed knowledge of these early developments.

A Dutch ship landed the first enslaved Africans at Jamestown, Virginia, in 1619. Before the end of the seventeenth century, African American fiddlers are reported performing at European American dances. In addition to the fiddle, African American musicians continued to make and play the banjo, which, according to Epstein, appears in Martinique as early as 1678 as the banza.[7] Dance music was also provided by the quills, or panpipe, and the mouth bow, both of which have survived into this century, and a wide variety of improvised percussion instruments including the jaw-bone, blacksmith's rasp, horse bits, and the castanet-like bones, as well as "body music" in the form of foot-stamping, handclapping, and the complex syncopated body-slapping technique known as "patting Juba" or "hambone."[8] Though large drums were banned by the Slave Laws of 1740, small tambourine-like drums were used to accompany plantation dances. The fiddle, however, appears to have been the most popular instrument played at the time by African Americans and European Americans for dancing.

Just as European instruments and melodies were adopted and fused with West African rhythms and instrumental techniques, it also appears that the enslaved Africans did the same thing with British step dancing, resulting in the creation of the first distinctly American genres of instrumental music and dance, the "hoedown" or "breakdown." As early as 1760, the English traveler Reverend Andrew Burnaby gave the following account of a fashionable ball in Williamsburg, Virginia:

"Towards the close of an evening, when the company are pretty well tired with country dancing, it is usual to dance jigs; a practice originally borrowed from the negroes. These dances are without method or regularity: a gentleman and lady stand up, and dance around the room, one of them retiring, the other pursuing, in an irregular, fantastic manner."[9]

Thus by the time of the American Revolution, the distinctive features of North American dance music—the coexistence of formal tutelage and aural transmission in addition to synthesis between European and African tradition—had already emerged.

FIDDLING AND DANCING IN A NEW COUNTRY

The early American passion for dancing continued to flourish after the Revolution. In the cities and towns, reels, jigs, and contra dances were extremely popular. French cotillions, danced in a square formation, were gaining favor. As in Great Britain during the same period, formal balls and assemblies were favored by the elite. Impromptu kitchen dances and "hops" were common among all classes of Americans.

American music publishers in the late eighteenth century issued a stream of dance instruction books and dance tune collections. Between 1794 and 1800, no less than thirty dance tutors were published in the new republic, including tunes commonly played today by country dance musicians. These included "Fisher's Hornpipe," (composed by a German, Johann Christian Fischer, who settled in London in 1790), "Chorus Jig," "Money Musk," "Speed the Plough," "The Devil's Dream," and "College Hornpipe," more commonly known as "Sailor's Hornpipe."[10] Hugh Wiley Hitchcock makes mention of a collection of instrumental music published in 1796 with the exhaustive title, *Evening Amusement Containing fifty airs, song's, duett's, dances, hornpipe's, reel's, marches, minuett's, &c., &c., for 1 and 2 German flutes.*[11] This volume contains two widely known dance tunes, "The Irish Washerwoman" and "Soldier's Joy." Joy Van Cleef's survey of late eighteenth-century New England dance manuscripts discloses other currently encountered titles, including "The Cuckoo's Nest," "The Dusty Miller," "Flowers of Edinburgh," "Stony Point," "Ways of the World," "The Waggoner," and "The White Cockade."[12]

Dancing was not only a popular form of social entertainment during the Federalist period but also played a prominent role in the circuses and popular theater of the day, both in America and Great Britain. John Durang, the first renowned American dancer, rose to fame as a hornpipe specialist in New York and Philadelphia. The tune composed in 1785, "Durang's Hornpipe,"[13] is still commonly found in repertoires of North American dance musicians. Its inclusion in dance tune collections transported it to the British Isles almost immediately after its initial publication in America. The same is true of the well-known tune, "Rickett's Hornpipe," which is associated with John B. Ricketts, a Scottish circus master and theater owner who was Durang's dancing partner between 1796 and 1799. So by at least the end of the eighteenth century, the influence was mutual on both sides of the ocean.

Competitive and exhibition step dancing occurred in Britain and North America long before the turn of the nineteenth century.[14] The publication of dance tutors and tune books on both sides of the Atlantic maintained a high degree of continuity in British and American dance and instrumental music styles. Touring show people working out of New York, Philadelphia, Boston, Baltimore, Richmond, and Charleston also helped to carry popular urban forms of music and dance into the hinterlands where they, in turn, were exposed to the emerging indigenous styles from which the blackface minstrel show would be developed only a few decades later.[15]

Fiddling and dancing were popular in the frontier areas due to lack of other diversions. However, when preachers during the Great Awakening of 1800 denounced fiddling and dancing as evil, many in the southern back country, filled with newfound religious fervor, gave up these pastimes. Many of their counterparts in the backwaters of Great Britain followed suit.[16] But the pressure that church people brought to bear on their neighbors was never strong enough to eradicate these traditions completely.[17] Some people compromised by developing the so-called "singing games" or "play parties," which were dances in every respect except that they were accompanied by rhymes rather than fiddle tunes.[18]

According to S. Foster Damon, it was during the early nineteenth century that square dances, based on the French cotillion, began to supplant the old longways or contra dances in most of the United States except New England. These new dances, employing simple figures called by a prompter, required little formal tutelage. This simplicity made them particularly suitable to frontier conditions, although they were first in vogue in the East and remained popular in urbane circles until replaced by the more formal and elegant quadrilles of the 1830s.[19] Unlike the quadrilles, which employed specially composed music and sedate gliding steps, the early nineteenth-century square dance was accompanied by reels, hornpipes, and breakdowns mostly played on the fiddle, entailing a good deal of loud, elaborate step dancing which offended the refined sensibilities of cosmopolitan observers.[20]

MINSTREL SHOWS: EXCHANGE BETWEEN THEATRICAL AND FOLK DANCE

A distinctively American style of dancing and instrumental music, reflecting a high degree of cultural interchange between European Americans and African Americans, emerged in the antebellum period, though its roots, as already noted, can be traced back to colonial times. Minstrels, who were African American as well as European American, incorporated authentic folk music and dance into their public performances, and, in turn, their own folk-inspired compositions were taken up by amateur performers who made them part of an ongoing, evolving tradition of step dancing and dance music. In addition, American hoedown steps and tunes were prominently featured along with hornpipes and jigs derived from the step dancing of the British Isles.

Entertainers in blackface had been presenting "Negro" music and dances as early as 1805, and the stepdancing "Negro Boy" was a well-established stock character in

American dance hall and circus routines by 1810. This character became a cross-cultural phenomenon when it was adopted by British circus entertainers in the 1840s, who in turn introduced the blackface dancing clown into France and Belgium in the 1860s.[21]

In the United States, the blackface comedians, accompanied by fiddle, banjo, tambourine, and bones, were commonly heard during the 1820s, along with dances and steps variously referred to as "hoedown," "breakdown," "buck dance," "buck and wing," "pigeon wing," and the "double shuffle."[22] However, it was only after Thomas Dartmouth "Daddy" Rice created a sensation with his characterization of a raffish African American roustabout named "Jim Crow" in 1829 that blackface minstrelsy became a full-fledged genre of vernacular entertainment in its own right.[23]

The first minstrel troupe to receive widespread acclaim was the Virginia Minstrels, who made their debut in New York City in 1842. Their instrumental ensemble included fiddle, banjo, tambourine, and bones, a format that was followed, with minor variations and substitutions, by the many other blackface ensembles who followed in the wake of their initial success. As in John Durang's day, step dancing to instrumental accompaniment was one of the staples of British and American entertainment (and the tradition would be maintained in an elaborated form by the soft-shoe and tap dance artists who flourished during the heyday of vaudeville).[24]

One of the most notable minstrel show dancers in America during the 1840s was an African American man who went by the name of Juba. Charles Dickens was only one of the journalists of his day who praised Juba's extraordinary, innovative style of step dancing. According to Emery,[25] Juba had succeeded in fusing elaborate African-derived shuffle steps with British-American jig and hornpipe patterns. He carried himself from the waist up with the characteristic rigid torso of an Irish jig dancer,[26] but from the waist down, his movements were strongly West African. The bowing patterns of the hoedown fiddling that accompanied his dancing likewise merged syncopated shuffle strokes with traditional harmonic and melodic formulas characteristic of British reels and hornpipes.

Like the Virginia Minstrels, Juba found himself dancing before enthusiastic audiences in England, where a transplanted minstrel show tradition thrived after it had become unfashionable in America. Indeed, in J. F. and T.M. Flett's invaluable study of North British dancing academies, *Traditional Step-Dancing in Lakeland*, it is interesting to learn that what they called the "Nigger Dance," performed by boys in blackface and ragged costumes, was part of the standard repertory of North British exhibition dancers, along with the jig, hornpipe, and clog dance, up to the early years of this century.[27] It is worth noting that American minstrel show dancers did not completely restrict themselves to native forms like the buck dance and hoedown but also performed these older genres of British step dancing as well. Precision team dancing by dancers wearing clogs or other types of noise-making footwear is not necessarily a recent development. Apparently some minstrel show troupes were performing elaborate synchronized clog routines as early as the 1880s.[28]

Quickly incorporated into the American square dance repertory, minstrel show tunes are a good example of the movement of material from the popular to the traditional or folk level. "Turkey in the Straw," still known in New England by the old minstrel show title, "Old Zip Coon," was allegedly composed by Dan Emmett, who is also credited with "Dixie" and "The Boatman's Dance," a less common tune still found in the repertories of old-time fiddlers and banjoists. Some other common dance tunes with minstrel show roots include "Cindy," "Whoa Mule," "Old Dan Tucker," "Buffalo Gals," "Liza Jane," "Lynchburg Town," "Year of Jubilo," "Climbing Up the Golden Stairs," and "Golden Slippers," which was composed by James Bland, an African American minstrel musician who also wrote "Carry Me Back to Old Virginny." A survey of the repertoires of contemporary American folk instrumentalists would undoubtedly reveal a significant number of tunes composed or popularized by minstrel show performers.

TRANSFORMATION OF COUNTRY MUSIC AND DANCE IN THE LATE NINETEENTH AND EARLY TWENTIETH CENTURY

Upwardly striving nineteenth-century Americans looked toward Europe for guidance in matters of fashion. When country dances were banished from polite society in England in the 1850s, fashionable urbanites on this side of the Atlantic followed suit. Square dances were still performed at fashionable American balls during the 1860s, but had practically disappeared from upper class urban social life by the 1890s. The same is apparently true of the country dance in the British Isles. Throughout the Western world, group dances were giving way to couple dances. The first popular couple dance was the waltz, which first appeared in France at the time of the Revolution and had become widely adopted in Europe and America by the 1820s. The polka craze swept Europe and America in the 1840s, followed by a succession of popular couple dances such as the mazurka, varsouvienne, redowa, galop, and schottische.

While the fashionable cosmopolitan social dances on both sides of the Atlantic by the turn of the century were the two-step and the waltz, older dances—both group and couple—did not disappear altogether.[29] According to Cecil Sharp, country dance, which had been the predominant social dance in England for the past two centuries, was relegated to the rural, old-fashioned areas.[30] Older dances—ranging from the relatively ancient contra dance and step dances to the comparatively modern square dance and couple dances such as the polka, schottische, mazurka, and varsouvienne—were still being danced and played in various sections of rural North America.

By 1900, sixty percent of the population of the United States was still living and working in rural communities. Diverse cultural and socioeconomic conditions resulted in the emergence of highly varied local and regional performance styles and repertoires that appear to have followed the same general patterns as dialects or material culture.[31] Social and cultural insularity was greater in some regions than others. Transportation and communication patterns imposed limits on rural life in North America which supported these varied traditions of music and dancing. Though some country dance music appeared on phonograph records as early as 1909,[32] the primary contexts in which most rural Americans were exposed to dancing and dance music still entailed direct face-to-face communication and interaction. It is important to recognize, however, that there has been a continuous history of musical literacy in America, at least in some circles, since colonial times, and the publication of dance tune folios and dance instructional manuals has been a major influence on old-time musicians and country dancers, particularly in the northern and western sections of the United States.

While dance music performance styles and repertoires were highly localized and varied, the instruments on which that music was played increasingly came from mail order merchandisers. These merchandisers were important agents for the dissemination of a national material culture. Virtually all of the instruments we associate with North American dance music—fiddles, banjos, guitars, mandolins, accordions, harmonicas, triangles, hammered dulcimers, bass fiddles, pianos, and pump organs—could be found in the catalogues of merchants such as Sears-Roebuck and Montgomery Ward. The 1910 Sears catalogue carried no fewer than forty-two pages given over to musical instruments; the 1990 Sears catalogue included only four pages of musical instruments, tucked away between many pages devoted to electronic entertainment devices.

The decade between 1910 and 1920 witnessed revolutionary changes in American society and culture. The 1920 census showed that for the first time in its history, the United States was a predominantly urban rather than a rural nation. Jazz, an exciting new musical style fusing African and American styles, was sweeping the country. Freed from the constraints of wartime austerity, many Americans were indulging in unlaced, freewheeling behavior, which shocked old-school conservative types, including automobile magnate Henry Ford, who devoted several years of his life to reviving his version of old-time music and dance.

There was an undeniably xenophobic element in Ford's attempts to revive old-time music and dance. His privately owned newspaper, *The Dearborn Independent*, published articles with titles like "Jewish Jazz Becomes Our National Music," and "How the Jewish Song Trust Makes You Sing."[33] Having begun recording old-time fiddlers in 1922, Ford set out in earnest in 1924 to standardize and revive the old tunes and dances. He engaged the services of a Hudson, Massachusetts, dance master named Benjamin B. Lovett and also put together an eclectic instrumental ensemble, including fiddle, hammered dulcimer, cimbalom (an Hungarian zither, also played with hammers), and a sousaphone (a larger version of the tuba), which was to record under the name of Henry Ford's Old Time Dance Orchestra. Between 1923 and 1927, major fiddling contests involving thousands of fiddlers were sponsored by Ford, and extensive efforts were made to promote old-time dancing, including the publication of *Good Morning*, a dance manual issued under the names of Mr. and Mrs. Henry Ford but actually ghostwritten by Benjamin Lovett.[34]

As with dance trends of earlier centuries, this revival/standardization process was simultaneously occurring on the other side of the ocean, in Scotland. As in the United States, the impetus to revive Scottish country dancing stemmed from the belief that older indigenous traditions were in danger of being overwhelmed by tasteless, vulgar novelties emanating from the urban underclasses, specifically jazz music and dancing. Miss Jean Milligan, the founder of the Royal Scottish Country Dance Society, set out to document the country dances still surviving in Scotland, much like Benjamin Lovett, Ford's dancing master, in the United States. Like Lovett, she did much more than simply preserve an existing tradition: she produced an authoritative canon of figures and steps that eliminated local and regional variants in favor of a transregional style that could be easily taught and performed.[35] It is probable that in both cases, elements of the revival forms fed back in to traditional dance.

Such revivals and inventions of traditional music and dance raise intriguing questions. It is essential that we consider the historical evolution and contemporary revivals of traditional music and dancing in global perspective, rather than thinking of them as isolated developments. Reconsidering the history of old-time fiddling and country dancing in trans-Atlantic perspective, we find very little difference in the chronology of dance fashions in North America and the British Isles; specific dance styles seem to have come in and gone out of fashion at approximately the same time. According to Colin Quigley, old-time fiddling and country dancing in North America are localized and regionalized expressions of more extensive western music and dance traditions.[36] Tangible evidence of mutual influence between North American and British music and dance styles dates back to the late eighteenth century and possibly earlier. Pervasive African influences in American society have continually spawned innovative syntheses. The rural areas of North America and the British Isles may have been *relatively* conservative as far as music and dance fashions are concerned, but at no point were they ever *absolutely* insulated from cosmopolitan fads and trends.

The evolution of the forms of country music and dance often described as "traditional" is the result of a continuing dialogue between popular and traditional styles, between elite and folk influences, and between the past and the present. A comparative approach is needed that reflects the intricacies of these pluralistic and dynamic subjects.

NOTES

1. See David Boyden, "The Violin," in *Musical Instruments Through the Ages*, ed. Anthony Baines (Baltimore: Penguin, 1961), 97–122. This information is from pp. 97–116.

2. See Boyden, "The Violin," pp. 97–116.

3. See S. Foster Damon, *The History of Square Dancing* (Barre, Massachusetts: Barre Gazette, 1957), 1–2.

4. A. P. Oppé and Cecil J. Sharp, *The Dance* (1924; Rpt. Totowa, New Jersey: Rowman and Littlefield, 1972), 24–25.

5. Damon, 3-4. For a more recent discussion of Puritans and dance, see Joy Van Cleef, "Rural Felicity: Social Dance in 18th Century Connecticut," *Dance Perspectives* 65, ed. Selma Jeanne Cohen, Spring 1976, vol. 17 (New York: Marcel Dekker, Inc., 1976), 4-8.

6. Hugh Wiley Hitchcock, *Music in the United States: An Historical Introduction* (Englewood Cliffs, N.J.: Prentice-Hall, 1969), 35.

7. Dena J. Epstein, *Sinful Tunes and Spirituals: Black Folk Music to the Civil War* (Urbana: University of Illinois Press, 1977), 359.

8. See Epstein, *Sinful Tunes*, 141-144, and Lynne Fauley Emery, *Black Dance from 1619 to Today*, 2nd ed. (Princeton, N.J.: Princeton Book Co., 1988), 27-28 and 96-98.

9. Edmund S. Morgan, *Virginians At Home* (Charlottesville: University Press of Virginia, 1952), 80.

10. Damon, *Square Dancing*, 16.

11. Hitchcock, *Music in the United States*, 26.

12. Van Cleef, *Rural Felicity*, 41-42.

13. See Lillian Moore, "John Durang, The First American Dancer," in *Chronicles of the American Dance*, ed. Paul Magriel (New York: Henry Holt and Co., 1948), 21.

14. See Breandan Breathnach, *Folkmusic and Dances of Ireland* (Dublin: Browne and Noland, Ltd., 1971) for Ireland; George S. Emmerson, *A Social History of Scottish Dance: Ane Celestial Recreatioun* (Montreal and London: McGill-Queen's University Press, 1972) for Scotland; and J. P. and T. M. Flett, *Traditional Step-Dancing in Lakeland* (London: English Folk Dance and Song Society, 1979) for Northern England.

15. Irving L. Sablosky, *American Music* (Chicago: University of Chicago Press, 1969), 47-49.

16. See Prys Morgan, *The Eighteenth Century Renaissance* (Llandybie, Dyfed, Wales: Christopher Davies Ltd., 1981), 49.

17. Jane R. Jenkins, "Social Dance in North Carolina Before the Twentieth Century—An Overview," (Ph.D. dissertation, University of North Carolina-Greensboro, 1978), 101-122.

18. W. K. McNeil, "Play-Party," in *Encyclopedia of Southern Culture*, eds. Charles Reagan Wilson and William Ferris (Chapel Hill: University of North Carolina Press, 1989), 514.

19. Damon, *Square Dancing*, 22-29.

20. See Damon, *Square Dancing*, 22.

21. Marian Hannah Winter, "Juba and American Minstrelsy," in *Chronicles of the American Dance*, ed. Paul Magriel (New York: Henry Holt and Co., 1948), 40 and 53.

22. Emery, *Black Dance*, 179-199.

23. Winter, "Juba and American Minstrelsy," p. 40. See also Emery, *Black Dance*, 181-199, and Hans Nathan, *Dan Emmett and the Rise of Early Negro Minstrelsy* (Norman: University of Oklahoma Press, 1962), 50-52.

24. Marshall Stearns, *Jazz Dance: The Story of American Vernacular Dance* (New York: Macmillan, 1968), 75-84.

25. Emery, *Black Dance*, 190.

26. See Breathnach, *Folkmusic*, 55-56.

27. See facsimile programs in Flett, *Traditional Step-Dancing*, 84-103.

28. Winter, "Juba and American Minstrelsy," p. 57.

29. See Loretta Carillo, "Dance," in *Handbook of American Popular Culture*, ed. Thomas Inge, 2nd ed. (Westport, Connecticut: Greenwood Press, 1989), 262.

30. Oppé and Sharp, *The Dance*, 31.

31. Richard Blaustein, "Traditional Music and Social Change: The Old Time Fiddlers Association Movement in the United States" (Dissertation, Indiana University, 1975), 26.

32. Archie Green, "Commercial Music Graphics: Thirteen," *John Edwards Memorial Foundation Quarterly* 6, part 2, no. 18 (Summer 1970): 70–73. This information is from p. 70.

33. Seymour M. Lipset and Earl Raab, *The Politics of Unreason* (New York: Harper & Row, 1970), 136.

34. Mr. and Mrs. Henry Ford, *Good Morning* (Dearborn, Michigan: The Dearborn Publishing Company, 1926).

35. Emmerson, *A Social History of Scottish Dance*, 297–301.

36. See Quigley, "Anglo-American Dance in Appalachia and Newfoundland," in this volume.

Chapter 17

Dance, Our Dearest Diversion: Historical Dance Reconstruction in Colonial Williamsburg

Merry Feyock

It is 1770 in Williamsburg, the small, neat, but prosperous capital city of the British colony of Virginia. It is April. Along with the bright spring flowers, Virginians from all parts of this vast colony—from the eastern Tidewater to the Blue Ridge and beyond, perhaps even from the Ohio territory far beyond the mountains[1]—are appearing in town for the biannual Publick Times to combine work and pleasure.

The General Assembly is in session in the Capitol, discussing taxation and other political controversies with the mother country. The Exchange is full of men of business engaged in their occupation; the well-supplied merchants are doing a brisk trade. In the taverns—places of lodging as well as places of entertainment—at the theater, and at the Capitol, the tavern keepers and the dancing masters are feverishly planning balls, assemblies,[2] plays, and other public entertainments for these visitors, who will more than double the population of the town for the next fortnight or so. Toward sunset, as the work of the day draws to a close, the candles are lighted, and the serious business of diversion begins.

In the Raleigh Tavern, for example, the dancing master—complete with powdered wig, brocaded suit, and silk stockings—is anxiously seeing to last minute details for tonight's subscription ball as his slaves idly tune their fiddles in the corner, readying music for the dance. Soon the elegantly attired company will arrive, adorned not only with their finest silks, satins, and laces but also with that aura, that immeasurable quality known as "good breeding"—a combination of finely polished manners, style, fashionable clothing, and innate dignity. The ball will begin at six with the minuets, as is customary in the genteel worlds of London, Paris, Boston, Charleston,

New York, and Williamsburg. And thus the stage is set for dance, an occasion for entertainment, certainly, but also for the public display of social status.

For eleven years it was my privilege and pleasure to explore the world of eighteenth-century Virginia gentry with the specific goal of learning what role the dance played in their lives. The sponsor of this research and the forum for the results was Colonial Williamsburg. Colonial Williamsburg's goal was, and continues to be, to show the importance of dance as an integral part of the rich fabric of colonial Virginia life. It attempts to attain that goal by continually researching the dance itself, including the social life of the period, and then by training Colonial Williamsburg's corps of dancers to present the results of this research as meaningfully and accurately as possible to the public.

DANCE RESEARCH

Determining the Time Frame

The first and most immediate consideration for research on dance in eighteenth-century Virginia is to determine the time frame. The logical starting point is to concentrate on the period between 1699 and 1780 since those are the years that Williamsburg served as the capital of Virginia. There are, however, some problems inherent in such a limit since there were, first of all, no known *published* American dance sources for this period. In fact, the first American dance manual was not published until well after the Revolution. Also, references in this particular period regarding different steps used in the various dances are seemingly nonexistent, compelling us to search outside of, but as close as possible to, this time frame. Finally there is, frustratingly, only one known Virginia dance named at all in this period, although a wealth of information about balls, assemblies, and other dances exists. It is known that Virginians were famous for being "immoderately fond of dancing."[3]

Another important practical consideration was identifying the most useful sources dealing with historical dance. The dance experience of the twentieth-century dancers at Colonial Williamsburg consisted of the modern, Cecil Sharp version of the Playford dances, supplemented by several important dance manuals published during the Bicentennial. Specifically, these manuals were Kate Van Winkle Keller and Ralph Sweet's *Choice Selection of American Country Dances of the Revolutionary Era, 1775–1795,*[4] and James Morrison's *Twenty-four Early American Country Dances, Cotillions & Reels for the Year 1976.*[5]

All these sources are useful. All of them are problematic in some way. It would have been tempting simply to take Cecil Sharp's versions of the Playford dances he had so thoroughly studied in England and assume them to be in their "original" form since the late seventeenth and early eighteenth centuries.[6] The dances Sharp observed in early twentieth-century England reflect two centuries of metamorphosis from the time of Playford. Thus, although Sharp's interpretations of Playford's dances are most enjoyable, these studies are a hindrance rather than a help for the serious historical dance researcher. They do not, in fact, show the dances as Playford must have known them, even though Sharp's versions have the same name and identical figures as the dances in Playford's collections. Despite the fact that Keller and Sweet as well as Morrison are all too far on the post-Revolution side of our ideal time frame, they are useful because they show *American* dances as they were in the last decades of the eighteenth century. This makes these manuals an invaluable reference tool.

As the research program has evolved over the course of several years, we have endeavored to narrow our focus, and in recent years have begun to concentrate primarily on the dances—admittedly still British—published between 1750 and 1770. The rationale for this lies in the fact that most programs we present as living history are dated at 1770.

Dance and the Gentry

The next pressing research consideration involves what aspect of society should be studied. Since there is very little information available about anyone else, we have settled by default on the "gentry," the wealthiest five to ten percent of Virginia's population who lived very much as their English counterparts and prided themselves on being at least as English as Englishmen, although admittedly slightly more distant from London than other English provinces. An early Virginia historian, Hugh Jones, wrote in 1722 that "the habits, life, customs, computations, etc. of the Virginians are much the same as about London, which they esteem their home,"[7] and "they live in the same neat manner, dress after the same modes, and behave themselves exactly as the gentry in London."[8]

What did dance mean to the English? It has been well established that dancing was very much in vogue all over Europe during the eighteenth century and that it was an important, almost ubiquitous element in all levels of society. Simply put, it was *the* thing to do. It was "the Darling or favourite diversion of all Ranks of People from the Court to the Cottage in their different manners of Dancing."[9] Yet its function in the social lives of the upper classes was radically different than we would assume today, based on contemporary attitudes toward dance.

Clearly, people danced for the sheer pleasure of it then, just as they do today. Yet for the gentry, the dance assumed another, more significant role. Fine dancing became the great *un*-equalizer, a means, much like the ostentatious flaunting of wealth, by which the gentry could distinguish themselves from the lesser or middling sort. The reasons for this were many: only the leisured upper classes had both the time and the money to invest in perfecting the dance in conjunction with social behavior, for "good breeding demands that pleasing and easy manner which can only be gained by dancing."[10] And the dancing master was the person to teach both. To learn to dance, then, not only meant mastery of complex figures and steps to the point of assured proficiency, but also mastery of the complex protocol involved: how to greet someone of varying social degrees properly; how to converse; how to carry and use a fan or a walking stick; how to give and receive objects in the proper manner. The diligence with which the gentry applied themselves to this task is evident in the fact that dance was a major component in the education of any person of quality and that, particularly in Virginia, dancing was considered "an innocent and an ornamental, and most certainly, in this province . . . a necessary qualification for a person to appear even decent in company!"[11]

Written documentation tells us that there were numerous occasions for dancing, both in town and in the Virginia countryside. Subscription balls, like the one described at the beginning of this chapter, were sponsored by various dancing masters, who could be either men or women, both to make a profit and to advertise their skills. Those who were permitted to attend were, of course, the gentry as well as those of "genteel appearance"—apparently a judgment on clothing and manners. These dancers of "genteel appearance" were members of the rapidly increasing middle classes who could afford the price of a ticket; so there was at these subscription balls and assemblies a degree of mingling between classes. During the Publick Times in April and October, these dances were held in taverns with great frequency (sometimes more than one per night), often with intense competition among dancing masters as to who could attract the most patrons.[12] Dancing masters also sponsored another kind of dance, called an assembly, sometimes at the Capitol or possibly also at a larger tavern. The distinction between a subscription ball and an assembly in Williamsburg is not yet clear.[13]

Dances were not only given to promote the talents of various dance masters. Balls were also given to celebrate a significant political event, such as the King's birthnight or the arrival of a new governor.[14] For example, in 1746 the English victory over Bonnie Prince Charlie at the battle of Culloden was celebrated by an elegant ball at the Capitol.[15] And, of course, balls were given at the Governor's Palace by special invitation for the politically and economically influential. An interesting note about these balls is that at least one governor (Botetourt, who was governor from 1768-1770) had a master of ceremonies, a Mr. Stark, to govern the conduct of the dance, as was customary in England.

Dancing also appeared on the Williamsburg stage as "entr'acts"—between-act entertainment in plays. Occasionally, balls were also held after a concert. Outside of town, on the plantations, balls were held for almost any reason: a wedding, christening, house-raising, boat race, or barbeque. They occurred during any season, even in the sweltering heat of a Virginia summer; they were particularly frequent during the Christmas season. Balls were known to last for days. It seems that whenever a "goodly company" of Virginians gathered together, it was likely that dancing was an important part of the festivities, even if the company consisted of nothing more than the family sharing a quiet hour at home.

Seeking out such facts as these requires extensive delving into a great variety of sources. For Williamsburg society, diaries are an important source of information. William Byrd II, a wealthy and very influential third-generation Virginian whose plantation, Westover, can still be seen only thirty miles up the James River from Williamsburg, wrote several diaries in secret code between 1710 and 1740.[16] Philip Vickers Fithian, a young tutor from New Jersey who spent a year with the Carter family in Northern Virginia, left a lengthy and detailed description of his experiences in the colony in 1774. Likewise, articles and advertisements exist in the local newspaper, the *Virginia Gazette*,[17] concerning dances such as subscription balls and assemblies, dancing masters advertising their trade, and—on more than one occasion—rewards for runaway slave musicians. These newspaper archives add to our knowledge of the period and the people. Other Virginia sources include inventories (of a person's estate after death for probate purposes) and wills. In addition to these sources, we are now beginning to look at published literature of the period, such as novels, to better enhance our understanding of this complex society and the position of dance in it.

Dance Genres in Eighteenth-Century Williamsburg

With regard to the dance genres of the time, information—especially information specific to America—has been difficult to find. However, we at Colonial Williamsburg are much indebted to Kate Van Winkle Keller, Chrystelle Bond, and Wendy Hilton for their most gracious assistance with our endeavors. Keller has been a staunch supporter of eighteenth-century American dance and has aided us greatly with her enthusiasm and assistance in finding sources. Along with Carolyn Rabson, she compiled the 1980 publication, *The National Tune Index*[18]—an invaluable resource tool for anyone interested in early American music and dance. Chrystelle Bond, professor of dance at Goucher College and longtime historic dancer and advocate of dance in museum settings, provided valuable outside support for establishing dance at Colonial Williamsburg. I have also had the great privilege of having Wendy Hilton as a teacher of baroque dance at several workshops, and have frequently used her excellent work, *Dance of Court and Theater*.[19] We are indebted as well to the research and/or methodology of dance scholars Shirley Wynne,[20] Ingrid Brainard, James Morrison, Margaret Daniels, Janis Pforsich, Christine Helwig, Charles Hendrickson, and many others who have written about eighteenth-century dance forms. These scholars are continually finding evidence of the importance of dance in the colonial and early national eras.

As primary sources, we are most fortunate to have in the collections of Colonial Williamsburg a copy of many of Playford's dance collections (which went through twenty-eight editions between 1650 and 1728). There is also a good collection not only of British country dances from 1700 to 1810, but also several collections of English and French baroque dance. In addition, there are works on manners and behavior, which, as I mentioned before, were also the province of the dance master. The lack of appropriate American sources would have been more disquieting if it were not for the fact that so much of the American colonial experience, apparently including dance, was so closely patterned after British counterparts. Here, as in many other areas of interest to Colonial Williamsburg where we have found American evidence scanty or inconclusive, we have of necessity reverted to British sources.

PERFORMING EIGHTEENTH-CENTURY DANCE IN
TWENTIETH-CENTURY WILLIAMSBURG

The final purpose of all this dance research in a museum such as Colonial Williamsburg is, of course, to bring its results before the public. There is, however, a very important intermediate step that must be taken; that is, to train those who will be communicating dance to the public—the dancers/interpreters themselves. When the period of intense research began more than ten years ago, Colonial Williamsburg had two groups of dancers: a small group of junior and high school students and the group of adults mentioned above who were learning some of the "old" dances for fun and recreation.

The "Student Dancers," later called the "Juvenile Performers," were all local young people who, by choice or by parental coercion, studied dance at Colonial Williamsburg intensively for at least one year. Before they were hired as dancers, they had to demonstrate proficiency in the dance repertoire, deportment, and basic social skills. Older students could become interpreters, that is, those who supplement the visual impact of the dance with verbal explanation.

The adult ensemble still contains many of the people who began dancing for fun. These performers evolved out of a core of assorted Colonial Williamsburg employees, none of whom were professional dancers. (Currently there are such diverse museum professions represented as curator, printer, interpreter, graphic artist, musician, and milliner.) When the commitment to an expanded dance program was made, this group became the first group of dancers to be trained in eighteenth-century dance according to the latest research being done in the field. It was never a goal to achieve a professional corps of trained dancers in the technical sense, but rather to acquire the presumed level of expertise of the gentry who actually danced here.

Although there are no precise references other than to good or bad minuets (see minuet section below), the fact that the gentry were able to dance minuets, cotillions, and other "French dances," as well as jigs and reels, seems to indicate a rather high level of expertise. Learning such dances as these has not always been an easy proposition for dancers used to the much simpler walking and skipping called for in Sharp's interpretation of Playford. We have, however, developed some proficiency in steps such as pas de bourre (in different rhythms), minuet (several different kinds), and, at last count, eight reel steps. These steps have been incorporated into our dance choreographies, either as notated in the original Feuillet notation[21] or as reconstructed.

One of the most difficult things for dancers to master has been the fine art of matching the steps to the music. No matter what is being danced, the music establishes the framework. It has been consoling to note that this problem is not new, as this excerpt from an eighteenth-century poem demonstrates:

Wou'd you in Dancing ev'ry Fault avoid,
To keep true Time be your First Thoughts employ'd;
All other Errors they in vain shall mend
Who in this one important Point offend.[22]

Tempo has posed another interesting problem for us in that dancers frequently rehearse and perform to recorded music with a steady, nonvariable beat. We are most fortunate to have *real* musicians accompany us in performance. Since people are certainly not machines, the tempo can vary occasionally within a dance. The moral in all of this is that we have learned to listen to the music, confident that the "music will tell us what to do."

As has been indicated, the dance and the rules of social interaction are as complex and difficult to master now as they must have been two centuries ago, but a knowledge of both together is, I believe, crucial to the re-creation of eighteenth-century life. For example, in a living history setting, it is imperative that performers know how to greet each other properly and to converse in proper eighteenth-century terminology. For visitors to get a feeling for the scene being presented, it is important that performers know how to carry themselves, how to stand, sit, and walk as well as perform the dance. Instructions for all this can be found in numerous dance masters' explanations of "polite behavior." For instance, Pierre Rameau in *The Dancing Master*, published in 1725, was quite explicit in explaining how the gentleman *doffs* his hat before a bow: it took Rameau *two pages of text and two illustrations* just to explain that simple procedure. Likewise, references such as "what are children before they have had instruction in the dance?"[23] and "dancing gives to every one who has learnt the Art, a proper Deportment, a genteel Behavior and an easy Address,"[24] solidify the connection between proper social behavior and dancing.

The technique of dance along with the social expectations surrounding it have helped to contribute to the evolution of style. Clothing is another element which absolutely must be taken into account. To recreate eighteenth-century dance as accurately as possible, it is critically important to be equipped with authentic clothing. At Colonial Williamsburg, we have been fortunate in having a costume department provide us with beautiful and increasingly accurate costumes, from stays, hoops, and fashionable silk ball gowns for the women to well-tailored suits, wigs, and hats for the men. We also have ample opportunity to practice wearing the clothing—a necessary experience since dancing is noticeably different when performed in the confines of proper eighteenth-century dress. Again, excerpts from various books on manners have helped us create the feeling of actually being in an eighteenth-century person's shoes.

Putting on a costume such as a ball gown and all the necessary accoutrements for the first time is definitely a novel experience. For those of us who did not grow up used to such confined clothing, being laced into stays is very restrictive at best, and uncomfortable at worst. Dancers find that simple movements such as getting up and sitting down, become quite complicated when they wear high heeled shoes and heavy brocade gowns with long trailing skirts. To dance within these confines takes constant practice, for balance is very different and has to be relearned. For the gentleman, the costume is not quite so restrictive, except that it is always a suit and therefore very warm. Also, the cut of the coat across the shoulders is quite narrow, so that the jacket serves much the same function as stays do in women's clothing, namely, to improve posture.

Our costume affects others as well. We have all noted that visitors' reactions to us change dramatically when we are in costume—especially in our ball finery—performing in the Governor's Palace by candlelight to some well-played music. The visual impact of the scene inspires deference bordering on awe on the part of spectators. This helps us achieve our goal of making our visitors' experience at Colonial Williamsburg educational and pleasurable.

Structures and Types of Dances in Eighteenth-Century Williamsburg

The next question to be addressed involves the structure and types of dances found most often during this period. In the absence of American sources, it became necessary to turn once more to British sources. However, comparing what Virginia accounts we have with contemporary English sources provides substantial evidence that dance in Virginia was basically the same as in England. For example, William Byrd writes of a ball he attended in London in 1719: "About 8 o'clock I went to a private ball . . . We had a fine supper . . . We danced till 2 o'clock."[25] A year later, he wrote about a ball held in Williamsburg: "We . . . then went to the governor's assembly, where was abundance of company. We danced till ten . . ."[26] He seemed to be as at home at a dance in London as he was in Williamsburg. The most detailed account, however, comes from Fithian in a description of a ball held at a neighboring plantation. He relates the order of dances: "About Seven the Ladies & Gentlemen begun to dance in the Ballroom—first Minuets one Round; Second Giggs; third Reels; And last of All Country-Dances."[27]

At more formal affairs, such as those at the Governor's Palace, the dance would be governed by a rigid formality, again closely following the English prototype. This protocol decreed that there be a Master of Ceremonies who was in charge of the evening. Most often this was a local dancing master, naturally considered the most knowledgeable in managing such an occasion. His tasks were many, but by far the most important and potentially nerve-wracking one was to establish the social ranking for the minuet. This dance always began a ball or assembly and was always danced by one couple at a time, in strictest observance of their social rank. On occasion, this tortuous duty was expanded to establish who was dancing with whom for the entire evening—clearly a task for a true diplomat. During the course of the century, sets of rules were developed to regulate the public balls or assemblies, as they were sometimes called. An example from the Richmond Assembly in 1790 will give an idea of the particulars:

2d. The Dancing shall commence with minuets, of which there shall not be more than four.

3d. That every couple in set dances shall stand according to the number which the lady may draw, unless she may chuse [sic] to stand lower or exchange her place; and every lady intending to dance, must draw.

6th. That the couple which may have last led a dance, must thereafter stand at the bottom, and no couple may call two dances.[28]

As mentioned before, it was customary to begin each ball or assembly with the minuet. The aesthetic performance of this dance was incredibly important, because the minuet was considered "the Ground work of all other dancing, being so well calculated and adapted as to give room for every person to display all the beauties & Graces of the body which become a genteel carriage."[29] The proper way of dancing a minuet was with "great ease and propriety,"[30] which everyone admired. To dance badly, however, was to make oneself an object of absolute ridicule such as poor maligned Captain Grigg, who according to Fithian in 1774 "hobled most dolefully."[31] Captain Grigg appears again several years later. In 1782, a young lady indulges in a bit of gossip in a letter to a friend: "I don't think I ever laught so much in my life as I did last night at Captain Grigg's minuet. I wish you could see him. It is really the most ludicrous thing I ever saw; and what makes it more so is, he thinks he dances a most delightful one."[32]

The minuet was considered both the most important and, since the arm movements were simplified, the easiest of the baroque dances for a nonprofessional dancer of the time to learn. These dances in the baroque style, the step vocabulary for which is the antecedent of our modern ballet, were written in Feuillet notation. While it cannot be proven that any other baroque dances were in the Virginians' repertoire, the fact that Charles Stagg, the dancing master in Williamsburg, owned copies of both John Weaver's and John Essex's translations of Feuillet is surely significant. There are also eighteenth-century Virginia references to "French dances," which may indicate a dance of this type since minuets were usually named as such. William Byrd wrote: "About 7 o'clock the company went in coaches from the Governor's house to the capitol where the Governor opened the ball with a French dance with my wife."[33]

Since the minuet's function was to establish the formality required by the occasion and also to delineate social order, the dance was done couple by couple in order of descending rank until everyone who was "able" had had a chance to dance. In Williamsburg, the master of ceremonies' duties in this regard were made somewhat easier with the publication of the "Rules of Precedency."[34] The minuet, then, was not merely a dance performed for the pure joy of movement, but a ritual as well. Although it was the easiest of the baroque dances, it was nevertheless both technically and socially demanding, especially for untrained dancers; it was most certainly a fearsome rite of passage for a young man or woman of the gentry standing up to dance it for the first time in front of the doubtless very imposing and proper company.

No such descriptions are available of the most important dance genre of the period, however—the longways or country dance. The numerous collections of eighteenth-century country dances, published primarily in London or in France, are both fantastically rich in information and frustratingly sparse in detail. For example, the typical collection of these dances may contain from a handful to several hundred country dances, some possibly original to that particular source or freely "borrowed" from another collection. A page typically contains the title of the dance, then the music (sometimes conveniently delineated with repeats and other necessary or helpful musical devices; sometimes not), then a brief description of the figures of the dance, which relates the floor pattern of the dance, usually in a cryptic and very general manner. Only rarely do these descriptions give specific steps, other than specifying use of the minuet step, if required, or other ambiguous steps, most called simply "setting" or "footing it."

In its most basic form, the country dances consisted of couples arranged in two lines up and down the room—men on one side, women on the other—and organized into "sets," typically consisting of eight to ten couples. Most of the time these dances would be progressive: always beginning at the top of the set, the head couple would dance the figures with the second or both the second and third couples, changing places with the second couple somewhere in the course of the dance. After completing the figures of the dance once, the head couple would repeat those figures with the next couple or couples, thus eventually having the opportunity to dance with every other couple in the set.

As noted in the Richmond Assembly rules, the place of the head couple was regulated so that each couple would have a chance to "call" a dance. There was no calling in the modern sense; during the eighteenth century, to call a dance meant that the couple chose and possibly explained their favorite dance before the dance actually began. Many of these dances had interesting names, such as "Hunt the Squirrel," "We'll Wed and We'll Bed," "Now or Never," "Lord Frog," and "An Old Man is a Bed Full of Bones." "Hunt the Squirrel" seemed to be especially popular—it was published in several dance collections through most of the century. No doubt its "chase" figure—during which the lady first wove through the set, chasing the man and then vice versa—contributed to its popularity.

> A thoughtful Head, and a reflecting Mind,
> Can in each Dance an useful Moral find:
> In *Hunt-the-Squirrel* thus, the Nymph we view,
> Seeks when we fly, but flies when we pursue. [35]

By the third quarter of the century, at least three new and lively dance genres were coming into vogue in London, and therefore, also in Virginia: the Scotch reel, the cotillion, and the jig.

The Scotch reel, a dance based on long-extant Scottish dance tradition, rapidly became so fashionable that even sophisticated London dancing masters traveled north to Edinburgh to receive the best instruction where they "undertook a rigorous course of three lessons a day to learn the steps of the Scotch Reels, signifying 'the importance they thought a right knowledge of the dance in question might do them on their return to London.' "[36]

This dance took on at least two forms, generally meaning the simple longways done in reel (common) time, or the complex dances for two, three, or four people who would alternately "reel"—dance an extended figure eight pattern around and by each other—for a certain amount of music and then "foot it": dazzle the onlookers with a variety of fancy steps more or less in place. Some reels seemed to be improvised on the spot; some were more carefully choreographed. Occasionally, they probably featured changing partners like jigs. All, however, involved a complex set of steps and a lot of stamina.

Although cotillions are not specifically mentioned in any of the earlier Virginia sources, there is no doubt that this dance was of great importance in England and therefore, by conjecture, in Virginia. This dance genre is also a very visible part of our American dance tradition since it evolved into square dancing. Like the square dance, the cotillion set was composed of four couples facing each other along the sides of the square. The cotillion was composed of a series of movements described as "Changes" and "the Figure," corresponding to the verses and the chorus of a song. The changes were the customary introductions to the dance, beginning with the basic Le Grand Rond, a circle to the left and then back and including such picturesque names as Le Grand Chaine (grand chain), Moulinet (literally *mill*, although we might know it as a *star*), Le Petit Quarre (the small square), and La Queue du Chat (the cat's tail). The Figure was the basic choreography of the cotillion, that which distinguished one dance from another. Cotillion figures are often more specific in the use of steps, in this case French ones, since the dance in its particular square form had been first perfected in that country before becoming wildly acclaimed in Britain in the 1760s (Figures 17-1 and 17-2).

The last and most elusive dance form mentioned in eighteenth-century Virginia is the jig. This dance seems to have been quite difficult to define, having been described as everything from a simple longways dance in jig (6/8) time to an improvised dance for one couple: "A couple gets up and begins to dance a jig (to some Negro tune) others comes and cuts them out, and these dances always last as long as the fiddler can play. This is . . . more like a Bacchanalian dance than one in a polite assembly."[37] Finally jigs were named as dances done by the black slaves in Virginia society and apparently emulated by their masters. Although as a general rule no steps were specified in individual dances, ample documentation is at hand indicating possible steps or step combinations that could be used in the reconstruction of a dance. In 1710, it was observed that

The most ordinary Steps in Country Dances (those excepted that are upon Minuet Airs) are Steps of Gavot, drive sideways Bouree step and some small Jumps forward of either Foot in a hopping manner or little hopps in all round figures . . . one may make little hopps or bouree steps but little hopps are more in fashion. . . . As it is ordinary that every figure of a Dance ends at every cadence or end of the Aire, it will be proper to make a small Jump upon both feet.[38]

By 1752 Nicholas Dukes observes that "according to the present method of dancing they keep continually footing, as in Casting of, Crossing over, or any other part of Figuring, you may foot it forwards or backwards or sideways as the Case requires."[39]

Of course, we are left with questions such as "what is footing?" Since step definitions are rarely found in the dance collections themselves, it is necessary to research other primary source material. Among the richest sources I have found to date are the baroque step vocabulary, mentioned above, and a series of Scottish dance steps

Figure 17-1. "The Cotillion Dance" by John Collett. This variation on a square-formation dance came into vogue in England and America in the last third of the eighteenth century. Note the fancy footwork. Colored engraving by James Caldwell from a painting. Copyright Colonial Williamsburg Foundation.

214

Figure 17-2. The Colonial Williamsburg Dancers dancing "le Grand Chaine" in a cotillion. Copyright Colonial Williamsburg Foundation.

published by a famous dancing master from Edinburgh, Francis Peacock. Some of these Scottish dance steps bear a surprising resemblance to some baroque steps, and some include "little hopps." Although Peacock's steps were not published until 1805, he was then at the end of an illustrious career spanning almost sixty years, which fortunately places him well back into our period. It might seem questionable to use his steps since he is Scottish, but the fact that a large percentage of the Virginia tobacco trade went to Scotland rather than England and that the English dancing masters themselves were traveling to Scotland to take lessons in the reel from Peacock made me look on this as a feasible source. Another source, Giovanni Andrea Gallini's book, *Critical Observations On The Art of Dancing,* published around 1770, provides us with some steps and figures from the latter part of the period, whereas his work, *New Collections of Forty-Four Cotillions,* also from 1770, has provided rich material for reconstructions.[40]

THE RECONSTRUCTION PROCESS

Given the abundance of background material and some knowledge of the dances, let us briefly look at the reconstruction process itself. In my case, the procedure has followed precisely defined steps geared toward the end product of a meaningful visual experience by which the public can be made more aware of this aspect of eighteenth-century life. These steps are as follows:

1. Determine what genre of dance and what date is required. Since there are currently a lot of longways dances in the repertoire, look for a cotillion this time.
2. Focus on a particular source—for cotillions, unquestionably Gallini.
3. Read through the material, visualizing the dance and playing the music on the piano. This will give a sense of how pleasing each part of the dance is, how aesthetically the individual parts fit together, what the effect of any repeats might be, and how the figures of the dance may fit with the musical strains.
4. Pick the most promising material and work through the phrasing choreographically, trying out appropriate eighteenth-century steps that work well within the musical phrasing and meter as well as within the time frame of the dance itself.
5. Write down possible interpretations of the dance, taking into consideration such variables as the complexity of the steps; for example, is it realistic to expect the dancers to master these particular step sequences? Also consider the "fit" of the dance phrase to the music and the visual impact to the spectator.
6. Try it out. Subject a "guinea pig" group of dancers to the new dance, and let them experiment with it. Dancers are not known for their shyness in offering suggestions in interpretation, and they help considerably with the fine tuning of a dance.
7. If the new dance meets with general acclaim, then learn, rehearse, and polish to performance level.

Since factual evidence is so fragmentary, an absolutely authentic reconstruction of even an English eighteenth-century country dance as it may have actually been danced in its time is surely impossible, even with resources such as Feuillet's notation system. Very few country dances were notated—and those few that were written down come from too early in the century for our purposes. Therefore, it is the task of the historic dance reconstructor/choreographer to assemble the parts of the dance into a meaningful and contextually believable whole from information gleaned from different and sometimes conflicting sources. I am personally convinced—although others, I am sure, will disagree with me—that there are as many interpretations of a given dance as there are modern dance historian-choreographers to interpret it, each in his or her own way.

Indeed, it must have been so in the eighteenth century. The dancing masters of the time must themselves have used the collections of dances to teach the figures and learn the music. Just as we do today, they would have used the steps they had learned from their dancing master or from published sources such as Feuillet and numerous collections of dances. For them as well, the success of their "reconstructions" would have been measured by how suitable, aesthetic, and just plain fun their students found the dances to learn and to perform for others.

For those of us who dance for Colonial Williamsburg, participating in the dance group has broadened our horizons in several different ways. First of all, it has given us the opportunity to meet people from different departments of our very large museum. This experience is not only beneficial in itself, but has also meant that each person's knowledge of eighteenth-century dance can be integrated and correlated with other historic research areas. On a social level, the dancers—more than half of whom are young unmarried museum professionals—have naturally enjoyed each other's company, meeting not just to dance, which for us is also *work*, but also for birthday parties, picnics, and other jovial occasions. Also, dancing is a good extra job for us.

Are these the only reasons? No. On a professional level, dancing enriches our own comprehension of eighteenth-century life. When one is dancing by candlelight at the Palace or the Capitol, there is a profound feeling of being part of all that happened in Williamsburg two hundred years ago, as if a shuttered window to the past were somehow opened slightly, if only for an instant. Remembering that feeling, we can use it to add to our visitors' breadth of experience by showing them why and how dance was important to the inhabitants of eighteenth-century Williamsburg.

And of course, now as then, dancing allows us to have fun. Now, as then, we follow the tradition.

Research will continue to change the way we view eighteenth-century dance in Virginia, but the motto today remains the motto noted by Fithian in 1774: "Blow high, blow low . . . *Virginians* are of genuine Blood—They will dance or die!"[41]

NOTES

1. See Emily J. Salmon, ed., *A Hornbook of Virginia History*, 3rd ed. (Richmond: Virginia State Library, 1983). Virginia was Britain's largest and richest colony. Prior to 1784, Virginia claimed lands from the North Carolina border north and west to the Great Lakes and the Mississippi.

2. It seems that there is no readily discernible difference between a subscription ball and an assembly. Both were given by dancing masters or tavern keepers for profit. Both were held in various locations at Williamsburg, at the Capitol, in a tavern, or occasionally in the dancing master's own home. Both could be held at any time of the year, although practically speaking most were held in conjunction with the Publick Times in April and October.

3. Andrew Burnaby, *Travels through the Middle Settlements in North-America. In the Years 1759 and 1760. With Observations upon the State of the Colonies*, 2nd ed. (London: T. Payne, 1775), 35.

4. Kate Van Winkle Keller and Ralph Sweet, *Choice Selection of American Country Dances of the Revolutionary Era, 1775-1795* (New York: Country Dance and Song Society, 1976).

5. James E. Morrison, *Twenty-four Early American Country Dances, Cotillions & Reels for the Year 1976* (New York: Country Dance and Song Society, 1976).

6. John Playford was the seventeenth century English publisher who is credited with beginning the country dance craze in England with his publication in 1650 of *The English Dancing Master*, a collection of some fifty country dances, each of which included the title of the dance, the music specific to it, and a brief description of the "figures" or patterns of the dance. This work was so enthusiastically received by the dancing public that he, and later his son, published sixteen more editions of this country dance collection. The last edition, published in 1728, contained almost nine hundred dances. See John Playford, *Playford's English Dancing Master 1651: A Facsimile Reprint with an Introduction, Bibliography and Notes*, ed. Margaret Dean-Smith, (London: Schott and Co., 1957).

Cecil Sharp was a highly regarded English dance researcher and historian in the early 1900s who collected folk dances from the English (and later the Appalachian) countryside. One of his most famous works, produced with Maud Karpeles, is *The Country Dance Book* (London: Novello and Co., Ltd., 1918; rpt. East Ardsley, England: EP Publishing, 1976). This is a six volume set of the dances he observed still being danced in England. These dances were originally found in the publications of John Playford. Sharp's versions of Playford's dances are still being danced avidly today by English country dancers all over the world.

7. Hugh Jones, *The Present State of Virginia. From Whence is Inferred a Short View of Maryland and North Carolina*, ed. Richard Morton (Chapel Hill: University of North Carolina Press, 1956), 80.

8. Jones, 71.

9. Kellam Tomlinson, *The Art of Dancing Explained by Reading and Figures; Whereby the Manner of Performing the Steps is Made Easy By a New and Familiar Method* (1735; rpt. Westmead, England: Gregg, International, 1970), as quoted in George S. Emmerson, *A Social History of Scottish Dance: Ane Celestial Recreatioun* (Montreal: McGill-Queen's University Press, 1972), 287.

10. Pierre Rameau, *The Dancing Master*, trans. Cyrill Beaumont (1725; rpt. Brooklyn: Dance Horizons, 1970), 2.

11. Philip Vickers Fithian, *The Journal and Letters of Philip Vickers Fithian, 1773-1774. A Plantation Tutor of the Old Dominion*, ed. Hunter Dickinson Farish (Williamsburg, Va.: Colonial Williamsburg, Inc., 1957), 33.

12. Two dancing mistresses, Mrs. Stagg and Mrs. DeGraffenriedt, engaged in an intense advertising campaign for their assemblies and balls (which included raffles and "Grotesque Dances, never yet perform'd in Virginia" during Publick Times, but they were very careful not to schedule them on the same evenings—except once as a benefit. *Virginia Gazette*, Williamsburg, 1736-1780 (Williamsburg, Virginia: Colonial Williamsburg Foundation Library, 24

March 1738). Other advertisements on 25 February; 22 April; 7, 10 and 14 October 1737; 13 October 1738; 20 April 1739.

13. In the *Virginia Gazette*, 15-22 April 1737: "To the Gentlemen and Ladies—That Mrs. Degraffenreidt intends to have a ball, on Tuesday next, being the 26th Instant, and an Assembly on Wednesday the 27th, at her house in Williamsburg; for which, Tickets will be delivered by her at her House at any Time before the Ball or Assembly begins."

14. *Virginia Gazette* for Thursday, 26 October 1769: "Yesterday being the day appointed for celebrating the anniversary of His Majesty's Birthday, his Excellency the Governor gave an elegant ball at the Palace, where there was a numerous and very brilliant assembly of Ladies and Gentlemen."

15. *Virginia Gazette* for 18 July 1746, p. 4: "On receiving the news, in this City, of the glorious victory gain'd over the Rebels . . . an universal Joy seem'd diffus'd among all Ranks of Persons . . . a Grand Entertainment was made at the Capitol . . . suitable to the extraordinary Occasion. . . . In the Evening, a very numerous Company of Gentlemen and Ladies appear'd at the Capitol, where a Ball was open'd and after dancing some Time, withdrew to Supper, there being a very handsome Collation spread on three Tables, in three different Roomes, consisting of near 100 dishes, after the most delicate Taste. . . . The whole Affair was conducted with great Decency and good Order, and an unaffected Chearfulness appeared in the Countenances of the Company. All the Houses in the City were illuminated . . . and the whole concluded with the greatest Demonstrations of Joy and Loyalty."

16. See for example, William Byrd, *The London Diary (1717-1721) and Other Writings*, eds. Louis B. Wright and Marion Tinling (New York: Oxford University Press, 1958), and William Byrd, *The Secret Diary of William Byrd of Westover, 1709-1712*, eds. Louis B. Wright and Marion Tinling (Richmond, Virginia: Dietz Press, 1941). Also William Byrd, *Another Secret Diary of William Byrd of Westover, 1739-1741. With Letters & Literary Exercises 1696-1726*, ed. Maude H. Woodfin and trans. Marion Tinling (Richmond, Virginia.: Dietz Press, 1942).

17. Fiddler Billy was the slave of the dancing master William Fearson. *The Virginia Gazette* for 4 November 1773, lists him as a runaway: "Run away from the Subscriber [Fearson], the Negro Boy so well known in this city by the Name of FIDDLER BILLY . . . I hereby forewarn all Persons from harboring him. Wm Fearson."

18. Kate Van Winkle Keller and Carolyn Rabson, *The National Tune Index* (New York: University Music Editions, 1980).

19. Wendy Hilton, *Dance of Court and Theater. The French Noble Style, 1690-1725*, ed. Caroline Gaynor (Princeton, N.J.: Princeton Book Company, 1981).

20. Shirley Wynne, "From Ballet to Ballroom: Dance in the Revolutionary Era," *Dance Scope* 10, no. 1 (Fall/Winter 1975-1976): 65-73.

21. Feuillet notation is a system of choreographic notation first publicized by Raoul Auger Feuillet in 1700 in his *Choreographie*. This notation system made possible a kind of standardization of the dance since it made choreographed dances accessible to any dancing master who had been taught to decipher it. John Weaver in *Orchesography or the Art of Dancing ye Characters and Demonstrative Figures . . . Being an Exact and Just Translation from the French of Monsieur Feuillett*, 2nd ed. (London: John Walsh, [ca. 1715]), and John Essex in *For the Further Improvement of Dancing* (London: Walsh, 1710) both translated this work into English almost immediately (1706 and 1710, respectively).

22. Soame Jenyns, *The Art of Dancing &c. A Poem in 3 Cantos*, (London: 1729), 31-32.

23. Curt Sachs, *World History of the Dance*, trans. Bessie Schönberg (New York: W. W. Norton & Co., Inc., 1937), 400.

24. Matthew Towle, *The Young Gentleman and Lady's Private Tutor. The First Part* (London and Oxford, circa 1770), 179.

25. Byrd, *The London Diary*, 5 August 1719, 301.

26. Byrd, *The London Diary*, 10 November 1720, 473.

27. Fithian, 57.

28. Richmond Dancing Assembly, manuscript (Richmond, Virginia: Virginia Historical Society, 1790).

29. Nicholas Dukes, *A Concise & Easy Method of Learning the Figuring Part of Country Dances by way of Characters. To which is Prefixed the Figure of the Minuet, by Nicholas Dukes, Dancing Master*, (London, 1752), p. 1.

30. Fithian, 33.

31. Fithian, 52.

32. Lucinda Lee Orr, *Journal of a Young Lady of the Old Dominion, 1782*, ed. Emily V. Mason (Baltimore: John Murphy and Co., 1891), 37.

33. Byrd, *Secret Diary*, 6 February 1711, 297.

34. The "Rules of Precedency," as published by the *Virginia Gazette* on 26 May 1774, are as follows:

"RULES of PRECEDENCY," compared and adjusted from the several Acts and Statutes made and provided in England, for the Settlement of the Precedency of MEN and WOMEN in AMERICA, by JOSEPH EDMONSON, Mowbray Herald.

GOVERNOUR of the Colony, or Province,	Governor's Wife.
President of the Council,	his Wife.
Counsellors,	his Wife.
Speaker of the Commons House of Assembly,	his Wife.
Chief Justice,	his Wife.
Treasurer,	his Wife.
Secretary of the Colony,	his Wife.
Gentlemen of the Assembly,	their Wives.
Mayor,	his Wife.
Alderman,	their Wives.

The Gentlemen of the Assembly, Crown Officers, &c. of any particular Colony, or Province, have no other Rank out of their Colony, or Province, than what belongs to them in their private Capacity as Men.

35. Jenyns, 49.

36. Evelyn Hood, *The Story of Scottish Country Dancing* (Great Britain: William Collins and Sons Co., 1980), 82.

37. Nicholas Cresswell, *The Journal of Nicholas Cresswell, 1774–1777* (New York: Dial Press, 1924), 52–53.

38. Essex, 15.

39. Dukes, V.

40. Giovanni Andrea Gallini, *Critical Observations On The Art of Dancing* (London, 1770), and *New Collection of Forty-Four Cotillions, With Figures properly adapted; Also the Music for Six select Dances, Two of which may be used as Cotillions* (London, 1770).

41. Fithian, 177.

Chapter 18

Yuppies Invaded My Tradition at Midnight: A Sociological Study of a Contemporary American Contra Dance

Richard Carlin

This chapter began, appropriately enough, over wine and cheese at a dance conference. I was talking to dance ethnologist Susan Spalding, one of the conference coordinators, when I said to her in jest: "You ought to have a chapter on the *real* people who do traditional dancing."

"Who's that? The mountaineers?" she asked. "We have a lot of studies about them."

"No," I said. "Yuppies! They're the real people that are keeping this dance alive."

"And what would you call this [chapter]?"

" 'Yuppies Invaded My Tradition at Midnight.' "

Susan immediately decided this was a wonderful idea, despite my protestations that I was just kidding. And the more I thought about it, the more it seemed that I was in a unique position, as a yuppie myself, to give an insider's insight into the contra dance boom that has taken place over the last decade.

Contra dance traces its heritage back to the seventeenth century's *contre danse*, popular in both England and France. In the United States, contre danse became *contra* or *country dance*, predominantly a progressive longways form. In a progressive longways dance, two lines of dancers face each other. Generally, every other or every third couple is designated as an "active" couple, with the remaining dancers termed "inactive." At the conclusion of the execution of each figure, the active couples progress toward the bottom of the set, while the inactives move in the opposite direction. Active couples become inactive once they reach the bottom of the set, while the inactive couples undergo a similar conversion experience once they reach the top.

Spearheaded by the Country Dance and Song Society of America (CDSS), the contra dance revival has spread to the rest of the country since its beginning in New
England more than ninety years ago (Figure 18-1).[1]

I chose the Princeton dance because I have been dancing and playing music there
for over twelve years. Based on my own experience contra dancing in Charlottesville, Virginia, and Washington, D. C., as well as on conversations with people
from around the country, I have come to the conclusion that the issues and trends
in Princeton are very similar to those that surface in the contra dance world elsewhere, that geographic location matters less in contra than it does in other forms
of traditional dance.

My interest was twofold: one, to conduct a demographic survey of the Princeton
contra dancers—to find exactly *who* was attending the dances. Secondly, I was interested in knowing more about *why* they danced and how the involvement of these
yuppies was changing the contra dance scene. I wanted to map the changes that have
occurred in this group over the last fifteen or so years.

AN APOLOGY AND DEFINITIONS

I define a yuppie as a college-educated (or more) person with a "professional" job.
First and foremost, I must candidly admit that no one in this study liked being called
a yuppie. There is a definite negative connotation to the term. Many people told me
they associated yuppies with materialistic, grasping folk who do not care about the
fate of the earth, let alone spend any time worrying about the survival of "the Lady's
Chain." Actually, the subjects of my study might be characterized more accurately as
yuppies (young, upwardly mobile professionals) during the day; hippies at night. The
title of this chapter is totally misleading, although it is a good title. I am not from the
"tradition" myself. My forebears were Eastern European Jews who were busy being
chased out of central Europe just a few years before Cecil Sharp got on his bicycle
and began collecting English traditional dances.[2] And as I have already admitted, I
am a yuppie. So perhaps it is best to say that this contribution is an insider's view
of how the contra dance revival has grown. As such, it gives insights into the way
traditional dance has spread through our society and the issues that the process
has raised along the way.

John Playford, in his landmark series of books called *The English Dancing Master* (published in various editions from 1651 to 1725), called these dances "longways for as many as will," and by the ninth and last edition of his work, this form
of dance predominated.[3] These dances traveled from England to the New World,
settling in New England where they entered into the traditional life of the small
town.

The ninetieth anniversary of the founding of the CDSS by May Gadd was celebrated in 1990. The founding of CDSS was the beginning of the contra dance
revival, but there were other subsequent waves of revivals. In the thirties during
the Depression, Ralph Page in New England got the notion that he could earn a liv-

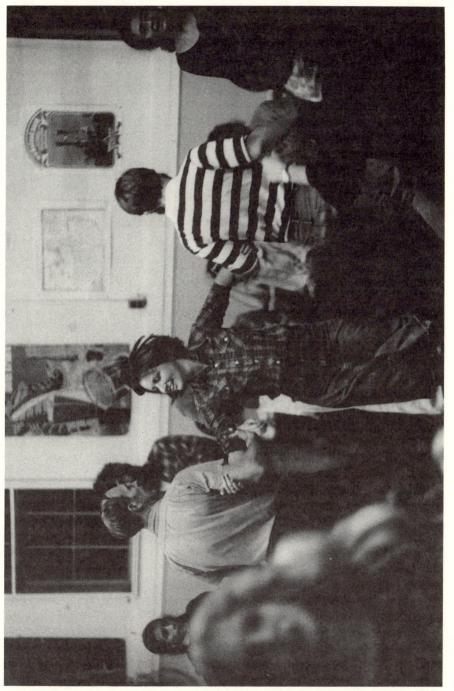

Figure 18-1. Contra dancing at Berea College, Berea, Kentucky, 1980s. Photograph by Kenneth Murray.

ing by calling dances.[4] He was tied into the recreational and international folk movements so that a lot of his dances entered into those arenas. In the sixties, two men, Dudley Laufman and Bob McQuillen, drove around from college town to college town in a big bread van reintroducing contra dance in New England.[5] Contra dance then spread down the East Coast and around the country.

The Princeton Contra Dance straddles both worlds. It started out as a group that came out of international folk dance. There were two international folk dances through the mid-sixties and seventies in Princeton. Some of those people, including my parents, hired a young caller named David Chandler to teach contra dancing in 1975-1976. They got interested in contra after dancing in New York and at the Hudson Guild Farm contra dance weekends in northwest New Jersey sponsored by the CDSS. The first group consisted primarily of fifty- and sixty-year-olds dancing to records. A few university students came along, and in 1978 after struggling for some years in search of a permanent home, the group located at Princeton University. Suddenly a large number of students were attending the dances, among them musicians who were interested in playing for dancing. A pick-up band drawn largely from the Princeton Folk Music Society was formed, growing to over thirty members. A few of the older folk continued to attend, but within a year or two the group was made up predominantly of students and young professionals.

The Princeton Dance remained affiliated with the university for a few years. As its members got older the student population diminished, and the dance was forced to find a new home. It first settled at a local church, then at a Catholic school in Princeton. For the last half decade, the group has actually not been located in Princeton. It is currently meeting in South Brunswick, about eight miles north of Princeton. Therefore, members have had to have access to transportation. Still, the Wednesday night dances attract an average of seventy to eighty people, of whom about ninety percent attend week after week. Special events draw several hundred people. The group is run by a loosely structured board of directors and, since about 1985, has been affiliated with CDSS.[6] Related groups have sprung up in surrounding neighborhoods, including the slightly more hip Lambertville Dance (meeting every other Friday), with dances coming and going in Pennington, Titusville, Trenton, Yardley, and Highland Park. Many of the same people attend these other dances.

PURPOSE AND METHODOLOGY

The purpose of this study was to determine "who are these folk?" In other words, who exactly is attending the weekly Princeton dances, and what is it about contra dancing that appeals to them? My methodology was relatively simple. I designed a questionnaire (Figure 18-2) to obtain basic information on the dancers. I then interviewed several "key players" in the community, including people who had served on the board of directors, callers, musicians, and regular dance attendees.

CONTRA DANCER SURVEY

Name (Optional): _____Age:_____ Sex: _____

Telephone Number: _____

Marital Status: ___Single ___Married ___Divorced ___Widowed
        Did you meet your spouse/significant other contra dancing?
                        ____Y   ____N
Education: _____High School _____College-Major_____ Degree_____
        Grad School - Major _____ Degree _____
        Other Education _____

Employer:

        Job Title: _____ Years at Current Job: ____
I have been contra dancing _____ years. I contra dance _____ times per
month. I travel _____ miles, on average, one way to attend a dance. I was
introduced to contra dancing by:
        _____ Girl/Boyfriend   _____ Co-Worker
        _____ Family Member   _____ Newspaper/radio
                                      announcement
        _____ Housemate   _____ Word of mouth
I have _____ years of dance training in _____ ballet, _____ modern, _____
jazz dance. I regularly dance:
        _____ Square dance   _____ Flatfoot/clog dance
        _____ Ballroom   _____ Playford dance
        _____ Aerobics   _____ Morris/ritual dance
        _____ International Folk   _____ Scottish
        _____ Pop/disco dance _____ Other (Specify:
                                _____)
I dance because: _____ it's good exercise
                   _____ it's a good way to meet people
                   _____ I want to improve my dance skills
                   _____ to relieve stress
                   _____ to socialize
                   _____ other (specify:_____)
In addition to dancing, I play the following musical instruments:

I play _____ times per month for dances.
I enjoy dancing to: _____ live music _____ recorded music.
In addition to dancing, I have:
                        _____ called for dances
                        _____ taught dances
                        _____ served on the board of directors
                        _____ organized special dance events

Other comments about contra dance:

Figure 18–2. *Contra dancer survey.*

STATISTICAL FINDINGS FROM THE CONTRA DANCER SURVEY

Survey Participants

The 118 responses to my survey were gathered at two different dances and represent approximately three-quarters of the attendees at each dance. Sixty-three of the
respondents were male, while fifty-five were female. For practical purposes, this is

close to even (fifty-three percent male to forty-seven percent female) and represents the general trend of men often slightly outnumbering women at the dances. I also did some follow-up surveys, talking to people I knew—callers, musicians, and others—to get more in-depth information.

Educational Status

One of the first things that interested me was the dancers' educational level. Not surprisingly for a town like Princeton, the educational level was unusually high. Only five respondents did not have college degrees, and three of them were still in high school. Nearly half (forty-seven percent) had multiple degrees, and many others had advanced training.

Despite the common feeling that "techies" and science-oriented people—the sort of people who wear pens in their pockets—predominate at the dances, about a third (twenty-nine percent) had B.A. degrees. About a fifth had B.S. degrees, with smaller numbers of M.S., M.A., and Ph.D. degrees (one respondent reported having *two* Ph.Ds). Assorted other degrees took up the rear (Table 18-1). There was only one music degree, although there were a lot of musicians. There were also planning degrees, B.F.A.s, and law, C.P.A., M.F.A., M.L.S., nursing, forestry, engineering, and an M.Ed. So there was a good spread of all types of professional degrees.

Employment History

In the employment category, there was a much wider variety than one would have expected (Table 18-2). Again, the common myth is that computer jocks make up the largest percentage of the contra dance community. Actually, the greatest number (15 percent) was found in the teaching professions, primarily high school and college teachers. Computers took a close second, however, with 9 percent, and if you put

Table 18-1
Highest Education Degrees Achieved by Princeton Contra Dancers

No.	Degree	No.	Degree
3	Still attend high school	2	J.D. (Law)
2	High school	1	C.P.A.
34	B.A.	2	M.B.A.
23	B.S.	1	M.F.A.
11	M.S.	1	M.L.S.
7	M.A.	1	M.D.
14	Ph.D.	2	Nursing
1	Music	1	Forestry
1	MCRP (Planning)	1	Engineering (E.E.)
1	B.F.A.	3	M.Ed.
		4	No response

Table 18-2
Employment Status of Princeton Contra Dancers

No.	Education (18) –Teachers	No.	Sciences (28)	No.	Medical (12)	No.	Professions (16)
3	Elementary	11	Computer programmers	4	Psychologist	2	Lawyer
10	High School	3	Biologist	1	Psychotherapist	1	Librarian
5	College	3	Physicist	2	Massage Therapist	2	Banker
		3	Engineer	1	Physical Therapist	2	Planner
		1	Product Sales Engineer	2	Nurse	1	Development officer
		2	Chemist	1	Medical doctor	1	Architect
		1	Research technician	1	Nutritionist	1	Art director
		1	Sen. research scientist			1	Buyer (dept. store)
		3	Statistician			1	Scientific writer
						1	Journalist
						2	CPA
						1	Labor relations mgr.

No.	Trades (11)	No.	Unskilled Workers (6)	No.	Students (7)	No.	Miscellaneous (8)
1	Forest ranger	1	Housecleaner	3	High School	2	Self-employed (undefined)
1	Dispatcher	1	Driver	4	Graduate School	1	Storyteller
1	Recording eng.	1	Printer			1	Homemaker
2	Secretary	1	Railroad ticket taker			3	Unemployed
1	Horologist	2	Clerk			1	Caterer
1	Bookkeeper						
3	Carpenter						
1	Electrician						

Note: There were eleven nonrespondents.

together all the sciences (including engineers, physicists, chemists, biologists, and so on), you would account for about a quarter of the total. The professions (for example, lawyers, C.P.A.s, and managers) accounted for 14 percent, medical workers (doctors, nurses) and the trades (electricians, carpenters, and so on) were nearly even (10 and 9 percent respectively). Unskilled workers, such as clerks and house cleaners, totaled 5 percent.

Surprisingly, the number of self-employed people was small, with very few respondents in the arts or more "far-out" professions, although there was quite a range in actual responses. Included were two massage therapists, a house cleaner, a printer, two lawyers, a horologist, a forest ranger, a storyteller, an architect, a recording engineer, three bank employees, one nutritionist, and four psychologists, to mention a few. There were only seven full-time students—three in high school and four in graduate school—and only three people who reported themselves as unemployed. There were five self-employed people in the group, including a lawyer, a caterer, a musician, and two undefined. Only one person reported herself as a full-time homemaker. Eleven people, or 9 percent, did not respond.

Marital Status

Marital status was defined as single, married, divorced, or widowed. As you might expect, about half of the attendees were single (47 percent) with married and divorced individuals running neck and neck at about a quarter each (25 and 23 percent, respectively). There were only five widowed people, which was not surprising, since most members of the group were in their mid-twenties and mid-thirties.

When asked if they had met their spouses or "significant others" contra dancing, thirty-one, or about a quarter, said yes. Surprisingly, the majority of these respondents reported themselves as single (sixteen), with nine married individuals, five divorced persons, and one widow.

Years Dancing

The responses to this part of the survey reveal that the Princeton area dancers are part of a "mature" group: the median number of years dancing was 5.5, with the average at 5.1. Nineteen respondents reported dancing over ten years, with one dancer having twenty-two years experience—the longest reported. New dancers (dancing less than a year) were the second highest respondents numerically (14 percent), and a number responded that it was their first night—a good sign for the future of the group. Undoubtedly, these numbers vary from week to week. (For a complete tally, see Table 18–3.)

Distance Traveled

In this category, I was interested to see how many dancers were "locals" and how many came from a greater distance. The larger, underlying question, of course, is

Table 18-3
Years of Contra Dance Experience

No.	Years	No.	Years
16	Less than one year	11	Six years
8	One year	5	Seven years
14	Two years	13	Eight years
10	Three years	5	Nine years
5	Four years	19	Ten years or more
10	Five years	2	Nonrespondents

whether the dance is an outgrowth of the community or whether the dance itself made the community. And the latter is very clearly true.

The Princeton Dance attracts people from all over the greater Princeton area, many of whom began dancing when the dance was located more centrally and conveniently in Princeton. Very few people (three respondents) traveled less than five miles to the dance. The average travel distance was sixteen to twenty miles, one way, to attend a Wednesday night dance. (And don't forget, most respondents work.) Six people travel more than forty-one miles one way. See Table 18-4 for a complete breakdown.

Times Per Month

In this category I was curious to see how "fanatical" the average Princeton dancer was when it comes to contra dancing. The average dancer dances about once a week or better, with the average number of times per month pegged at 4.64 and the median times at 4.25, which of course means that people on average attended every Princeton dance. A high number of respondents (14 percent) said they dance six times a month, indicating that they must attend more than one dance (since Princeton meets only once a week). However, the majority attend between one and four times a month (54 percent). Some married respondents reported a drop in attendance following marriage or, most notably, parenthood. See Table 18-5 for the complete breakdown.

Table 18-4
Average Travel Distance One Way to Dance

No.	Travel Distance	No.	Travel Distance
3	1-5 miles	6	26-30 miles
19	6-10 miles	2	31-35 miles
26	11-15 miles	7	36-40 miles
27	16-20 miles	6	41 plus miles
10	21-25 miles	12	Nonrespondents

Table 18-5
Average Times per Month Attendance at Contra Dances

No.	Times per Month	No.	Times per Month
18	1 or less	2	7 times
19	2 times	9	8 times
12	3 times	1	9 times
15	4 times	7	10 or more
11	5 times	10	Nonrespondents
17	6 times		

How Did They Learn About Contra Dancing?

Word of mouth seems to be the most effective way that people learn about contra dancing, with about a third of the respondents citing this as their first source of information. Boy/girlfriends accounted for about a quarter, with other sources, including family members, housemates, coworkers, and newspaper/radio/billboard announcements, about equally divided. One might argue that all these sources, excluding newspaper/radio/billboards, constitute "word-of-mouth" advertising.

Other Dance Experience

I was interested to know whether contra dancers had extensive background in ballet, modern, or jazz dance, or participated in other dance activities such as other types of folk or popular dance. Very few (15 percent) had training in classical dance, although in this group several had multiple training in ballet, modern, or jazz. This training, however, seemed to have little influence on their enjoyment of or participation in contra dancing and was probably a natural part of a middle-class upbringing which often includes ballet training at young ages (particularly for girls). College attendees often take a dance course as part of their liberal arts education.

The group was split about fifty-fifty between those who only contra dance and those who participate in other dance activities. And it was interesting that a number of people wrote emphatically on the form: *I only contra dance*, as if any other form of dancing would be unthinkable. Those who dance other styles, participate in two other dance forms on average. Princeton's own Morris team originated among the contra dancers, so it was not surprising that Morris dancing[7] led the number count, with square dancing close behind.

There were some other interesting juxtapositions. I'll give the remaining categories in order of response; dance forms that were tied are listed together. Aerobics was tied in popularity with swing dancing—the current yuppie/nostalgia craze among Princeton area contra dancers. Clog dancing and Playford/English dance tied at ten apiece, and international folk, ballroom, and pop/disco tied at eight. Scottish (down considerably from what it would have been a decade ago when Princeton had an active Scottish group), was followed by Cajun, Irish, and French

Canadian (Table 18-6). The eclecticism of this response reflects the dance-literacy of the Princeton contra dancers and their own far-flung interests. One person listed T'ai Chi under "other dance forms," arguably a legitimate categorization.

Why Do They Dance?

In this category the respondents had a chance to speak for themselves, as well as checking off several options. The options offered were: "it's good exercise"; "it's a good way to meet people"; "I want to improve my dance skills"; "to relieve stress"; and "to socialize." About one-third of the respondents (29 percent) checked all options, and the majority checked more than one. Among these options, "good exercise" and "socializing" accounted for slightly more than three-quarters of the respondents, with "meeting people" close behind at 67 percent and "relieving stress" at over half. Interestingly, "improving dance skills" ranked the lowest at 42 percent. Apparently, people do not contra dance to become star performers.

Under "other," the leading write-in was "it's fun" at 16 percent. Many people scolded me for not including this in the prepared categories. (As a true sociologist, I don't know if I can admit enjoyment as a legitimate category.) Five respondents said they "love the music," three gave as a reason "promoting the tradition," two said they "enjoy meeting men," and one said he was "addicted" to contra dancing. Five people responded, "Contra dancing is my life"; it was hard to tell how serious they were in making this statement. Two people also commented that contra dancing was "one of the few sports one can totally participate in without any previous training," and two others said they "appreciated the fact that more advanced dancers helped the beginners by leading them through the dance."

Live Music versus Recordings

Not surprisingly, no one said they preferred dancing to records over live music. The folk music community has been a major force at Princeton contra dances. There are two semi-professional bands, Tripping Upstairs and Hold the Mustard, plus a

Table 18-6
Participation in Other Dance Forms

No.	Dance Forms	No.	Dance Forms
16	Morris dance	8	Ballroom
15	Square dance	8	Pop/Disco
11	Aerobics	5	Scottish
11	Swing dance	4	Cajun
10	Clog dance	3	Irish
10	Playford/English dance	1	French Canadian
9	International Folk	1	T'ai Chi

Note: 61 respondents said they participate in other dance activities; 57 said that they only contra dance.

pick-up band that plays for dances once a month. The annual Halloween dance features a mammoth pick-up band called Rum and Onions that has achieved some fame up and down the East Coast. Live music is a major attraction that sets this dance apart from other traditional and pop dances.

Extra-dance Experiences

In the last question on the survey, I wanted to see how many dancers called dances, taught dances, served on the board of directors, or organized special events, in order to gauge the level of involvement in the greater mission of the dance community. A quarter of the respondents had served on the board of the dance—showing the high level of involvement in the management of the dance—with about one fifth involved in organizing special events. About one sixth of the respondents had called or taught contra dances.

COMMENTARY: GROWTH AND CHANGE

Many concerns were raised in my discussions with the dancers that reflect some of the issues raised by the contra dance revival.

Repertoire

Many of the people surveyed have been involved with the Princeton group for ten or more years, and I have played music and danced with the group off and on throughout this period. One of the major changes commented on by a number of participants was the change in repertoire. When the group first started, everyone was a novice: the callers were just learning to call, the musicians were just learning to play music, and the dancers were just learning to dance. People relied on references, such as the *Community Dance Manuals*, which were published by the English Folk Dance and Song Society between 1947 and 1967 and have established the standard contra repertoire for many years. Originally, the Princeton group focused on the "traditional" contras—such as "Petronella" (which was performed every week), "Rory O'Moore," "Lady of the Lake"[8]—and every dance featured at least one English or Playford dance ("Hole in the Wall," "Picking Up Sticks," "The Black Nag"), and one or two square dances. In the early years, the dance always ended with "La Bastringue," a French-Canadian circle dance that was popular at the local international folk dance group. As a musician, I was often chided if I refused to play that number. Once when I introduced the "Burger King" theme in the middle of it, I was in particularly deep trouble.

If you tried to play "La Bastringue" today, you would be run out of the place on a rail; it would be totally unacceptable. Today, a majority of the dances are newly composed, either by the callers themselves or by other young callers throughout the country. Playford/English dances are rarely called and are usually greeted with much grumbling from the regulars. In fact, those who enjoy English dancing broke away to form their own monthly dance, which is usually sparsely attended by only about ten or twenty people. Square dances are also rarely on the program. In fact, one caller recalled an evening when she announced a square only to be faced by a recalcitrant group of dancers formed in contra lines. Only by waiting them out was she able to proceed with the dance.

Style

One of the "burning issues" in the Princeton area is an outgrowth of repertoire and focuses on dance style. There is a group of dancers, the "zesty contra crowd"—dancers who favor energetic contras, dancing with great gusto. The zesty contras take their name from a collection[9] made by caller Larry Jennings of the more progressive, modern contras: high-energy, more complicated figures done to fast music, with a lot of tossing about of women in various directions. They are intolerant of any "sissy" stuff, such as squares, English dances, or even waltzes and less high-powered contras. When Dudley Laufman came to Princeton (one of the founding fathers of the contra revival, as you will recall), the group was impatient with his slow teaching style, simple figures, and the length of each dance, which seemed to go on forever. They prefer the more complex calls of younger dance leaders, and they want each dance to move quickly.

Some of the survey respondents commented on this phenomenon. Interestingly, the zesty versus nonzesty camps seem to divide along sexual lines, with males accounting for most of the zesty contra dancers. One woman called these people the "contra police," presumably because they seek to enforce their rules of performance on everyone else. She objected to their rough handling when they "push or shove people into place." Another woman commented, "I used to think [contra dancing] taught cooperation, but dancers are getting a little cheeky these days . . . a whole bunch of solo dancers instead of a bunch of people dancing with each other, responding to each other." Is this a function of increasing popularity? One well-traveled caller objected to the "movement of contras towards aerobic stimulation and away from a social event."

One zesty contra dancer succinctly expressed this camp's position: "Let's have more and dance harder."

Community

The sense of community is something that has not changed at the Princeton dance. The dance originally centered on a group of college students and town folk who were part of the more left-leaning, politically conscious people pursuing alternative lifestyles. Even in the 1970s, such people felt "different," and the dance helped them find a group of like-minded folk where they could feel comfortable.

Caller Dudley Laufman observed how contra dance in his native New England seemed to attract people from this alternative lifestyle: "Mainly, it's filling the needs of young people. I think it has to do with the Back-to-the-Earth movement and all that; and that they feel they are rejecting the 'plastic society.' "[10]

Many participants in the survey commented on the continued sense of community in the Princeton group. A fiddler said, "The Princeton Country Dance organization has been one of the most open and innovative I have seen in terms of encouraging participation," and his wife said, "It has been a great way to meet people to do things besides dancing: i.e., making quilts, gardening, playing music, hiking, cross country skiing, movies, dinner, cutting wood, hauling manure, and attending concerts."

A musician/dancer said, "It is the closest thing I have found to a neighborhood or community." A woman who has organized many special events and served several times on the Princeton Board said, "The people I have met contra dancing have formed the core of the most wonderful, generous, imaginative, supportive *community* I have ever had the joy to be part of" [her emphasis].

Much has been made in the popular press of the breakdown of the traditional "community." It is undoubtedly true that like-minded people now have to seek each other out through special interest groups like the Princeton contra dance. Although they may have to travel twenty, thirty, or forty miles to attend a dance, the trip brings them back into contact with their natural community.

The core group of dancers socialize together quite frequently. There have been contra dance weddings (the tenth anniversary booklet[11] published by the group claimed over thirty weddings coming from the dance itself), picnics, and other social events. People who met at the Princeton dance have formed other dance groups, such as the local Morris, garland,[12] sword,[13] and Scottish dance groups. Other nondance spin-off groups include a singing group and a new mothers group that meets every Tuesday to share concerns about their babies.

CONCLUSION: TRADITION AND CHANGE

One of the comments I heard from several dancers was that they enjoyed contra dancing because it was "traditional." When I asked a dancer if she would continue to attend the Princeton dance if the same people came but they performed disco dancing, she replied indignantly, "They wouldn't do that!" When I pressed the issue, she still insisted that the people and the dancing went together, that it was impossible to imagine the Princeton group performing nontraditional dance.

Leaving aside the issue of whether contra dancing is truly "traditional," it seems that it is at least important for the dancers to believe it is. They like the notion that they are upholding some "ancient art" and carrying it forward in the face of terrible odds, despite the pressures of the twentieth century. The fact that most of the dances were created recently—and many of the traditional ones have been rearranged beyond recognition—does not seem to have much of an impact on their thinking. In fact, few dancers seem to be aware of the history of the contra revival.

The yuppification of contra dance is not necessarily a bad thing. When I first began contra dancing in New York, many of the older CDSS members took the attitude: "Where were you when we started this tradition?" I can remember many occasions when May Gadd would pull dancers off the floor if they were not performing in the Cecil Sharp-approved manner. There were few other young people at the New York dances, and the general atmosphere was off-putting. CDSS was in shambles, and did not look like it would survive. Certainly, the infusion of young blood has helped spread the contra dance style; there are now 115 CDSS affiliate groups throughout the country.

Perhaps tradition in its broadest sense has been served. The young dancers of Princeton have created new dances, new tunes, and a new dance style, built on what came before. The yuppies have invaded and conquered, but they have also become a part of the traditional process.

NOTES

1. For general background on contra dancing, see Pauline Norton, "Country Dance," *The New Grove Dictionary of American Music*, eds. H. Wiley Hitchcock and Stanley Sadie (London: Macmillan Publishers Ltd., 1986), 1:515, and Richard Nevell, *A Time to Dance: American Country Dancing from Hornpipes to Hot Hash* (New York: St. Martin's Press, 1977), 20, 137-148.

2. A pioneering English collector, Cecil Sharp was the folklorist who spearheaded the traditional dance and music revivals in England. He also made several field trips to Appalachia between 1916 and 1918. He was one of the founders of the English Folk Dance and Song Society (EFDSS).

3. A reprint of the 1651 Playford volume with modern music notation is John Playford, *The English dancing Master or Plaine and easie Rules for the Dancing of Country Dance, with the Tune to each Dance*, eds. Hugh Mellor and Leslie Bridgewater (London: Dance Books Ltd., 1984). A representative cross-section of Playford material, along with a history of the dances, is given in Kate Van Winkle Keller and Genevieve Shimer, *The Playford Ball: One Hundred Three Early English Country Dances* (Pennington, N.J.: a cappella books, 1990).

4. See Beth Tolman and Ralph Page, *The Country Dance Book: The Best of the Early Contras and Squares, Their History, Lore, Callers, Tunes and Joyful Instructions*, rev. ed. (Brattleboro, Vermont: The Stephen Greene Press, 1976). Tolman and Page share their thoughts about country dance (especially on pp. 3–25) and give instructions for various forms, including contra, quadrilles, squares, jigs, reels, horn pipes, polkas, schottisches, and other assorted dances.

5. See Nevell, 100–116.

6. The CDSS has grown as local groups have formed. These smaller groups can gain greater legitimacy by "affiliating" with the national organization.

7. Morris dancing is an English dance form, danced in a set or side of six dancers (two lines of three).

8. Douglas Kennedy, ed., *Community Dances Manual* (Princeton, New Jersey: Dance Horizons/Princeton Book Co., 1986), 60–61.

9. Larry Jennings, *Zesty Contras* (Boston: New England Folk Festival Association, 1983).

10. Nevell, 105.

11. Sue Dupré, *Princeton Country Dancers 10th Anniversary Booklet* (Princeton, New Jersey: Self-published, 1989).

12. Garland dancing is a traditional women's dance performed with large garlands of flowers to welcome in the spring.

13. Sword dancing comes from ritual drama and is performed either with flexible or rigid metal "swords."

Part 4

Practical Suggestions for the Documentation of Dance

Musician Mike Seeger and dance caller Bob Dalsemer have spent considerable time and energy documenting traditional Appalachian dance. Both base their collecting of traditional dance on a philosophy that respects the dancer. Both emphasize the crucial importance of asking the vernacular dancers what is important to them and how they view the place of dancing in their lives. Seeger and Dalsemer remind us that before hoping to achieve any reasonably valid understanding of such fluid and subjective concepts as aesthetics and tradition, researchers must heed the insider's point of view. In line with current practice in disciplines such as folklore and anthropology, they recommend recording context as well as the dance material itself.

Together, they provide a practical manual of dance documentation: ways to preserve the experience of a traditional dance form on videotape and by means of descriptions and through material gleaned from interviews. These are necessary first steps in the effort not only to record a vernacular dance form for posterity, but also to provide contemporary and future scholars with the raw materials for in-depth analysis and comparative study.

Chapter 19

Collecting Traditional Appalachian Square Dances

Robert G. Dalsemer

I am a caller, dancer, and musician who has been interested enough in rural folk music and dance forms to seek them out in an effort to educate myself. As part of this effort, I have visited more than a dozen traditional dance communities—mostly between 1972, when I attended my first "traditional" square dance at the Maryland Line, Maryland, Fire Hall, and 1982, when my book *West Virginia Square Dances* was published by the Country Dance and Song Society. In addition to Maryland and West Virginia dances, I have also observed dances in Pennsylvania, Tennessee, and Virginia.

I define "traditional" dance communities as those where the following conditions exist: 1. there is a continuous tradition of dancing in the community that has spanned several decades or longer, often with the same caller, musicians, and dancers; 2. there is a limited repertoire of dances and/or figures (most often, less than a dozen) that are danced every time a dance is held; 3. it is not customary to teach or walk through dances beforehand; and 4. dancing is performed to live music. These criteria serve to distinguish the kinds of dances I study from modern club square dancing and from those folk revival dances that nowadays tend to be associated with New England contra dancing. By *country dance* I mean a social dance for two or more couples in a set.

I wrote *West Virginia Square Dances*, which contains detailed descriptions of dancing in five West Virginia communities, because I saw a rich living folk tradition from which I and others could learn. Also I was frustrated with the minuscule amount of informed documentation we have about traditional American country dance forms.

The books that did exist left many unanswered questions about dance style, form, structure, and ambiance.

I think that if we are going to understand more about where American folk dance comes from in all its forms, we need to have more collecting done in those communities where there is a strong and relatively unbroken tradition of old-time social dance. There are a number of strong traditions inside and outside Appalachia that should be explored in depth (Pennsylvania, Ohio, Michigan, Missouri, and many parts of Canada come to mind). Collectors should approach such traditions with as wide a knowledge as possible of folklore, folk music, and dance history. Today's traditional dance researchers will have better technology at their disposal: truly portable and affordable audio and video equipment, word processors, and computers, to name a few. But they need to supplement all of this technology with a broad knowledge of square dance. The broader their personal knowledge, the better their observations will be.

As a way of encouraging those people who might want to do some collecting, I want to share some of my recommendations for fieldwork—recommendations based on my general observations and perceptions of some of the common themes I saw running through the different communities I visited. By reading this, you might come to know a little bit more about what I found and what you might wish to look for yourself.

Become as knowledgeable as possible about as many different forms of dance as you can. Be wary of relying on secondhand knowledge. Popular writing about square dance has tended to perpetuate the same myths over and over again. For example, the big circle form of Southeastern square dance is a unique regional style. Many popular articles mistakenly refer to it as "the running set" and imply that it is an ancient form of English country dance, a concept that is unverified and oversimplified. English collector Cecil Sharp observed square dancing on several occasions in Kentucky in the early 1900s and dubbed what he saw "the Kentucky running set."[1] However, the running set was performed in a four-couple square set. The big circle style as we know it today, in which all the dancers are continuously active, appeared to develop in the period between the two World Wars when dances began to take place in public halls rather than private homes. The origins of square dancing in general are perhaps English, but perhaps not. It is an area that requires scholarly study.

Be sure to document all dances, even those you feel are not "traditional." The hallmark of most of today's traditional dances is variety. You will find that there is usually a mixture of square and couple dances, sometimes called *round dances*, in most traditional dance communities. The idea is to have something for everyone. The dances I used to attend at the Maryland Line Fire Hall had a set program: a big circle mixer (popularly called a "Paul Jones"), and a pair of four-couple square dances followed by three round dances. The round dances included such old-time couple dances as the waltz, polka, and schottische, 1950s rock and roll, and novelty dances like the Mexican Hat Dance and Alley Cat, the latter two mainly for children. Then the whole cycle would repeat throughout the evening.

You may not find so broad a range of traditions as I found at Maryland Line, but you will learn a lot about how a community entertains itself and interacts through dance. It is important to take in everything and not just what you came to see.

Note the overall structure of each dance. In square dances, the structure of a dance plays an important part in the learning process, and it is an important element to note. What I mean by structure is the way the individual square dance is built, how it follows a certain pattern.

The overall structure may vary widely from community to community, but it usually remains the same within a given community even though different figures may be introduced into the structure by the caller. For example, in Dunmore, West Virginia, the structure of each square dance (which is in the big circle style) is as follows:

1. Couples make a big circle, then circle left and right.
2. Couples divide into two-couple subsets, then circle left and right.
3. Couples dance a figure of the caller's choice.
4. In the two-couple set, dancers swing the person of the opposite sex who is *not* their partner, then swing their own partner.
5. Move on to another couple and repeat steps two through four.
6. After six to nine repetitions of steps two through five, couples return to a big circle, then circle left and right.
7. Giving right hands to partners, dancers pull past each other (all the men going one way, all the women the other) and dance a "grand right and left" or "grand chain" around the circle. The first time partners meet again, they pass by and continue the chain.
8. The second time partners meet, they turn by the right hand halfway, pull past each other, and grand chain in the reverse direction.
9. When partners meet again, they promenade as couples counterclockwise around the hall.
10. One couple, designated by the caller, stops promenading, faces each other, reaches across taking each other's hands, and makes an arch. The others go under and similarly make arches. When the last couple has gone through, the first couple follows them through the tunnel, and when they emerge they lead the others in a promenade. This ending is locally called "build a bridge" and occurs at the end of every dance.

Each square dance is virtually the same except for the caller's choice of figures in the two-couple subset.

In published works on Southeastern square dance, there is a tendency to emphasize dance figures at the expense of overall structure. They are equally important. The structure of a traditional square dance provides important clues to the community's stability and its relationship to other dance communities.

Expect a limited repertoire of dances and/or figures. In my experience, a community that has a repertoire of ten to twelve figures or dances that most of the dancers can execute has a very highly developed tradition. There are many communities that get by with a much smaller repertoire. Often, as fewer dancers are able to properly execute the more intricate figures, those figures are dropped from the repertoire.

The dancers are quite content to dance the same dances week after week because they are there to enjoy the physical energy and the movement to music. They come to dance, not to perform dances.

This consistency of figures and callers is crucial to the learning process. Together with the stability of the overall dance structure, they make it possible for new dancers to learn the local style without any formal instruction. Most traditional callers do not view teaching as part of their role. In traditional square dancing, particularly in those styles where there is no direct relationship between the figures and the musical phrases, the caller's job is mainly to keep the dancers moving and keep enthusiasm high.

Note the quality of movement—both at a particular traditional dance and as you travel from region to region. In communities with a long, continuous tradition of dance, movements like circles and swings tend to be vigorous but fairly effortless and smooth. The familiarity of the dances promotes smooth transitions, for example, from swings to circles to swings—the staple of Appalachian dance styles. Also note how dancers express the rhythm of the music in their shoulders and upper bodies as well as their feet.

When you move outside an individual community, you will want to take special notice of regional variations. In West Virginia, for example, there is much variation in dance structure. While there are communities that dance in a big circle set, others do four-couple squares. It seems that they either do one or the other, but not both. Look for details. How do people swing? Do they use a walking step (rhythm: right and left and right and left), a two-step (left-right-left and right-left-right, and so on), or a pivot step (right and right and right and right, with weight mostly on the right foot and the left used for balance). Do the dancers use any clogging steps? Sometimes? All the time? What sort of promenade hold do they use? (There are quite a few different ones.) In big circle traditions, how do they get from the big circle into two-couple subsets? Do they number off before the dance, or do they just couple up in seemingly random fashion? Are there any two-couple figures that belong to the southern "do-si-do" family?[2] Have any terms or figures that are not native to Appalachian square dancing been incorporated from other styles? Some examples of these imported figures are the "allemande," "ladies' chain," "right and left through," and "do-si-do" (the latter figure when it refers to a back-to-back movement for two people).

Record whether the dancers frequently change partners or keep the same partner for most of the evening. At folk revival dances, particularly contra dances, it is common for dancers to ask a new partner for each dance. Dancers in traditional rural communities may tend to keep the same partner for most of the evening. In those communities in northern Appalachia (West Virginia, western Pennsylvania) where dancing is still being done in a four-couple square, you may well observe the same four couples dancing together all evening at the same spot on the floor.

Be sure to document the language of square dance calling carefully. Expect to find a variety of square dance terminology. Different communities may have different names for essentially the same figure. For example, "Cowboy Loop" in Kentucky may be called "Lace-the-Shoe" in Tennessee or "Ocean Wave" in North Carolina.[3] You may also find the same name for completely different figures. One observer who seemed oblivious to such nuances complained when "ladies right and left through" was called in New Creek, West Virginia, and the women did another figure instead. Naturally, the ladies at New Creek did precisely what was called; it just meant something different to them than to a New England contra dancer or a modern club square dancer.[4]

Calls are a method of conveying directions to dancers as well as a self-contained art form that has its own rhythm, expression, cadence, rhyme, musicality, melody, and humor. You may find that traditional callers, like traditional singers, occasionally use language they do not fully understand; they just learned it that way. For example, the callers at New Creek, West Virginia, have a call that goes "four hands up and dotsey dice, first to the left and then to the right."[5] None of them could tell me anything about the derivation or meaning of the term *dotsey dice*.

Avoid preconceived notions about the type, style, or instrumentation of music. Live music is perhaps the most important distinguishing element. But the music at long-established traditional dances is more varied and more influenced by modern music than you might expect. For example, despite the fact that during the 1970s it was common among folk revivalists like myself to dismiss amplified music as "not traditional," I found that amplified instruments were the rule rather than the exception in traditional square dance communities. After all, amplified instruments had been around for almost half a century so they had plenty of time to become firmly established in a community's repertoire of dance music.

If you want to learn about traditional country dance fiddle and guitar styles at many rural square dances, listen to country music records of the 1940s, 1950s, and 1960s. Traditional musicians have always been influenced by music that was popular in their formative years. Thus, among fiddlers you may find the influence of Tommy Jackson, a Nashville-based sideman and recording artist of the 1950s, greater than that of Tommy Jarrell, the Mt. Airy, North Carolina, fiddler who was highly influential in the old-time music revival of the 1970s. In fact, I visited some excellent dances where there was no fiddler at all—the lead, even for square dance tunes, was played on electric guitar. Besides fiddles and guitars, I have found drums, accordions, pianos, and horns.

Remember to conduct interviews with callers, musicians, and long-time dancers. They are very useful sources of all kinds of background information. Ask them, for example, how long the dance event has been going on at this location? Where might it have taken place before this? How does the dancing and music today differ from ten, twenty, or thirty years ago? Who are the dancers? Are they local, or do many drive long distances to get there? What organization runs the dances: a volunteer fire company, community association, or grange? Do they hire callers and musicians?

Musicians and callers are often the major promoters of dancing in the area as well as outgoing, informed sources of information. The longevity of a community's dance traditions usually depends on one or more energetic callers and some strong musicians who play on a regular basis and have a following.

I urge those with interest and access to video equipment to record as much old-time dancing as possible. To be able to make relatively inexpensive visual records of traditional folk dance style is something no other generation of dance collectors has been able to do. And style is something that can never really be deciphered from the printed word alone. The data so collected will be indispensable to researchers, folk dance teachers, folk musicians, and of course, future generations of dancers. Besides data we need scholarship: independent, critical thinking based on broad knowledge. Collectors, folklorists, dance ethnologists, historians, and sociologists working together will then be able to give us a far more informed view of our rich folk heritage.

NOTES

1. See Cecil J. Sharp and Maud Karpeles, *The Country Dance Book, Part V: The Running Set* (London: Novello and Company, Ltd., 1918).

2. Two examples of southern "do-si-do" figures are the "Georgia Rang Tang" and the Kentucky "do-si-do." In the "Georgia Rang Tang," the dancers turn their opposites by the right hand and then turn their partners by the left hand, repeat the first two turns and then swing their opposites. The Kentucky "do-si-do" is similar to the "Georgia Rang Tang," except that dancers begin by turning their partners by the left hand and end with a partner promenade.

3. This family of two-couple figures begins in a circle. The active man drops hands with the opposite woman, then leads his partner in a clockwise direction under an arch made by the arms of his partner and the opposite man. He then circles around his partner's original position and leads his partner and the opposite man under an arch made by the arms of the opposite couple. He continues circling clockwise until all are back in their original positions.

4. At New Creek, "ladies right and left through" means ladies change places with each other, usually turning by the left hand following the call "left hands across," also known as a "left hand star." For definitions of other right-and-left-throughs, see, Ted Sannella, *Balance and Swing* (New York: Country Dance & Song Society, 1982); Larry Jennings, *Zesty Contras* (Wellesley Hills: New England Folk Festival Association, 1983); Betty Casey, *The Complete Book of Square Dancing* (Garden City, New York: Doubleday and Co., Inc., 1976); or Jane A. Harris, Anne M. Pittman, and Marlys S. Waller, *Dance A While* (New York: Macmillan College Publishing Co., 1994).

5. Robert G. Dalsemer, *West Virginia Square Dances* (New York: Country Dance & Song Society, 1982), 15.

Chapter 20

How To Document Dance: From the Notes to *Talking Feet*

Mike Seeger

Talking Feet is an eighty-seven minute video documentary produced by Mike Seeger and Ruth Pershing on the subject of percussive footwork, known variously in the Southern United States as flatfooting, buckdancing, hoedown, or rural tap dancing.[1] It is the first such documentary and is designed for students, dance enthusiasts, dancers, and the general audience. *Talking Feet* was funded by the Smithsonian Institution and the Folk Arts program of the National Endowment for the Arts.

Following are excerpts from the 142-page book that accompanies the documentary. The book provides background on the project, general information about the dances, an analysis of the various styles of percussive dance, descriptive tablature for several of the dances, background on the dancers, and excerpts from interviews with them. In addition, it includes the following suggestions for the individual undertaking film or video documentation of traditional dance. I would like to pass on some suggestions for those of you who might want to document dance. I will make suggestions for two basic groups: the home recordist and the professional.

AMATEUR VIDEOGRAPHERS

Use as good a camera as you can afford. Currently, technology is changing so rapidly that I cannot recommend a certain type of camera/recorder. Before you purchase a camcorder, consult a variety of stores, "consumer report" type magazines, or call someone at an audiovisual center at a nearby college or university. I suggest buying at discount mail order stores. If you cannot afford to purchase a video recording camera and are unable to borrow one, they are sometimes available from colleges, universities, or arts organizations.

Refer to a couple of good texts that will help you in your documentation. These include *Field Work* by folklorist Bruce Jackson,[2] and *Home Video Production* by John Melville Bishop.[3] Jackson devotes an entire chapter to "movies" in which he talks briefly about the various pieces of equipment and techniques involved in filming and videotaping; Bishop's book discusses very helpful techniques for the nonprofessional video-documentor.

Practice using the camera before you go into the field. Anyone can learn to use a video camera, but it takes practice to be really effective.

What To Film and How To Film It

- Identify the dancers, musicians, tune titles, and date audibly on the tape.
- Use your viewfinder to compose the shot.
- For solo dancing, you want to see the dancer in the screen from head to toe, with a little room to spare on the top and bottom.
- Use two cameras at the same time if you can, one for full-length shots and one for close-ups. Film the close-ups from the knees down, especially if the feet are important, as they are in Appalachian clogging, flatfooting, or buckdancing. Otherwise, use the second camera for any details that are crucial to the dance form you are recording.
- The dancers should mostly face the full-length camera, while the close-up camera should be from the side. If you and your dancers have plenty of time, reverse these and shoot from various angles. If you do not have sufficient distance to film a dancer from head to toe (usually about twenty-five feet), focus on the feet for a while, then slowly move the camera up so that you show the essence of the entire body movement.
- It is best to focus on one dance event or on one community rather than to attempt many superficial visits to a number of dance events or communities.
- If you can, record at the actual locations and occasions where the dancing naturally takes place, such as at dances or at home. This can be difficult because it is an intrusion into a social situation. On the other hand, the film crew's presence can transform the dance into a special event.
- Try to get your dancers' favorite musicians for your sessions. If that is not possible, use their favorite records.
- When recording a dance event, film as many dances as you can. Most southern dancers do not have arranged pieces. They improvise as moves occur to them, and each dance can be quite different.
- You might want to ask dancers and musicians to come to a dance a little early or stay a little late on the night of a public dance so that you can record. Film as long as you can before and after, as comments and context are important. Take your time; videotape is cheap. If you can manage it, other aspects of the dance should be recorded as well for their context value.

- Talk with your dancers, at their homes if possible. Ask them how dance fits into their lives, what it means to them, and so forth. If appropriate, ask them to demonstrate some of their steps or movements slowly for you.
- You have to use your judgment—and social skill.

Technical Considerations

- It is best to use a tripod under your camera.
- Filming inside a home can be a challenge because of poor lighting, bad acoustics, and the lack of sufficient room to get full-length shots of dancers.

Lighting can pose some special challenges when filming dance:

- If possible, film outside but not in direct sun.
- Lighting at indoor dances is usually dim. You can try to work around this problem in several ways: You might try to get dancers to come over to a corner where you have set up a couple of lights; you might get permission to use brighter lights at a dance for at least a portion of the evening; or you might use one of the new cameras that have the capability of shooting in low light. If you do need to use lights, you can set a couple of flood-lights at a forty-five degree angle to the subject. It is possible to get special lights and bulbs for this purpose. They should cost about fifty dollars a pair.

There are also special technical considerations when it comes to recording sound at dances:

- If inside, try for a live wooden floor. By a "live" wooden floor, I mean one that gives a little and is not on concrete. This provides good sound and protects the legs and back from injury. If outside, have the dancer perform on a porch, a plywood sheet or, even better, a platform supported by two-by-fours. Whether inside or outside, be sure that the background is as plain and uncluttered as possible.
- If your camera has provisions for external microphones, you can improve recorded sound immensely by recording in stereo, using one channel for music and the other for dance sounds. With careful placement of musicians around a single microphone, you can get a good musical sound. You will, of course, need to have the dancer fairly close to the music. This proximity is what makes recording foot sounds so difficult since the music will obscure the sound of the feet on the foot-sound microphone. A hand-held ultradirectional mike aimed at the feet is best, but a directional mike similarly aimed will usually do. Sometimes laying the mike on a cloth foam pad or "mouse" on the stage close to the feet will work. Experiment, but try to keep the feet sound separate from the music by getting the mike close to and aimed at the feet.

FOR THE PROFESSIONAL

For the professional, I add the following the suggestions:

- Engage a dance specialist, and plan carefully the intent and execution of the project.

- In order to avoid problems with copyright clearance, do your best to have musicians play traditional pieces.

- Have fair contracts with your musicians and dancers; pay them, and give them video copies of their dancing.

- Have sufficient personnel at the recording session to deal with the artists, with technical matters, and to document the session.

- We encourage using 16mm film rather than videotape since it has superior resolution quality and permanence. There are, however, advantages to videotape. Videotape is cheaper, gives you the option of viewing the material immediately, is easier to edit in some ways, and does not necessitate the cutting of the master, so that all recorded material remains intact. Hollywood professionals enjoy the best of both worlds by using a video-recorder simultaneously with a film camera so that the performance may be viewed immediately.

- When recording, be very sure that your camera operator is filming the appropriate material in the appropriate way as suggested above; that is, filming a dancer full-length, staying with each shot a good long while.

- Similarly, when editing, do not cut quickly from shot to shot. Stay with each shot awhile so that the viewer can get a solid feel for the subject. As much as possible, cutaways should be to other shots of the dance, not just reaction shots designed to prevent viewer boredom.

- Whatever you do, remember that the film you shoot has permanent archival value. Keep all master recordings or films. Even better, donate them to an archive. Under no circumstances should you cut up the only negative in the editing process. Either make a duplicate negative or print for archival purposes, or copy onto videotape the segments that you expect to use and then edit your production on video. If you edit on film, a cheaper option is to make a duplicate of those takes that will actually be used in the final cut so that a film version of all material may be archived. Archives such as The Archive of Folk Culture at the Library of Congress, the Southern Folklife Collection at the University of North Carolina-Chapel Hill, the Dance Collection at the New York Public Library, or the Archives of Appalachia at East Tennessee State University would be interested in receiving copies of your recordings.

- Use your art to communicate the art and integrity of the dance.

NOTES

1. Mike Seeger and Ruth Pershing, *Talking Feet: Solo Southern Dance: Flatfoot, Buck, and Tap*, 87-min., color, VHS and Beta 1/2-inch video documentary (El Cerrito, California: Flower Films, 1988).

2. Bruce Jackson, *Field Work* (Urbana: University of Illinois Press, 1987).

3. John Melville Bishop, *Home Video Production: Getting the Most from Your Video Equipment* (New York: McGraw-Hill, 1986).

Conclusion

What is tradition? What is community? How do tradition and community shape dance, and how does dance help to shape tradition and community? These are the central issues that emerged as we listened to vernacular dancers and shared research with them and with dance researchers.

The definition of tradition is a work-in-progress. At times, scholars have understood tradition to be "lore," a body of knowledge that is the exclusive property of pre-literate oral cultures. In contrast, some apply *tradition* to the whole culture, not just certain facets of that culture. In other instances, writers equate tradition with performance, or regard it as a set of rules, standards, and symbols governing human behavior. Finally, some have viewed tradition as being essentially a transmission process by which a body of knowledge and beliefs from the past is passed down relatively intact from generation to generation, largely by oral means or by example. Tradition has been placed at the opposite end of the spectrum from creativity, change, popular culture, elite culture, civilization, and literacy. The list could go on. Because *tradition* tries to describe such a complex reality and is so commonly used by so many people in so many contexts, it may always be a work-in-progress.

Nevertheless, although we are not prepared to settle the long-running debate over the definition of tradition, we do feel qualified to participate in the ongoing discussions about the nature of tradition. One of our discoveries is that dance forms widely regarded as traditional—forms such as old-time square dance or indigenous preservation attempts—have much in common with the outsider "revivals" often dismissed as non-traditional. In fact, we were far more struck by their similarities than by their differences.

Very few of either the "traditional" or "outsider" forms have been passed from generation to generation in an unbroken line. Continuous traditions, such as old-time dance in Fancy Gap in Virginia's Blue Ridge Mountains, are rare. More commonly, the popularity of vernacular dance ebbs and flows. Old-time square dancing in Chilhowie, Virginia, footwork dancing in Dante, Virginia, Cherokee tribal dance in North Carolina, and contra dance revivalists and historical reconstructionists all over the country are all examples of vernacular dance resumed after a period of relative dormancy.

Placing "traditional" vernacular dance in opposition to civilization or to popular and elite cultures is unrealistic. As folklorist Richard Blaustein notes, it is difficult to find a tradition so isolated and conservative that it has not been affected by cosmopolitan, national, or international trends. For example, the Green Grass Cloggers integrate elements of Western club square dance, a highly organized, twentieth-century form of square dance, and the Dante old-time dancers incorporate elements of the Charleston.

As is often the case in modern America, these dance traditions are disseminated by means of printed materials, as well as by oral transmission and instruction by example. Cherokee revivalists, contra dancers, and historical reconstructionists have all been known to use manuals that provide a blueprint for the dance in question, but they then proceed to fill in the details. Those details reflect a combination of cultural aesthetics, beliefs, values, personal taste, and the creative interplay between the individual and the community.

In "Dance, Our Dearest Diversion," Merry Feyock comes to much the same conclusion about the crucial relationship between written text and interpreter as a result of her work with historical dance reconstruction. Historical dance reconstructors attempt to be as faithful as possible to the original structure and style of the dance in question. However, Feyock notes how few country dances were notated during the eighteenth century; she explains that the eighteenth-century dance reconstructionists of necessity try to assemble the bits and pieces they can find into a "meaningful and contextually believable whole." This is not a process that she sees confined to twentieth-century reconstructionists working with sketchy materials. "I am personally convinced—although others, I am sure, will disagree with me—that there are as many interpretations of a given dance as there are modern historian-choreographers to interpret it, each in his or her own way. Indeed, it must have been so in the eighteenth century."[1]

Dancers, then, are certainly in the habit of altering and elaborating on the dance elements they find in written texts. They also can, and often do, change any and all dance elements, including those that have been transmitted orally or by example. All such received traditional elements potentially undergo the same process as the one Feyock describes. After comparing similar social dance traditions in Appalachia and Newfoundland, similarities that cannot be explained by any form of direct or indirect influence, Colin Quigley concluded that this process of taking certain expressive forms and elements from the past and then tailoring them to fit current circumstances is common. "Dancers of the past and of isolated rural areas have been no less active and creative in devising movement responses to their particular experience than the urbanites generally represented by surviving dancing masters' collections or today's revivalists," he asserts.[2]

Vernacular dances, according to our definition, are all community based. Communities in modern America take a variety of forms. Some are rooted in a particular geographic area. More often, in today's complex, highly mobile society, communities are based on shared interests, values, ideals, or memories. For example, Eileen Carson is a "revivalist" clogger who was raised in the Washington, D.C., area by parents who left their East Tennessee home in search of better paying jobs. She poses the question, "Where is the community? I have found my whole community on the road, not in the neighborhood where I live. My community is at festivals. It's those festivals that have shaped me. We live in a different time. People are able to travel and pick their community."[3] Consequently, the task of explaining the relationship among tradition, community, and dance is not simple.

Again, it is the old-time dancing in the Blue Ridge community of Fancy Gap that fits a common conception of traditional dance. The community is rural and fairly well defined. Change occurs slowly, and square dancing has a long history of being an important means of social interaction for the community.

Again though, Fancy Gap is the exception rather than the rule. As we see with square dance in Hoagland, Indiana, even where the dance form is fairly stable, the community itself has loosened from its moorings in a specific place.

In these chapters, we see communities, or at least certain segments within a particular community, using vernacular dance to make a statement about who they are. Striking miners, the Cherokee, African American steppers, and mountaineers all employ their chosen dance forms to proclaim their unique history, their belief that they are perpetuating that particular heritage and the special cultural identity that grows out of that history and heritage. While we have much in common with mainstream society, their dance says, we also have much that is different, and we are proud of those differences. Internally, dance can sometimes quite literally help the dancers to create a sense of cohesion, to help form the group. At other times, the dance expresses tensions within the community.

Finally, in many cases people come together in seemingly random groups to perform old-time square or Green Grass-style clogging, to re-enact historical dances, or to participate in contra groups. These individuals generally do not have as conscious or well-articulated a cultural identity as do the striking miners or fraternity members. However, although we cannot be certain until we conduct surveys such as the one developed by Richard Carlin, we suspect that certain types of people bound together by similar views and values are attracted to specific types of vernacular dance that they associate with those perspectives. These people often seem to be relatively younger—often, though not always, professionals—who work in competitive workplaces and live in neighborhoods that function simply as places to live. Or they are older people, retired or nearing retirement, who no longer automatically connect with society through their children or by means of their roles as workers.

Although it is a function of vernacular dance in all manner of communities, for these people the sense of being a part of something larger than themselves is partic-

ularly important. Dance creates this sense of community through the personal relationships formed by becoming part of the group and by the very act of dancing itself.
Furthermore, a particular dance form demonstrates through its structure and style
the type of community that the dancers define for themselves. For example, the
African American steppers' unified, highly synchronized dance style directly parallels the very cohesive, conformist ethos of their fraternities and sororities. Dance can
generate this sense of community regardless of whether it is a social form, such as
old-time square or contra, or a performance form such as stepping or Green Grass
Clogging.

We return to the point that communities of dancers do not just passively hand on
the dance forms as they have received them. They may be attracted to a particular
form of dance because it is consistent with their culture or because it mirrors how
they see themselves. They then proceed to fine tune that dance form in accordance
with their experience, values, ideals, and needs. Spalding notes that Chilhowie
dancers, in both their square dance and their clogging, prize variety and skill more
than their Blue Ridge neighbors. She speculates that this results from their faster-
paced lifestyle in a location better positioned to be affected by the crosscurrents of
mainstream culture. Modern Cherokee simplify and tame the once bellicose eagle
dance, eliminating the tales of war exploits. Contra dancers start out with relatively
simple country dances found in historical sources and over time show a preference
for a more rapid, more complex and challenging style requiring considerable mental
concentration.

Dance changes as communities change. And tradition is the process by which
communities strike a balance, attempting to create vernacular dances that manage
simultaneously to keep faith with the past and to reflect current beliefs and needs.
Ironically, when proponents of a particular dance form become so intent on preserving the "pure" and correct version of vernacular dance that they fail to allow the
communities of dancers to make any modifications, they may, in fact, be contribut-
ing to its demise. The Bidstrups' efforts to introduce Scandinavian dance to the
southern Appalachians is a case in point. Tradition involves conservation and invention, change and creativity (both individual and group), and continuity. Tradition,
as folklorist John Bealle so aptly put it, is "a verb, not a noun."[4]

NOTES

1. See Merry Feyock, "Dance, Our Dearest Diversion," in this volume.

2. See Colin Quigley, "Anglo-American Dance in Appalachia and Newfoundland," in
this volume.

3. Eileen Carson, concluding discussion of the 1990 Southern Dance Traditions Conference, East Tennessee State University, Johnson City, Tennessee, 2 March 1990.

4. John Bealle, concluding discussion of the 1990 Southern Dance Traditions Conference,
East Tennessee State University, Johnson City, Tennessee, 2 March 1990.

Bibliography

PUBLICATIONS AND ARCHIVAL MATERIALS

Adair, James. *Adair's History of the American Indians.* Ed. Samuel Cole Williams. Johnson City, Tennessee: The Watauga Press, 1930.

Aldrich, Elizabeth. *From the Ballroom to Hell: Grace and Folly in Nineteenth-Century Dance.* Evanston, Illinois: Northwestern University Press, 1991.

Allen, Frederick Lewis. *Only Yesterday.* 1931. Reprint. New York: Bantam Books, 1959.

Babcock, Barbara A. "The Story in the Story: Metanarration in Folk Narrative." *Verbal Art as Performance.* Ed. Richard Bauman. Rowley, Massachusetts: Newbury House, 1977: 61–80.

Bateson, Gregory. "A Theory of Play and Fantasy." *Steps to an Ecology of Mind.* Ed. Gregory Bateson. New York: Ballantine, 1972: 177–193.

Bauman, Richard. "Differential Identity and the Social Base of Folklore." *Toward New Perspectives in Folklore.* Eds. Americo Paredes and Richard Bauman. Austin: University of Texas Press, 1972: 31–41.

Bellah, Robert, et. al. *Habits of the Heart: Individualism and Commitment in American Life.* New York: Harper & Row, 1985.

Bender, Thomas. *Community and Social Change in America.* Baltimore: Johns Hopkins University Press, 1978.

Benson, Norman. "The Itinerant Dancing and Music Masters of Eighteenth Century America." Ph.D. dissertation, University of Minnesota, 1963.

Beverely, Robert. *The History and Present State of Virginia.* Ed. Louis B. Wright. Chapel Hill: University of North Carolina Press, 1947.

Bishop, John Melville. *Home Video Production: Getting the Most from Your Video Equipment.* New York: McGraw-Hill, 1986.

Blaustein, Richard. "Traditional Music and Social Change: The Old Time Fiddlers Association Movement in the United States." Dissertation, Indiana University, 1975.

Bovbjerg, Viggo. *Swedish Schottische.* Chicago: Recreation Training School of Chicago, n.d.

Boyden, David. "The Violin." *Musical Instruments Through the Ages.* Ed. Anthony Baines. Baltimore: Penguin, 1961: 97–122.

Breathnach, Breandan. *Folkmusic and Dances of Ireland.* Dublin: Browne and Noland, 1971.

Brunvand, Jan Harold. *The Study of American Folklore: An Introduction.* 2nd ed. New York: W.W. Norton & Co., 1978.

Buckland, Theresa. "English Folk Dance Scholarship: A Review." *Traditional Dance, Volume I.* Ed. Theresa Buckland. Crewe, England: Crewe & Alsageer College of Higher Education, 1982.

Burchenal, Elizabeth, ed. and trans. *Folk-dances of Denmark.* New York: G. Schirmer, 1915.

——. *Folk-Dances and Singing Games.* n.p., 1909.

——. *Folk-dances of Finland.* New York: G. Schirmer, 1915.

——. *Dances of the People.* New York: Schirmer Music, 1913.

Burnaby, Andrew. *Travels through the Middle Settlements in North-America. In the Years 1759 and 1760. With Observations upon the State of the Colonies.* 2nd ed. London: T. Payne, 1775.

Burns, Thomas A. with Doris Mack. "Social Symbolism in a Rural Square Dance Event." *Southern Folklore Quarterly,* vol. 42, no. 4 (1978): 295–327.

Byrd, William. *Another Secret Diary of William Byrd of Westover, 1739–1741. With Letters & Literary Exercises 1696–1726.* Ed. Maude H. Woodfin and trans. Marion Tinling. Richmond, Virginia: Dietz Press, 1942.

——. *The London Diary (1717–1721) and Other Writings.* Eds. Louis B. Wright and Marion Tinling. New York: Oxford University Press, 1958.

——. *The Secret Diary of William Byrd of Westover, 1709–1712.* Eds. Louis B. Wright and Marion Tinling. Richmond, Virginia: Dietz Press, 1941.

Campbell, John C. *The Southern Highlander and His Homeland.* New York: Russell Sage Foundation, 1921.

Campbell, Olive D. and Cecil J. Sharp. *English Folk Songs from the Southern Appalachians.* New York: Putnam, 1917.

Carillo, Loretta. "Dance." *Handbook of American Popular Culture.* Ed. Thomas Inge, 2nd ed. Westport, Connecticut: Greenwood Press, 1989: 259–278.

Carson, Jane. *Colonial Virginians at Play.* Williamsburg, Virginia: Colonial Williamsburg Foundation, 1989.

Casey, Betty. *The Complete Book of Square Dancing (and Round Dancing).* Garden City, New York: Doubleday & Co., 1976.

Chaney, David. *Fictions and Ceremonies: Representations of Popular Experience.* London: Edward Arnold, 1979.

Coburn, Letitia. "Juba and Ring Shout: African-American Dances of the Antebellum South." Paper presented at the Southern Dance Traditions Conference, East Tennessee State University, March 1990.

Cooke, Benjamin G. "Nonverbal Communication Among Afro-Americans: An Initial Classification." *Rappin' and Stylin' Out: Communication in Urban Black America.* Ed. Thomas Kochman, Urbana: University of Illinois Press, 1972: 32–64.

Cooke, Peter. "The Bride's Reel in Cullivoe, Shetland." *Traditional Dance, Volume III.* Ed. Theresa Buckland. Crewe, England: Crewe & Alsageer College of Higher Education, 1982.

Cresswell, Nicholas. *The Journal of Nicholas Cresswell, 1774-1777.* New York: Dial Press, 1924.

Dalsemer, Robert G. *West Virginia Square Dances.* New York: Country Dance & Song Society, 1982.

Damon, S. Foster. *The History of Square Dancing.* Barre, Massachusetts: Barre Gazette, 1957.

Daniel, Jack L. and Geneva Smitherman. "How I Got Over: Communication Dynamics in the Black Community." *Quarterly Journal of Speech,* vol. 62 (1976): 26-39.

Dommet, Roy. "The Kitchen Lancers." *English Dance and Song,* vol. 41, no. 3 (1979): 7.

Duke, Jerry. *Clog Dance in the Appalachian Mountains.* San Francisco: Duke Publishing Co., 1984.

Dukes, Nicholas. *A Concise & Easy Method of Learning the Figuring Part of Country Dances by way of Characters. To which is Prefixed the Figure of the Minuet, by Nicholas Dukes, Dancing Master.* London, 1752.

Dundes, Alan. "The Devolutionary Premise in Folklore Theory." *Journal of the Folklore Institute,* vol. 6, no. 1 (January-April 1969): 5-19.

Dupré, Sue. *Princeton Country Dancers 10th Anniversary Booklet.* Princeton, New Jersey: Self-published, 1989.

Eaton, Allen H. *Handicrafts of the Southern Highlands.* 1937. Rev. ed. New York: Dover Publications Inc., 1973.

Ehle, John. *Trail of Tears: The Rise and Fall of the Cherokee Nation.* New York: Anchor Books/Doubleday, 1988.

Eller, Ronald D. *Millers, Millhands and Mountaineers: The Modernization of the Appalachian South, 1880-1930.* Ann Arbor, Michigan: University Microfilms International, 1976.

Emery, Lynne Fauley. *Black Dance from 1619 to Today.* 2nd ed. Princeton, New Jersey: Princeton Book Co., 1988.

Emmerson, George S. *A Social History of Scottish Dance: Ane Celestial Recreatioun.* Montreal: McGill-Queen's University Press, 1972.

Epstein, Dena J. *Sinful Tunes and Spirituals: Black Folk Music to the Civil War.* Urbana: University of Illinois Press, 1977.

Essex, John. *For the Further Improvement of Dancing.* London: Walsh, 1710.

Evans, J. P. "Sketches of Cherokee Characteristics." *Journal of Cherokee Studies,* vol. 4, no. 1 (Winter 1979): 10-20.

Feintuch, Burt. "Dancing to the Music: Domestic Square Dances and Community in South-central Kentucky (1880-1940)." *Journal of the Folklore Institute,* vol. 18, no. 1 (January-April 1981): 49-68.

Feuillet, Raoul Auger. *Orchesography or the Art of Dancing ye Characters and Demonstrative Figures . . . Being an Exact and Just Translation from the French of Monsieur Feuillet.* Trans. John Weaver. 2nd ed. London: John Walsh, ca. 1715.

Feyock Merry. "The Dance in English Society, 1500-1800." Research report for Colonial Williamsburg, 1982.

Finger, Bill. "The Limits of a Folk Hero." *Southern Exposure,* vol. 2 (Spring 1974): 27-37.

Finger, John R. *Cherokee Americans: The Eastern Band of Cherokees in the Twentieth Century.* Lincoln, Nebraska: University of Nebraska Press, 1991.

——. *The Eastern Band of Cherokees 1819-1900.* Knoxville: University of Tennessee Press, 1984.

Fithian, Philip Vickers. *The Journal and Letters of Philip Vickers Fithian, 1773-1774. A Plantation Tutor of the Old Dominion.* Ed. Hunter Dickinson Farish. Williamsburg, Virginia: Colonial Williamsburg, 1957.

Flett, J. P. and T. M. *Traditional Step-Dancing in Lakeland.* London: English Folk Dance & Song Society, 1979.

——. *Traditional Dancing in Scotland.* London and Boston: Routledge & Kegan Paul, 1964.

Ford, Mr. & Mrs. Henry. *Good Morning.* Dearborn, Michigan: The Dearborn Publishing Co., 1926.

Frazier, E. Franklin. *Black Bourgeoisie: The Rise of a New Middle Class in the United States.* New York: The Free Press, 1962.

French, Laurence and Jim Hornbuckle. "The Cherokees—Then and Now: An Historical Glance." *The Cherokee Perspective.* Eds. Laurence French and Jim Hornbuckle. Boone, North Carolina: Appalachian Consortium Press, 1981: 3-14.

——. "The Contemporary Scene." *The Cherokee Perspective.* Eds. Laurence French and Jim Hornbuckle, Boone, North Carolina: Appalachian Consortium Press, 1981: 26-43.

Friedland, Lee Ellen. "Traditional Folk Dance in Kentucky." *Country Dance and Song,* vol. 10 (1979): 5-19.

Gallini, Giovanni Andrea. *New Collection of Forty-Four Cotillions, With Figures properly adapted; Also the Music for Six select Dances, Two of which may be used as Cotillions.* London, 1770.

——. *Critical Observations On The Art of Dancing.* London, 1770.

Gates, Henry Louis Jr. *The Signifying Monkey: A Theory of Afro-American Literary Criticism.* Oxford and New York: Oxford University Press, 1988.

Gillespie, Angus K. "Pennsylvania Folk Festivals in the 1930s." *Pennsylvania Folklife,* vol. 26 (Fall 1976): 2-11.

Grant, John L. "Behavioral Premises in the Culture of Conservative Eastern Cherokee Indians." Masters thesis, University of North Carolina-Chapel Hill, 1957.

Green, Archie. "Commercial Music Graphics: Thirteen." *John Edwards Memorial Foundation Quarterly,* vol. 6 (Summer 1970): 70-73.

——. "Commercial Music Graphics No. 32: The National Folk Festival Association." *John Edwards Memorial Foundation Quarterly,* vol. 11 (Spring 1975): 23-32.

Gulick, John. *Cherokees at the Crossroads.* Chapel Hill: Institute for Research in Social Science, University of North Carolina, 1960.

Hall, Frank. "Improvisation and Fixed Composition in Clogging." *Journal for the Anthropological Study of Human Movement,* vol. 3 (1984-1985): 200-217.

Harris, Jane A., Anne M. Pittman, and Marlys S. Waller. *Dance A While.* New York: Macmillan College Publishing, Co., 1994.

Hilton, Wendy. *Dance of Court and Theater. The French Noble Style, 1690-1725.* Ed. Caroline Gaynor. Princeton, New Jersey: Princeton Book Company, 1981.

Hitchcock, Hugh Wiley. *Music in the United States: An Historical Introduction.* Englewood Cliffs, New Jersey: Prentice-Hall, 1969.

Hoffman, Richard L. "Community in Action: Innovative and Coordinative Strategies in the War on Poverty." Ph.D. dissertation, University of North Carolina, 1969.

Hood, Evelyn. *The Story of Scottish Country Dancing.* Great Britain: William Collins & Sons Co., 1980.

Hoyer, Raymond A., comp. *Games for Play Institutes.* Louisville, Kentucky: Community Council Recreation Committee, 1921.

Hudson, Charles. *The Southeastern Indians.* Knoxville: University of Tennessee Press, 1976.

Hunter, Robert Jr. *Quebec to Carolina in 1795-1786: Being the Travel Diary and Observations of Robert Hunter, Jr., a Young Merchant of London.* Eds. Louis B. Wright and Marion Tinling. San Marino, Calif.: Huntington Library, 1943.

Jackson, Bruce. *Field Work.* Urbana: University of Illinois Press, 1987.

Jackson, Florence. "Blocking: A General Overview." Course paper, Virginia Polytechnic Institute & State University, 1984.

Jakobson, Roman. "Closing Statement: Linguistics and Poetics." *Style in Language.* Ed. T. A. Sebeok. New York: John Wiley & Sons, 1960: 350-377.

Jenkins, Jane R. "Social Dance in North Carolina Before the Twentieth Century—An Overview." Ph.D. dissertation, University of North Carolina-Greensboro, 1978.

Jennings, Larry. *Zesty Contras.* Boston: New England Folk Festival Association, 1983.

Jenyns, Soame. *The Art of Dancing &c. A Poem in 3 Cantos.* London, 1729.

Jones, Hugh. *The Present State of Virginia. From Whence is Inferred a Short View of Maryland and North Carolina.* Ed. Richard Morton. Chapel Hill: University of North Carolina Press, 1956.

Jones, Loyal. "The Minstrel of the Appalachians: Bascom Lamar Lunsford at 91." *John Edwards Memorial Foundation Quarterly,* vol. 9 (Spring 1973): 2-7.

——. *Minstrel of the Appalachians: The Story of Bascom Lamar Lunsford.* Boone, North Carolina: Appalachian Consortium Press, 1984.

Kaeppler, Adrienne L. "Method and Theory in Analyzing Dance Structure with an Analysis of Tongan Dance." *Ethnomusicology,* vol. 16, no. 2 (May 1972): 173-217.

——. "Structured Movement Systems in Tonga." *Society and the Dance.* Ed. Paul Spencer, Cambridge: Cambridge University Press, 1985: 92-114.

Keller, Kate Van Winkle and Carolyn Rabson. *The National Tune Index.* New York: University Music Editions, 1980.

—— and Genevieve Shimer. *The Playford Ball: One Hundred Three Early English Country Dances.* Pennington, New Jersey: a cappella books, 1990.

—— and Ralph Sweet. *Choice Selection of American Country Dances of the Revolutionary Era, 1775-1795.* New York: Country Dance & Song Society, 1976.

Keller, Robert. *Dance Figure Index of American Country Dances, 1730-1810.* Sandy Hook, Connecticut: The Hendrickson Group, 1989.

Kennedy, Douglas, ed. *Community Dances Manual, Books 1-7.* Princeton, New Jersey: Dance Horizons/Princeton Book Co., 1986.

Kline, Michael. "Where the Ravens Roost." *Old-Time Herald,* vol. 2, no. 5 (August-October, 1990): 24-28.

Knott, Sarah Gertrude. "The National Folk Festival After Twelve Years." *Western Folklore,* vol. 5 (1946): 83-93.

Kochman, Thomas. "Toward an Ethnography of Black American Speech Behavior." *Rappin' and Stylin' Out: Communication in Urban Black America.* Ed. Thomas Kochman. Urbana: University of Illinois Press, 1972: 241-264.

Labov, William. "Rules for Ritual Insults." *Rappin' and Stylin' Out: Communication in Urban Black America.* Ed. Thomas Kochman. Urbana: University of Illinois Press, 1972: 265-314.

Langley, Joan and Wright. *Yesterday's Asheville.* Miami: E.A. Seeman Publishing, Inc., 1975.

Levine, Lawrence W. *Black Culture and Black Consciousness: Afro-American Folk Thought from Slavery to Freedom.* Oxford and New York: Oxford University Press, 1977.

Lewis, Helen et al. "Family, Religion, and Colonialism in Central Appalachia." *Growin' Up Country.* Ed. Jim Axelrod. Clintwood, Virginia: Council of the Southern Mountains, 1973: 131–156.

Lipset, Seymour M. and Earl Raab. *The Politics of Unreason.* New York: Harper & Row, 1970.

Malone, Bill C. *Country Music, U.S.A.: A Fifty Year History.* 1968. Rev. ed. Austin: University of Texas Press, 1985.

March Stephen, and David Holt. "Chase That Rabbit." *Southern Exposure,* vol. 5 (Summer/Fall 1977): 44–47.

Martin, Harold H. "Minstrel Man of the Appalachians." *Saturday Evening Post,* vol. 220 (May 22, 1948): 31.

Matthews, Gail. "Cutting a Dido: A Dancer's Eye View of Mountain Dance in Haywood County, North Carolina." M. A. thesis, Indiana University, 1983.

Matthews-DeNatale, Gail. "Kinesic Conversations: Statements about Identity and Worldview in Appalachian Dance." *Of, By, and For the People: How Dance Proclaims Political Ideals, Ethnicity, Social Class, and Regional Pride.* Riverside, California: Society of Dance History Scholars/Congress on Research in Dance, 1993.

McLeod, John A. "Minstrel of the Appalachians: An Interpretative Biography of Bascom Lamar Lunsford." Typescript, 1973.

McLoughlin, William G. *Cherokees and Missionaries, 1789–1839.* New Haven: Yale University Press, 1984.

——. *Cherokee Renascence in the New Republic.* Princeton, New Jersey: Princeton University Press, 1986.

McNeil, W. K. "Play-Party." *Encyclopedia of Southern Culture.* Eds. Charles Reagan Wilson and William Ferris. Chapel Hill: University of North Carolina Press, 1989.

"Memoirs of Bascom Lamar Lunsford." Typescript in the Lunsford Collection at Mars Hill College, Mars Hill, North Carolina.

Memorial University of Newfoundland Folklore and Language Archive (MUNFLA). Ms. 78–0003 and Ms. 72–155.

Merriam, Alan. "On Objections to Comparison in Ethnomusicology." *Cross Cultural Perspectives in Music.* Eds. Robert Falck and Timothy Rice. Toronto: University of Toronto Press, 1983: 174–189.

Mitchell-Kernan, Claudia. "Signifying, Loudtalking, and Marking." *Rappin' and Stylin' Out: Communication in Urban Black America.* Ed. Thomas Kochman, Urbana: University of Illinois Press, 1972: 315–335.

Moore, Lillian. "John Durang—The First American Dancer." *Chronicles of the American Dance.* Ed. Paul Magriel. New York: Henry Holt & Co., 1948: 15–37.

Morgan, Edmund S. *Virginians At Home.* Charlottesville, Virginia: University Press of Virginia, 1952.

Morgan, Prys. *The Eighteenth Century Renaissance.* Llandybie, Dyfed, Wales: Christopher Davies, 1981.

Morrison, James E. "Social Dance in Colonial Virginia." Report for Colonial Williamsburg, 1981.

——. *Twenty-four Early American Country Dances, Cotillions & Reels for the Year 1976.* New York: Country Dance and Song Society, 1976.

"Music, Songs and Folklore of the South." *Southern Tourist* (March 1926): 60 and 62.

Nathan, Hans. *Dan Emmett and the Rise of Early Negro Minstrelsy.* Norman: University of Oklahoma Press, 1962.

Nettl, Bruno. *The Study of Ethnomusicology: Twenty-nine Issues and Concepts.* Urbana: University of Illinois Press, 1983.

Nevell, Richard. *A Time to Dance: American Country Dancing from Hornpipes to Hot Hash.* New York: St. Martin's Press, 1977.

Northup, Solomon. *Twelve Years a Slave.* Auburn, New York: Derby & Miller, 1853.

Norton, John. *The Journal of Major John Norton, 1816.* Ed. with introductions and notes by Carl F. Klinck and James J. Talman. Toronto: Champlain Society, 1970.

Norton, Pauline. "Country Dance." *The New Grove Dictionary of American Music,* vol. 1. Eds. H. Wiley Hitchcock and Stanley Sadie. London: Macmillan Publishers, 1986: 515.

Oppé, A. P. and Cecil J. Sharp. *The Dance.* 1924. Reprint. Totowa, New Jersey: Rowman & Littlefield, 1972.

Orr, Lucinda Lee. *Journal of a Young Lady of the Old Dominion, 1782.* Ed. Emily V. Mason. Baltimore: John Murphy & Co., 1891.

Pedersen, Dagny and Neva Boyd. *Folk Games of Denmark and Sweden for School, Playground and Social Center.* Chicago: H. T. FitzSimons Co., 1915.

Pichierri, Louis. *Music in New Hampshire, 1632–1800.* New York: Columbia University Press, 1960.

Pine, L. G., ed. *Who's Who In Music.* London: I.B. Shaw Publishing Co., 1951.

Playford, John. *The English dancing Master or Plaine and easie Rules for the Dancing of Country Dance, with the Tune to each Dance.* Eds. Hugh Mellor and Leslie Bridgewater. London: Dance Books, 1984.

Playford, John. *Playford's English Dancing Master 1651: A Facsimile Reprint with an Introduction, Bibliography and Notes.* Ed. Margaret Dean-Smith. London: Schott & Co., 1957.

Quigley, Colin. *Close to the Floor: Folk Dance in Newfoundland.* St John's: Memorial University of Newfoundland Folklore & Language Publications, 1985.

Raitz, Karl B. and Richard Ulack. *Appalachia, A Regional Geography.* Boulder, Colorado: Westview Press, 1984.

Rameau, Pierre. *The Dancing Master.* Trans. Cyrill Beaumont. Paris, 1725. Reprint. Brooklyn: Dance Horizons: 1970.

Randolph, Vance. *Pissing in the Snow and Other Ozark Folktales.* Urbana: University of Illinois Press, 1976.

Richardson, Phillip. *The Social Dances of the Nineteenth Century in England.* London: Herbert Jenkins, 1960.

Robinson, Blackwell P. ed., *The North Carolina Guide.* Chapel Hill: University of North Carolina Press, 1955: 134–143.

Royce, Anya Peterson. *The Anthropology of Dance.* Bloomington: Indiana University Press, 1977.

Rust, Frances. *Dance in Society.* London: Routledge & Kegen Paul, 1969.

Sablosky, Irving L. *American Music.* Chicago: University of Chicago Press, 1969.

Sachs, Curt. *World History of the Dance.* Trans. Bessie Schönberg. New York: W. W. Norton & Co., 1937.

Salmon, Emily J., ed. *A Hornbook of Virginia History.* 3rd ed. Richmond: Virginia State Library, 1983.

Sanders, J. Olcutt. "Finding List of Southeastern Square Dance Figures." *Southern Folklore Quarterly,* vol. 6, no. 4 (December 1942): 263–275.

Sannella, Ted. *Balance and Swing.* New York: Country Dance & Song Society, 1982.

Schechner, Richard. "Towards a Poetics of Performance." In *Essays on Performance Theory, 1970–1976*. New York: Drama Book Specialists, 1977: 108–139.

Schneider, Gretchen. "Public Behavior at the Governor's Palace: A Look at 18th Century Gentle Persons." Research Report for Colonial Williamsburg, 1981.

Seeger, Charles to Adrian J. Dornbush. August 21, 1936. U.S. Farm Security Administration, *Miscellaneous Printed Matter*. 2 vols. (unpaged). Music Division, Library of Congress.

Seeger, Mike and Ruth Pershing. *Talking Feet: Solo Southern Dance*. Berkeley, California: North Atlantic Books, 1992.

Sharp, Cecil J. *English Folksongs from the Southern Appalachians*, 2 vols. London: Oxford University Press, 1932.

——. *Folk Dancing in Schools and Folk Singing in Schools*. London: English Folk Dance Society, 1920.

Sharp, Cecil J. and Maud Karpeles. *The Country Dance Book, Part V: The Running Set*. London: Novello & Company, 1918. Reprint. East Ardsley, England: EP Publishing, 1976.

Sharpe, Bill. *A New Geography of North Carolina*. Vol. 1. Raleigh, North Carolina: Sharpe Publishing Co., 1954.

Sider, Gerald. *Culture and Class in Anthropology and History*. Cambridge and New York: Cambridge University Press, 1986.

Social Plays, Games, Marches, Old Folk Dances and Rhythmic Movements: for Use in Indian Schools. Washington: Office of Indian Affairs, 1911.

Southern, Eileen. *The Music of Black Americans: A History*. New York: W. W. Norton & Co., 1971.

——, ed. *Readings in Black American Music*. New York: W. W. Norton & Co., 1971.

Spacek, Anna and Neva Boyd, comp. *Folk Dances of Bohemia and Moravia for School, Playground and Social Center*. Chicago: Saul Bros., 1917.

Speck, Frank G. and Leonard Broom in collaboration with Will West Long. *Cherokee Dance and Drama*. Berkeley: University of California Press, 1951.

Stearns, Marshall. *Jazz Dance: The Story of American Vernacular Dance*. New York: Macmillan, 1968.

Szwed, John F. and Morton Marks. "The Afro-American Transformation of European Set Dances and Dance Suites." *Dance Research Journal*, vol. 20, no. 1 (Summer 1988): 29–36.

Thomas, Robert K. "The Redbird Smith Movement." *Symposium on Cherokee and Iroquois Culture*. Ed. William N. Fenton and John Gulick. Smithsonian Institution Bureau of American Ethnology, Bulletin 180. Washington, D. C.: U. S. Government Printing Office, 1961: 161–166.

Timberlake, Henry. *Lieut. Henry Timberlake's Memoirs, 1756–1765*. Annotated, indexed and with an introduction by Samuel Cole Williams. Johnson City, Tennessee: The Watauga Press, 1927.

Tolman, Beth and Ralph Page. *The Country Dance Book: The Best of the Early Contras and Squares, Their History, Lore, Callers, Tunes and Joyful Instructions*. Rev. ed. Brattleboro, Vermont: The Stephen Greene Press, 1976.

Tomlinson, Kellam. *The Art of Dancing Explained by Reading and Figures; Whereby the Manner of Performing the Steps is Made Easy By a New and Familiar Method*. London, 1735. Reprint. Westmead, England: Gregg, 1970.

Torp, Lisbet, ed. *The Dance Event: A Complex Cultural Phenomenon*. Copenhagen: ICTM Study Group on Ethnochoreology, 1989.

Towle, Matthew. *The Young Gentleman and Lady's Private Tutor*. *The First Part*. London and Oxford, circa 1770.

Turner, Victor. *The Anthropology of Performance*. New York: PAJ Publications, 1986.

Van Cleef, Joy. "Rural Felicity: Social Dance in 18th Century Connecticut." *Dance Perspectives* 65, Spring 1976, vol. 17. Ed. Selma Jeanne Cohen. New York: Marcel Dekker, Inc., 1976.

Virginia Gazette. Williamsburg, 1736-1780. Williamsburg, Virginia: Colonial Williamsburg Foundation Library.

Wallace, Anthony. "Cultural Composition of the Handsome Lake Religion." *Symposium on Cherokee and Iroquois Culture.* Eds. William N. Fenton and John Gulick. Smithsonian Institution Bureau of American Ethnology, Bulletin 180. Washington, D. C.: U. S. Government Printing Office, 1961: 143-151.

Weede, Fred L. "Asheville Rhododendron Festival." Undated typescript, Asheville, North Carolina: Pack Memorial Public Library.

Weller, Jack E. *Yesterday's People.* Louisville: University of Kentucky Press, 1965.

Whisnant, David E. *All That Is Native and Fine: The Politics of Culture in an American Region.* Chapel Hill: University of North Carolina Press, 1983.

———. *Folk Festival Issues: Report From a Seminar.* Los Angeles: John Edwards Memorial Foundation, 1979.

———. *Modernizing the Mountaineer: People, Power, and Planning in Appalachia.* New York: Burt Franklin & Co., 1980.

Wiebe, Robert. *The Search for Order: 1877-1920,* a book in the series *The Making of America.* Ed. David Herbert Donald. New York: Hill & Wang, 1967.

Williams, Charles. *"Cotton Needs Pickin'": Characteristic Negro Folk Dances.* Norfolk: Guide Publishing Co., 1928.

Winter, Marian Hannah. "Juba and American Minstrelsy." *Chronicles of the American Dance.* Ed. Paul Magriel. New York: Henry Holt & Co., 1948: 39-63.

Witthoft, John. "Observations on Social Change." *The Cherokee Indian Nation: A Troubled History.* Ed. Duane H. King. Knoxville: University of Tennessee Press, 1979: 202-222.

———. "Will West Long, Cherokee Informant." *American Anthropologist,* vol. 50 n.s. (1948): 355-359.

Wolfe, Thomas. *Look Homeward Angel.* New York: Scribner's, 1929: 142-143.

Wynne, Shirley. "From Ballet to Ballroom: Dance in the Revolutionary Era." *Dance Scope,* vol. 10, no. 1 (Fall/Winter 1975-1976): 65-73.

VIDEOTAPES AND FILMS

Document Associates. *Cherokee.* 26 min. VHS 1/2 inch videotape. New York: Document Associates, 1976.

Johnson, Anne and Susan Spalding. *Step Back Cindy.* 30-min. VHS 1/2-inch video documentary. Whitesburg, Kentucky: Appalshop, 1990.

Lee, Spike (producer, director and screenwriter). *School Daze.* Distributed by Columbia Pictures, New York, 1988.

Memorial University of Newfoundland Educational Technology. *Jim Decker's Party.* 16mm film, 1967.

———. *Running the Goat in Harbour Deep.* 15-minute 1/2-inch VHS, #C 18, 1980.

———. *A Square Dance.* 30-minute 1/2-inch VHS, #361, 1980.

———. *Wedding Party on Fogo Island.* 16mm film, 1967.

Seeger, Mike and Ruth Pershing. *Talking Feet: Solo Southern Dance: Flatfoot, Buck, and Tap.* 87-min., Color, VHS and Beta 1/2-inch video documentary. El Cerrito, California: Flower Films. 1988.

Index

About the Contributors

RICHARD BLAUSTEIN is Professor of Sociology/Anthropology and Senior Research Fellow, Center for Appalachian Studies and Services, East Tennessee State University.

RICHARD CARLIN is the author of several books on traditional music and dance, including the forthcoming *Big Book of Country Music*. He was the founder-editor at a capella books, an imprint dedicated to books on the performing arts, and is now Senior Editor at Schirmer Books.

ROBERT G. DALSEMER is a square dance caller, dance collector, writer, and musician. He is coordinator of music and dance programs at the John C. Campbell Folk School in Brasstown, North Carolina, and since 1991 has served as President of The Country Dance and Song Society, an international association of groups and individuals interested in traditional dance and music.

DOUGLAS DAY is a folklorist and a musician who will dance only at gunpoint. Day earned his doctorate in folklore at the University of Pennsylvania. From 1988 to 1991, Day worked as a public folklorist at the John C. Campbell Folk School in Brasstown, North Carolina, documenting and presenting traditional artists in the region. His field recording sampler, "Mountain Valley Music: Grassroots Music from Western North Carolina and North Georgia," made the 1990 Library of Congress Selected List of Folk Music Recordings. He is currently director of the folk arts program at Allied Arts of Chattanooga and coordinator of the National Folk Festival in Chattanooga through 1995.

MERRY FEYOCK has been involved with the research, teaching, choreography, and performance of eighteenth-century theater and social dance at Colonial Williamsburg since 1979. Currently, as the Director of the Virginia Academy of Historic Dance, she has expanded her interests to include historic dance as diverse as the seventeenth-century Italian *ballo* and the early nineteenth-century waltz.

ELIZABETH FINE is Associate Professor at Virginia Polytechnic Institute and State University, where she holds a joint appointment in Communication Studies and the Center for Programs in the Humanities. She is Coordinator of the Appalachian Studies Program. Her books include *The Folklore Text: From Performance to Print*, which was selected by *Choice* as an Outstanding Academic Book of 1985 and received a Chicago Folklore Prize, and *Performance, Culture, and Identity*, co-edited with Jean Haskell Speer. In 1993, she received the Lilla A. Heston Award for Outstanding Scholarship in Interpretation and Performance Studies, awarded by the Speech Communication Association.

PHIL JAMISON is a musician and square dance caller who joined the Green Grass Cloggers in 1980. He is a frequent writer and dance editor for the *Old-Time Herald*, a magazine about old-time music and dance. He lives in Asheville, North Carolina with his wife and two daughters.

GAIL MATTHEWS-DENATALE is an independent educational consultant and author, who holds a Ph.D. in Folklore from Indiana University. She has published many articles on dance. Her educational materials have received several awards from the American Association for State and Local History, and the American Folklore Society recognized her "pathbreaking work in folklife education" with its 1993 Public Sector Fellowship. She has served as a dance and movement consultant for the National Endowment for the Arts, the Smithsonian Institution, and the Kennedy Center's National Initiative to Preserve American Dance (NIPAD). A traditional buckdancer, she learned how to dance from her father Dan Matthews, who grew up in Canton, North Carolina.

COLIN QUIGLEY holds a Ph.D. in Folklore and Mythology from the University of California, Los Angeles. He is the author of *Close to the Floor: Folk Dance in Newfoundland* and *Music from the Heart: Compositions of a Folk Fiddler*. Currently he is Associate Professor of Dance Ethnology in the World Arts and Cultures program at the University of California, Los Angeles.

MIKE SEEGER has devoted his life to singing and playing southern traditional mountain music, and producing documentaries and concert presentations of traditional musicians, singers, and dancers. He has toured North America and abroad since 1960 as a soloist or with the vanguard old-time music group, the New Lost City Ramblers. He has produced twenty-five documentary recordings and thirty-seven recordings of his own music for Folkways, Rounder, Flying Fish, Vanguard, Arhoolie, County, Homespun, Flower Films, and others.

SUSAN EIKE SPALDING is Coordinator of the Dance Initiative for the Minnesota Center for Arts Education. She holds her Doctorate in Dance from Temple University, is a Certified Movement Analyst, and is President of the Congress on Research in Dance. Her video documentary, *Step Back Cindy: Old-Time Dancing in Southwest Virginia*, appeared on Public Television in 1991. Recent research explores interethnic interaction in the development of aesthetics of Appalachian traditional dance.

PAUL L. TYLER, a native of Hoagland, Indiana, holds a Ph.D. in Folklore and American Studies from Indiana University. A fiddler and square dance caller, he is program director for Folk and Ethnic Music for the David Adler Cultural Center in Libertyville, Illinois.

DAVID E. WHISNANT is Professor of English at the University of North Carolina at Chapel Hill, where he also teaches in Folklore and American Studies.

JANE HARRIS WOODSIDE is Assistant Director of the Center for Appalachian Studies and Services at East Tennessee State University. She coordinated Center-sponsored conferences, workshops, and public programs on vernacular dance from 1989 to 1992. She has conducted research and lectured on traditional dance among the Eastern Band of the Cherokee in North Carolina.

ISBN 0-313-29428-3

90000>

9 780313 294280

EAN

HARDCOVER BAR CODE